FRIENDS IN YORK
THE DYNAMICS OF QUAKER REVIVAL
1780–1860

STUDIES IN PROTESTANT NONCONFORMITY
EDITED BY ALAN P. F. SELL

FRIENDS IN YORK
THE DYNAMICS OF QUAKER REVIVAL
1780–1860

Sheila Wright

KEELE UNIVERSITY PRESS

First published in 1995
Keele University Press
Keele, Staffordshire

© Sheila Wright

Composed by KUP
Printed by Hartnolls, Bodmin
Cornwall, England

ISBN 1 85331 051 4

Contents

GENERAL EDITOR'S PREFACE   6

ACKNOWLEDGEMENTS   6

ABBREVIATIONS   7

INTRODUCTION   9

CHAPTER 1   York in 1780   11

CHAPTER 2   The Evangelical Influence on York Quakerism   21

CHAPTER 3   Quaker Women's Role and Function in York Monthly Meeting   31

CHAPTER 4   The Structure and Pattern of Family Life   51

CHAPTER 5   Quakerism and Philanthropy in York   69

CHAPTER 6   Quakerism and Politics in York   85

CHAPTER 7   Demographic and Socio-Economic Profiles of York Monthly Meeting   109

CONCLUSION   133

APPENDIX I   138

APPENDIX II   146

APPENDIX III   147

APPENDIX IV   149

APPENDIX V   151

APPENDIX VI   152

APPENDIX VII   154

APPENDIX VIII   177

APPENDIX IX   179

APPENDIX X   180

APPENDIX XI   182

BIBLIOGRAPHY   197

NOTES   213

INDEX   249

General Editor's Preface

The volumes in this series will comprise critical evaluations of the Protestant Nonconformist heritage of England and Wales, with special reference to the historical development of the several groups and their contribution to modern Christian thought.

The series will include conference papers of The Association of Denominational Historical Societies and Cognate Libraries, a body established in 1993 to foster co-operative research in the field; and a sub-series entitled Protestant Nonconformist Texts. In the latter, significant texts from the several traditions will be edited and introduced.

The Reverend Professor Alan P. F. Sell

Acknowledgements

I wish to acknowledge the help and guidance of my many friends at the University of York, especially Dr Edward Royle, Dr Jane Rendall, Dr Treva Broughton, Dr David Scott and Sue Grace. Their friendship has supported me and the many hours of debate, argument and consequent stimulation have often led me to reconsider the direction and argument of this book. I also acknowledge the help of the staff of the Borthwick Institute of Historical Research, York, who patiently found obscure information on the Quakers of York, and also the staff of York Archives, especially Rita Friedman and Mary Fallon. I must also thank the descendants of William and Samuel Richardson for giving me access to his private papers. Not least, I wish to dedicate this book to Edward Wright, for without his sense of humour and support, which allowed him to share a house with five hundred of York's Quakers and me for three and a half years, it would never have been written.

Abbbreviations

York Monthly Meeting   (YMM)

York Men's Monthly Meeting Minutes   (YMMMM)

York Women's Monthly Meeting Minutes   (YWMMM)

Bristol Monthly Meeting   (BMM)

Bristol Men's Monthly Meeting Minutes   (BMMMM)

Bristol Women's Monthly Meeting Minutes   (BWMMM)

Bristol Archives   (BA)

Borthwick Institute of Historical Research   (BI)

British Library   (BML)

Brotherton Library, University of Leeds   (BL)

Friends' House Library, Euston Road   (FHL)

John Rylands Library, University of Manchester   (JRL)

York Archives   (YA)

York Public Library   (YPL)

Introduction

A great deal has been written about early Quakerism but very little serious attention has been paid to its development after 1750.[1] Of the work that has been carried out on seventeenth-century Quakerism, two studies of local meetings are the most relevant to this book, which is derived from my thesis on the Quakers in York, completed in 1991 at the University of York. David Scott's work on York Monthly Meeting and Nicholas Morgan's work on Lancashire Quakerism both cover the period from the Civil War to approximately the end of the reign of Queen Anne.[2] Recently, Christine Trevett has considered the role of women in early Quakerism.[3] Elizabeth Isichei's *Victorian Quakers* and Rufus Jones' *The Later Periods of Quakerism* are the most relevant works for a study of the later period of Quakerism.[4] Other work on English nineteenth-century Quakerism is thin on the ground and mostly consists of papers published in the *Journal of the Friends Historical Society* and booklets published by local Meetings for the consumption of their memberships, providing a limited view of the Meeting and no in-depth analysis of the dynamics, doctrinal changes, polemics or development of the Meeting.[5] Some relevant work on eighteenth-century American Quakerism exists, but has to be used with an awareness of the differences in development caused by the influences of colonialism.[6]

Because of the lack of any truly comparative work, this book has to stand alone until similar work is carried out. It is not yet possible to know how typical or atypical York Monthly Meeting was in this period. Geographically, the study is limited to York Meeting and its immediate environs, which excludes the outlying satellite Meetings in 1780 of Skipwith and Selby but includes villages such as Naburn and Fulford. This geographical line was drawn because Friends in the excluded Meetings were not an integral part of the social and economic life of the city of York. A limited amount of comparative material has been available from Bristol Monthly Meeting, and the evidence gathered has been particularly useful in the demographical analyses made in chapter 7, and in the chapter which considers women's role and position within the internal organization of the Meeting.

Fortunately, anyone working on the city of York is well supplied with secondary source material – the city has a complete volume of the *Victoria County History* devoted to it.[7] Alan Armstrong's work on the economic and social status of the population of York is an invaluable source of demographic information.[8] Religion in the city in this period has also caught the attention of historians, notably Edward Royle. Most of these works are of a general nature and only the Evangelical Anglicans and Methodists have received more detailed attention.[9]

John Stephenson Rowntree's figures, collected for his seminal essay on the decline in membership of the Society of Friends, show that, of all the Monthly Meetings within Yorkshire Quarterly Meeting, York was the only one which expanded its membership in the period between 1780 and 1860.[10] It was these figures which posed an important question to be considered in this book: what caused the rise in membership? Was it natural increase over decrease, or was it caused by some form of internal dynamic – and, if so, what form did this take? In chapter 7 I explore the possible demographic causes for the expansion, but before that a number of influences on York Quakerism are considered, all of which add up to the suggestion that the growth was largely due to a unique internal dynamic which developed within the Meeting over the period in question.

After a brief introduction to York in 1780 and to the position in the city of the Society of Friends, chapter 2 considers the influence of Evangelicalism on York Quakerism. In chapter 3 I argue that women were vital to the development and organization of the Meeting and, as ministers, were essential propagators and proselytizers of new or changed doctrines. Chapter 4 considers what effect the rise of a distinct middle-class culture and the influence of Evangelicalism might have had on women and the domestic and family life of York's Quakers. Furthermore, I propose that women's importance as socializers and educators within the sphere of the Quaker family was directly influential on the structure of the Meeting. Chapter 5 looks at the role that York's Quakers played in the social and philanthropic activities of the city, and in chapter 6 I consider their integration and involvement with the political structure of the city.

CHAPTER 1

York in 1780

Eighteenth-century York was run by a corporation consisting of a lord mayor, aldermen, sheriffs, a council of twenty-four, chamberlains and other minor officials. The city had thirty-two parishes and a considerable amount of local government was devolved through them. It had a large freeman franchise and elected two Members of Parliament. In 1780 the population was between sixteen and seventeen thousand, most of whom lived within the city walls. York's economy relied heavily upon its position as a market and service centre for the surrounding agricultural areas. In the 1720s and '30s the city had been a social centre, drawing in the landed gentry and aristocracy for the fashionable season, but by 1780 this side of life was in decline, largely owing to better transport to, and the attractions of, Bath and London. York remained a city of shopkeepers, dealers, merchants, mariners and brokers and failed to develop any major manufacturing industry. The guilds had lost much of their power and the status of their membership had declined. In the last decades of the eighteenth century, small-scale new manufacturing industry was introduced into the city, including comb-making, confectionery, wholesale drugs, toy manufacture and a glass works. At the same time there was an expansion in banking and by 1780 there were three banks in the city.[1] But trade and employment was dominated by small-scale manufacturing and tradesmen and it was amongst these men that the majority of Quakers were to be found. Four of York's industries had their roots in the activities of late eighteenth-century and early nineteenth-century Quaker manufacturers and tradesmen. The Tuke tea and coffee business, begun in 1725 as a grocer's shop by Mary Tuke, had expanded by 1780, under the guidance of her nephew William Tuke, to include a wholesale outlet in London. In 1862 the business was sold to Henry Rowntree and formed the basis for the present Rowntree confectionery company. The York Glass Works, founded by Charles Prince, was sold to Thomas Backhouse and Joseph Spence in 1835 and was not finally closed until the early 1980s. William Richardson's tannery/agricultural business, founded in the 1770s by his father, became Richardson's Agricultural Merchants and was only closed in

11

1973. Sessions, the printers founded by William Alexander in 1811, is still in existence in the city.

Politics in York from 1754 to 1783 were dominated by Rockinghamite Whiggism. After the death of the Marquis of Rockingham, a more radical, independent era dawned and amongst the new influences was the Revd Christopher Wyvill's Yorkshire Association. This was supported by the corporation, which also aligned itself to the Prince of Wales' party and supported Wilberforce (Member for Hull) and the anti-slavery campaign.

Although the city was a declining social centre, it still clung to the institutions of the social season, with the races and the Assize Balls forming the high points. Improvements were undertaken in street cleaning and lighting under the provisions of the 1763 Lighting and Cleansing Act, but no major new building works were undertaken until the 1820s, when the Yorkshire Museum, the Festival Concert Rooms and the York Subscription Library were built.

The poor were still cared for largely by the parishes, which had various charities under their control. A workhouse was established in Marygate in 1768 which, although increasingly inadequate, was not replaced until the middle of the nineteenth century. Education in the city was haphazard. For the poor, there was a Blue Coat Boys' School and a Grey Coat Girls' School, both of which had been established in 1705 and reorganized in 1785 by Evangelical Anglicans who also revamped the spinning and knitting schools. There were various other educational institutions, including Archbishop Holgate's Grammar School, where in 1764 twenty-four boys were taught English and Latin, and St Peter's School, which was in decline. A few schoolmasters ran their own establishments in the parishes.[2] The Bar Convent catered for Roman Catholic girls, but the only Protestant Nonconformist school was Esther Tuke's in Trinity Lane for Quaker girls, established in 1785 and which, although closed in 1814, was reopened in 1835 to become The Mount Girls' School.[3]

Although in 1780 both religious and civic life was dominated by the Anglican Church and the Minster, York also had a small Nonconformist community. The Anglican Church presided in twenty-two parishes, with seventeen incumbents in 1764, of whom only three had other livings outside York.[4] Roman Catholics probably numbered about eighty-two families in 1764 and, besides the chapel in the Bar Convent in Blossom Street, also held services in a house in Little Blake Street. Generally, they suffered very little harassment, although like most Nonconformists, they were excluded from civic life. Several served in their parishes and they appear to have had no difficulty in gaining their freedom. Protestant Nonconformists were represented by Quakers, Unitarians, Methodists, the Countess of Huntingdon Connexion and Moravians. Archbishop Drummond's visitation of 1764 shows that there were about sixty-six Nonconformist families out of a total of 2,701, of which thirty-three were Presbyterians and only six or so identified as Methodists. The Quakers numbered around a hundred individuals in 1780.

The nineteenth century saw many changes in York. Economically, the city continued to be a local market and a provider of goods and services for the surrounding countryside. But its importance as a market was declining as transport improved. Until local government reorganization under the Municipal Corporations Act of 1835, the city retained its freemen traders. The Ouse was still a main source for the transportation of goods into the city, but the failure of the Ouse Navigation Committee to keep it clear, deepen and widen it meant that, by the time work was carried out in the 1830s, the railways were poised to overtake it in importance.

The population of the city increased, but slowly in comparison with the industrializing towns of the West Riding. In forty years York's population rose by 71%, while Leeds' expanded by 186%, Bradford's by 444% and Halifax's by 125%.[5] Only in comparison with some other country towns did York appear not to have fared too badly: Chester grew by only 54% and Bath by 42%. This lack of expansion was in part due to the failure of the corporation to encourage industry, but it was also largely geographic. York, surrounded by the estates of large land-owners, is on a plain, with none of the water power that had attracted industrial expansion in the Leeds, Halifax and Bradford areas in the eighteenth century. Alan Armstrong's analysis of occupations shows how dependent the city was on small manufacturers, shopkeepers and domestic households as sources of employment.[6] In 1830 there were 492 firms involved in the food and clothing trade and York was still 'a city of small-scale handicraft enterprises on which the Industrial Revolution had made little, if any, direct impact'.[7] The economic situation of the city in 1833 was succinctly summed up by the Quaker Joseph Rowntree: 'While other towns have gone forward the people of York, relying too much on prescriptive rights and ancient importance had stood still; and that was but another term for going back.'[8]

Although in many ways the city altered little, the 1837 and 1851 religious censuses showed that changes had occurred in the religious affiliation of the population of York. The Anglican Church still had the greatest single share of attenders at its services: 37.9% in 1837 and 48.2% in 1851, but Nonconformity had greatly increased in the city since the late eighteenth century and in 1837 their numbers exceeded Anglican attenders by 18%.[9] Of these, Wesleyan Methodists were by far the largest group in both periods, followed by the Congregationalists in 1837 and Wesleyan Reformers in 1851. The Society of Friends accounted for 3.4% in 1837 and 2% in 1851, and Roman Catholics for 6.6% in 1837 and 9.3% in 1851, coinciding with the rise in Irish immigration into the city during the famine years of the mid-1840s. In all, only 55% of the population of the city attended a religious service, according to a count by the Manchester Statistical Society in 1837, but this rose to 61.2% on census Sunday in 1851.[10]

Although there were few outward changes in the Anglican Church during the later eighteenth century, it did produce two exceptional figures. William Richardson, vicar of St Michael le Belfrey, was an Evangelical Anglican who was often accused of being 'Methodistical' and who made St Michael's the most fashionable parish church in the city. The Revd John Graham was vicar of St Saviour's and St Mary's Bishophill Senior from 1796.[11] The Established Church was revitalized in the early nineteenth century by men such as these, and Evangelicalism became a powerful doctrine preached by vicars and curates from many of the city's parish pulpits. At the same time the Nonconformist denominations saw a dramatic rise in their congregations. Amongst the most active congregations were the Wesleyan Methodists, who opened New Street Chapel in 1805 and who expanded to such an extent that they opened the huge Centenary Chapel in 1840.[12] The Unitarian congregation at St Saviourgate Chapel also grew, and their minister, the Revd Charles Wellbeloved, was an influential figure in philanthropy and education. It was he who brought the Manchester College to York in 1803.[13] The Congregational minister, the Revd James Parsons, was one of the foremost preachers of his time and his congregation at Lendal Chapel (built in 1816) grew to such an extent that the new Salem Chapel had to be built in 1839. The Society of Friends also enlarged their Meeting House in 1816 to house a growing membership which included such new and lively individuals as Joseph and Sarah Rowntree, Joseph Spence, James and Thomas Backhouse and William and Ann Alexander, who joined an established, enterprising group of substantial tradesmen and merchants led by William and Esther Tuke, Henry and Samuel Tuke, Lindley and Hannah Murray, David Priestman and William and Samuel Richardson.[14]

The railways revitalized York's economy in the 1840s and '50s and, although maligned for his excesses, George Hudson has to be given credit for ensuring that York became one of the great railway cities of the Victorian age. It was not just railway lines that came to York. It was also carriage workshops and engine repair yards, all of which provided employment for the city's growing population. The census of 1841 shows only 41 railway workers, but by 1851 this had risen to 513, of whom 390 were immigrants, with 537 dependents.[15]

This was not the only major change in York's organizational structure. The 1825 local Police Act began the move towards local government reorganization and this was completed under the Municipal Corporations Act in 1835. York's social life also began to change. The races became less important as a social event and the Assize Balls, which had been weekly events in the eighteenth century when the courts were sitting, were by 1828 held only six times a year. But there were new social events: a music festival was established in 1823 and the Philosophical Society in 1822. Although not the fashionable centre it had been in the early to mid-eighteenth century, York still provided an active, if different, social calendar for its inhabitants.

The Society of Friends

After the verve and vigour of seventeenth-century Quakerism, the Society of Friends nationally had, by the opening of the eighteenth century, already begun to retreat inward from the world, no longer sending out large numbers of ministers to preach to convert. Instead, they sought merely to sustain rather than to expand their membership, and in many cases lost recruits as a consequence. At the same time, the number of accredited ministers fell, reducing Friends' ability to proselytize. The Quarterly Meeting of Bristol and Somerset was amongst those which reported in the 1760s that 'two-thirds of the meetings [under their jurisdiction] have no acknowledged minister' and sit in silence in Meeting week after week.[16] Esther Tuke of York Monthly Meeting complained about the lack of ministry and the inability of Friends '... to sympathise with the awakened or those who err or who are out of the way', commenting that there was a deadness and lack of spiritual life amongst Friends in the Meetings she visited.[17] Ministry, under the guidance of repeated Epistles from the Yearly Meeting, was exhorted to remain a spontaneous outpouring of words and warned not to prophesy '... none present to be wise above what is written', and the lack of premeditation often resulted in incoherent ramblings. In 1745 a more damaging Epistle warned ministers not to preach in Meetings where Friends '... are not themselves faithful against payment of tithes, and in observing other branches of our Christian testimony' – surely the Meetings which most needed ministerial guidance.[18]

The decline in ministry was accompanied by a growth in a cloistered psychology which intruded into the lives of all Friends. Increasingly, the Yearly Epistles from the Society became obsessed with plainness of dress and speech and pettifogging discipline and more concerned with outward form than inner spiritual vitality or growth.[19] Quakers eschewed theological thought as being a barrier to the reception of the Inner Light and this resulted in a failure to provide a religious training for Quaker youth and the enjoyment of education and knowledge for its own sake was shunned as being '... more frequently hurtful than helpful'.[20]

Although Quaker historians generally deny the existence of change, by 1780 Quietism was beginning to be challenged. Improved educational facilities, such as Esther Tuke's girls' school in York, founded in 1785, and Ackworth School, Pontefract, opened in 1778, started to provide a better standard of education for young Quakers. There was a growing awareness of the inadequate levels of ministry available in many Meetings and during the 1780s and '90s attempts were made to revitalize the Society.[21] At the same time, the economic and social standing of Friends was changing. Increasingly, the membership was becoming more middle-class and, although still predominantly tradesmen, artisans, merchants and shopkeepers, they were growing in wealth. It was their upward social mobility and the opportunities and demands of their increased status within society which, along with doctrinal changes introduced through greater contact with the wider world, helped to change the Society over the period from 1780.

One of the consequences of greater integration was that the Evangelical revival, begun within the Established Church, infiltrated Quakerism at the beginning of the nineteenth century. This, combined with the growth of humanitarianism encouraged by Enlightenment philosophy, inspired Quakers to take up the cause of the ill-treated: lunatics, prisoners and, most important of all for the future political and social progress of Friends, the slave.

York Monthly Meeting

York Meeting had its origins in George Fox's visit to the city in 1651. Apparently, there was already a group of 'severall people that was very tender', suggesting he had a few followers.[22] It was William Dewsbury who drew together the Yorkshire Quarterly Meetings, and visits to the Quarterly Meeting from George Fox in 1663, 1665, 1666 and 1669 reinforced his work. The first Meeting House in York, acquired in 1674, was in a tenement adjacent to Friargate. This was extended in 1718 and again in 1816.[23]

York Monthly Meeting was one of fourteen which formed the Yorkshire Quarterly Meeting. Each Monthly Meeting was entirely autonomous, but they all met together once a quarter to regulate the business of the entire area. Within each Monthly Meeting were four organizational groups, of which the most important was the Men's Monthly Meeting. This was responsible for the day-to-day running of the Meeting, including discipline, regulating marriages, certificating new members and those moving to other Meetings, looking after the sick and the poor, etc. The Preparative Meeting dealt with the finances, regulating legacies and charities. The Meeting for Ministers and Elders consisted of the élite and was concerned with the ministry and spiritual welfare of members.

The most distinctive aspect of the organization of Quakerism was the role it gave to women. The Women's Meeting was a completely separate group from the Men's, although it was ultimately responsible to them. Women's Meetings were established by George Fox and arose from the levelling and egalitarian ideas of the Civil War Sects.[24] Women, Fox argued, were the spiritual equals of men, because they too were just as able to receive the Inner Light. They were to be '... helps meet [within the Society] ... as they were before the Fall'.[25] He extended these ideas to make them an integral part of the organizational structure of the Society:

> ... what ye Lord had opened unto mee I declared unto him concerninge there [women] haveinge a meetinge once a weeke every 2 day [i.e. every Monday]: yet they might see and enquire into ye necessity of all ffriends whoe was sicke and weake and whoe was in wants or widdowes or fatherlesse: in ye Citty and suburbes.[26]

During the eighteenth century York Meeting, along with many others, appears to have lost its earlier verve and vigour. The Meeting for Ministers and Elders degenerated between 1720 and 1770, sending no women representatives to the Quarterly Meeting, and there were only twelve accredited ministers throughout the period from 1687 to 1768. By far the most active and dynamic ministers were Henry Frankland, Benjamin Stone and Mary Ellerton, all of whom had died by 1740. Between 1740 and 1768 only four ministering journeys were certificated, two by Ann Mercy Bell, who was the most active female minister.[27] This lack of ministry led to increasing references in the Monthly Meeting Minutes to drowsiness, unpunctuality and poor attendance, a clear indication of a lack of discipline and guidance.

By 1780, York Meeting was beginning to experience a revival in its ministry. This revival was led by a group of powerful and influential women who were to be responsible for the revitalization of the Meeting and its ministry. In 1765 Esther Maud became the second wife of William Tuke, who was already a leader within York Meeting and a prominent figure at Yearly Meeting. Esther Tuke, appointed a minister in 1778, was the source of the revitalization of York Meeting. Her powerful ministry and her many journeys within the environs of York Meeting and around England – in July 1785 she preached to over a thousand people in Berwick Town Hall – all helped to enliven the ministry and tighten up the lax discipline.[28] In 1781 she reported to Monthly Meeting that Friends were recommended not to put '... into offices [those] whose conduct and appearance is not consistent with what we profess nor appoint such to represent Meetings, whose outward appearance manifests too great a deviation from that plainness'. And Clifford Meeting was to be visited in 1785 to '... stirr [sic] them up to an exercise of the discipline and a more frequent attendance of their Meetings'.[29] She was joined in the ministry by her stepdaughters Sarah in 1781 and Elizabeth in 1787 and by her own daughter Ann in 1788. These young women, along with their brother Henry Tuke, formed the nucleus of ministers who began to restore the quality and quantity of York's ministry over the next twenty years. But it was not only the ministry which benefited from the attention of these women. In 1785 they and nine other Quaker women established the Quaker girls' school in Trinity Lane, specifically to train a future generation of women who could provide leadership and, if called to do so, good ministry within the Society. They also helped and encouraged the Quaker men involved in the foundation of the Retreat in 1796 and Ann Tuke was responsible for its name.[30]

However, the changes in religious practice and the growing social status of Friends in York Meeting did not find favour with all, and the conflicts which arose add confusion to any study of late eighteenth-century Quakerism. On the one hand, Esther and Sarah Tuke were aware that many wished to maintain the Quietist principles of early Friends, but they recognized the problems faced by late eighteenth-century Quakerism and tried to eradicate the sterility which was so well demonstrated by the opening lines of the Women's Quarterly Meeting Epistle for 1781: 'Dear Friends, We are sensible that to us as a people no new thing can be said ...'.[31] Esther and her daughters' attempts to provide strong ministerial leadership, and thus change, were often met with criticism by visiting ministers and were unhelpful to a Meeting trying to shake off the stultifying effects of Quietism. Susanna Boone visited York in August 1787 and complained that '... they broke up the Meeting too soon for me so I was in great trouble which has been my lot most of my time there for want of feeling more tender sympathy and unity of Spirit amongst them'.[32]

But the winds of change were beginning to blow through the Society and in York Meeting they found a ready response. Increasingly prosperous, well-educated members were not prepared to accept the stale platitudes and biblical symbolism of past ministry. Encouraged by the resurgence of a powerful women's ministry, intellectuals such as Henry Tuke and Lindley Murray began to scrutinize every aspect of Quaker doctrine. Intellectualism, encouraged by well-informed women such as Henry's sisters and stepsisters and his wife Maria, was no longer discouraged. Religious discussion and argument became a feature of the Quaker home and Esther Tuke encouraged her four-year-old grandson Samuel to read and discuss passages from the Bible with her.[33]

York Meeting never lacked weighty members who constituted an important element within the Yearly Meeting and who formed a prosperous section of York's business community.[34] Consequently, Quaker relationships with urban York suggest that, throughout the eighteenth century, there had been very little disharmony. Quakers were responsible, godly citizens who generally conformed to the expectations that the urban world of commerce held of its members. Vertical ties of patronage and oligarchic rule helped to ensure that Quakers observed the obligations that the social structure placed upon them, serving as officials in the parishes and on the corporation. As tradesmen and merchants, Quakers had to conform to the prevailing social and economic norms if financial ruin was not to result. Changes in the religious life of the city at the end of the eighteenth century, and in particular the decline of the domination of the Established Church, diluted Anglican corporate and parish control, which meant that, increasingly, citizens from other denominations were represented amongst those in authority. Quakers were less alone as Dissenters. At the same time they were moving spiritually and philosophically closer to Christians from other denominations, and as humanitarian and social contact grew they were drawn more and more into the philanthropic, cultural and political activities of York society.

CHAPTER 2

The Evangelical Influence on York Quakerism

The Evangelical revival, evident during the last decades of the eighteenth century, was to have a profound effect on Quakerism.[1] Quakerism by the 1780s had degenerated into a state of internalized apathy. Much of its original verve and vigour had disappeared. The stifling effects of Quietism had reduced many First Day Meetings to lethargic, uninspired silent worship only rarely interrupted by disjointed, incoherent rambling ministry. Evangelicalism was to be Quakerism's revival, but this was not achieved without resistance from old-style Quakers fearful that the new creed would destroy the nature of Friends' unique beliefs. The origins of what became a national revival had its intellectual roots in York Meeting. When William Tuke, a man of vision, leadership and forcefulness, married Esther Maud in 1765, her talents for leadership, ministerial work and educational advancement became a vital source of influence on William's son Henry, who was brought up to believe in the need for the revitalization of Quakerism through a greater attention to discipline, a reduction in sterile, formal ministry and a greater understanding of the human needs of the membership. As a result of his upbringing and education, the work of Henry Tuke was to be vital to the revival of Quakerism. He was joined in this work by Lindley Murray and they gradually promoted changes within the Quaker belief system which ensured that, under their influence, Evangelicalism became the dominant, doctrinal force upon Quakerism in the nineteenth century.

Quakerism was (and still is) an experiential, individualistic, internalized, even mystical, belief system which put primary emphasis on the Spirit, or the Inner Light, which had the power to guide and influence the individual. Because Quakers denied the outward forms of recognized Christianity, eighteenth-century contemporaries accused Quakerism of being neither Christian nor Protestant and of being both Deist and Unitarian.[2] One twentieth-century historian has suggested that seventeenth- and eighteenth-century Quakerism, because of its meditative, mystical qualities, had closer links to Roman Catholicism than to Puritanism.[3] The Scriptures for Quakers were a guide to knowledge of

God, not an arbiter of faith. They considered that scriptural knowledge was not necessary to receive knowledge of Christ. Robert Barclay's treatise, *An Apology for the True Christian Divinity*, laid emphasis on received rather than learned faith. *An Apology* laid the foundation of Quaker doctrine in respect to the Scriptures by placing them secondary to the Inner Light. Barclay wrote in Proposition III that whilst the Scriptures were '... heavenly and divine writings', they were not '... the principle foundation of all truth and manners; because the principal foundation of truth must be truth itself'.[4] He reinforced this statement with the declaration that '... the Scriptures' authority and certainty depend upon the Spirit by which they were dictated; and the reason why they were received as truth is, because they proceed from the Spirit. Therefore, they are not the principle ground of truth.'[5] His statements of belief had become such an integral part of the Quaker belief system that the idea of intellectual debate or study of faith was anathema to eighteenth-century Quakers. But it was the intellectual awakening developed under the influence of the Enlightenment which questioned Quietism and was eventually to face, and come into conflict with, the challenge of Evangelicalism. Friends would have to disavow Barclay's Proposition III before they could become true Evangelicals.

Rufus Jones has described Evangelicalism at the beginning of the nineteenth century as embodying the doctrinal belief that:

> Man is a fallen and ruined being, devoid of spiritual capacity, totally depraved by his own nature and sundered by an infinite chasm of separation from God. Two bridges only span or have spanned that chasm, both of them in every sense supernatural images. One is Scripture and the other is Christ.[6]

As David Swift has suggested, Evangelical Anglicanism was 'experimental Christianity' and the workings of the Holy Spirit were as essential to that faith as was the Spirit to the beliefs of Friends. Evangelical Anglicanism was a religion of the heart, described by Charles Simeon as being '... experienced in your own soul'.[7] Because, as David Bebbington and Geoffrey Best have pointed out, Evangelicals emphasized the importance of conversion over and above Baptism, Evangelicals were accused of making 'invalid distinctions between the more or less Christian among the Baptised ...'.[8] A reduction of emphasis on the importance of Baptism as the condition of a knowledge of Christ added to the areas of agreement in interpretation between Quakers and Evangelicals. However, Evangelicalism also emphasized a literal and deterministic reading of the Scriptures as a guide to earthly belief and behaviour and this was diametrically opposed to the traditional Quaker belief system, which regarded the Scriptures as secondary to the primary rule of the Spirit.

Despite differences in interpretation of Christian doctrine, sufficient areas of agreement already existed and it was these which allowed some Quakers to espouse Evangelicalism. This espousal of Evangelical mores should not be seen in isolation or as being entirely due to the Evangelical revival. Many of the areas of agreement which developed between these two Christian groups devolved from the non-religious, practical humanitarianism which sprang from the Enlightenment and which, by the 1780s, had already begun to infiltrate Quakerism. Despite the fact that York Meeting had been affected by the Quietism of the early to mid-eighteenth century, Quakers in the city had never retreated from the world and were influential members of the local community.[9] It was under the influence of innovative Quakers, such as those of York Meeting, that they became leaders of the anti-slavery movement, initiators of prison reform and in York, with the foundation of the Retreat, instigators of an eventual nationwide reform in the treatment of the insane.[10] It was men and women such as Elizabeth Fry, William Allen and William Tuke who were to be the initiators of Quaker involvement in practical schemes which led to changes in social emphasis within Quakerism.

Quakers were the first to express a sense of moral outrage and guilt over slavery, and the national and local anti-slavery campaign organizations formed a springboard for Evangelical Anglican and Quaker co-operation, bringing together the two creeds. In London, William Wilberforce, Thomas Clarkson, Granville Sharp and other members of the Clapham Sect drew Quakers such as William Allen into their sphere and this laid the ground for the different denominations to work together in pursuit of a common cause. But these alliances were not confined to London; in York, the anti-slavery movement drew Quakers such as the Tukes not only into the Saints' sphere, but also into the local Anti-Slavery Society.[11] The combination of co-operation and a widening network of connections forced intellectual Quakers onto a wider stage; no longer could they hedge themselves in with their own peculiarities, nor did they try to.

The intense interest in religion, spawned by the Evangelical revival and encouraged by newly founded journals such as the *Eclectic Review* and the *Christian Observer*, renewed and expanded areas for religious debate. Quakers, because they were Dissenters and, as such, anti-Establishment, became targets for abuse and accusation from articles in these journals and were forced to defend and explain their principles, beliefs and writings.[12]

Exposure to public scrutiny highlighted differences of opinion within Quakerism, although divisions between Quietists and Evangelical Quakers were never clear-cut. The majority of Quakers occupied the middle ground and their affiliation belonged to neither camp. However, despite the lack of a positive or definite swing in favour of either group, it was to be Evangelical Quakers who were slowly to win the high ground in the decades between 1800 and 1832.[13] Not until the Yearly Meeting of 1832, though, was any attempt made to articulate the changes which were beginning to be manifest within Quakerism.[14]

York Meeting already had a reputation for being progressive by the 1790s. The foundation of the Retreat, Trinity Lane School and, although not entirely a York Meeting project, Ackworth School all contributed to the perception that York Meeting was one of ideas.[15] These emanated largely from one extraordinarily talented family: William Tuke, his wife Esther, their children Ann, Sarah, Mabel, Elizabeth and Henry, and their grandson Samuel were amongst the leaders of the York Meeting and were all weighty members of the Society. By 1780 Esther, Sarah, Ann and Henry were four of its most active and outspoken Evangelical ministers who, deeply aware of the problems that the Society was facing, were involved in promoting its rebirth as well as encouraging its humanitarian interests.[16] Educated and influenced by his stepmother Esther and his sisters, it was Henry who provided the intellectual voice of the Meeting. Also of vital importance to his development and growth as a writer were the guidance, advice and stimulation of Lindley Murray, the American gentleman and grammarian.

When Henry Tuke and Lindley Murray met in York in 1784, they already shared similar backgrounds. Both were the sons of wealthy merchant fathers, although Lindley Murray's was much better-off than William Tuke. Lindley Murray was born in Swetara, Pennsylvania in 1745 and was one of twelve children. His parents, like Henry's, were long-established Quakers, but not strict in their behaviour or beliefs, having the Scriptures read each morning and evening in the family and ensuring that Lindley had a true and complete understanding of them. Neither did they or he use the 'thee' and 'thou' form of address. His father owned a flour mill and traded in the West Indies and became one of the wealthiest men in Pennsylvania. Lindley had a liberal education and was an intellectual who enjoyed his membership of a debating society. But as a Quaker, he was aware of the dangers that such activities posed for those without strong beliefs. At seventeen or eighteen he decided to practise law, having realized that he did not wish to pursue a merchant's life, and he was called to the Bar when he was twenty-two years old. Soon after this, he married Hannah and they purchased a country home on the banks of the Hudson river, three miles from New York. Because of his declining health, he came to live in England in 1784 and, after searching Yorkshire for a congenial place to live, settled in Holgate, near York. It is probable that his decision to settle there had more to do with the nature of York Meeting and its membership than with his health, since York did not and does not have one of the healthiest climates in England. With his background of liberal Quakerism, he was looking for a Meeting which was receptive to his style of beliefs and one in which he would find congenial and like-minded members. On his arrival in York, the wealth he had created in America provided him with sufficient income to enable him to settle into a life of writing and indulge his intellectual interests.[17] It was in York that he met Henry Tuke and their friendship and intellectual partnership dates from this period.

Henry Tuke was born in 1755 and was educated at a school run by Friends in Sowerby, near Thirsk. It was there that his intellectual interests developed, but because his father, whose philanthropic activities were expanding, needed him in his increasingly prosperous tea and coffee business, he was unable to take up his first choice of a medical career, joining the company instead in 1770. Although disappointed in having to give up his educational ambitions, he was still able to pursue his love of the Greek and Latin classics in his limited spare time and even started writing a book on the life of Archbishop Huss.[18] In 1781 he married Mary Maria Scott, the daughter of Favill Scott, a wealthy Norwich banker. She was not a Friend by birth, but had relatives in the Society and became convinced after several months of staying with William and Esther Tuke. Her broad education and intellectual interests, which included the reading of Evangelical writers such as Hannah More, Cowper and Felicia Hemans, helped to expand Henry's ideas.[19] By the last decade of the eighteenth century their family was growing up, and in 1804 their son Samuel was twenty years old and able to take an increasing role in the family business. This relieved Henry of some of his responsibilities, allowing him to devote more time to his writing and studying. It was at this time that he discovered the intellectual stimulus of disciplined thought about the nature of individual faith.

Lindley Murray and Henry Tuke were to tread with care a revolutionary path towards a change in spiritual emphasis within Quakerism. Both knew that traditional Quakers within the Society would not easily espouse such changes in spiritual emphasis, and both were aware that they would meet a level of resistance from Quietists such as Sarah Lynes Grubb and her husband, John Grubb.[20] Sarah Lynes Grubb wrote often and desperately of her fears that Evangelicalism was having a detrimental effect on the core beliefs of the Society. She particularly felt that ministers were 'sliding and others already gone' from the original source of their ministry and that, by adopting Evangelical notions of the supremacy of Scripture and rationalist religious debate, '... much of this [lack of originality] is to be traced to their adopting the views and sentiments of those ... [who] have sought to bring all things to the test of *reason*, instead of to that Spirit which searcheth all things, even the deep things of God'.[21] Although there might be resistance from some traditionalists, Henry Tuke and Lindley Murray were aware that they drew support from a section of young Quakers, including Elizabeth Fry and Joseph John Gurney. It was the latter who took the Evangelical interpretation of Quakerism to greater heights, not only openly advocating the rational study of the Bible but also believing, as David Swift has written, that '... thought about the nature of God and the scheme of redemption can be helpful preparation for a man's actual drawing near to God in Christian worship'.[22] However, the foundation of Gurney's future influence was laid down by the work of Lindley Murray and Henry Tuke and it was they who were to be the first to express the change in spiritual emphasis within the Quaker belief system.

Over a period of ten years from 1800, it is possible to chart the gradual influence of Evangelicalism on Henry Tuke's writing. His first publications appeared around 1800 and were replies to articles in the *Monthly Review*, the *Eclectic Review* and the *Christian Observer*, to which he said he subscribed because of its 'unbiased and Christian principles' and because it reflected his own developing theological interests and ideas.[23] He published his earliest defence of Quakerism in the volume of the *Christian Observer* for August 1803. Writing in response to an article entitled 'An Account of the Conversion of a Quaker', in which the writer suggested that Quakers did not believe in the Atonement, Henry defended Quakers by quoting from Barclay's *Apology*, which, as he emphasized, upheld Friends' belief in the Atonement.[24] Over the next couple of years Henry Tuke became a regular contributor to these journals. His articles were often in defence of Quaker doctrine and practice, but he also became involved in lengthy debates with other contributors on theological interpretation and biblical translation.[25]

In an unpublished manuscript written in 1804 there are the first indications that his theological ideas were drawing him closer to traditional Christians. In this he suggested that '... little essential difference would be found to exist between them [Quakers] and the members of the Established Church'. However, there is evidence that there was still some confusion in his mind as to the relationship between the Spirit and the Holy Scriptures and he felt it necessary to qualify this statement, adding that: 'There is however, this difference, that the former contend that the Spirit which dictated the Scriptures and not the writings themselves, are the primary rule of faith and manners whilst the latter maintain the converse of this proposition ...'. Evidence of his intellectual struggle with traditional Quaker interpretation lies in the same manuscript, in which he suggests that whilst Quakers may believe in the 'revealed religion of the Spirit', he himself makes the important personal distinction, stating that he believes that the Spirit exists in conjunction with the Scriptures, not in opposition to them.[26]

By September 1805 he had written his first definitive Evangelical article, setting out how he conceived the Spirit to relate to the Holy

Scriptures. Answering an anonymous letter in the *Christian Observer* in which the writer challenged the notion that Quakers could call upon two 'paramount courts of ultimate appeal ... viz. the Scriptures and the Inner Light', Henry Tuke replied that Quakers believed that '... the Scriptures were dictated by the Divine Spirit and that a portion of the same Spirit is given to men in the present day ...', and he added that since Christians had sanctioned the Scriptures for many generations, it was '... certainly reasonable to depend upon them more than on any pretended private revelation which contradicts them and which has not received the sanction and concurrent approbation of so many ages ...'.[27]

In 1805 Henry published his first full-length book, *The Principles of Religion*. This was written for the use of parents and teachers when instructing Quaker youth and was also intended as a guide for non-Quakers to the principles of Quakerism. Although based primarily on Barclay's *Apology*, it deviates from it in some important areas and there are two sections where he expands the Evangelical beliefs that he had begun to disseminate in his earlier articles. These influences are particularly evident in the passages where he expresses his views on the Last Judgement and the eternal damnation of sinners. He considered that if believers unite with God, then it is possible 'to conclude, that there is a part of man which is immortal: and that there must be a future state, in which virtue and vice will meet with their respective rewards, in a more signal manner than they appear to receive them in this life'.[28] It is in this passage that he expresses his belief in the Evangelical idea that earthly behaviour had a connection with heavenly rewards. Later in the book he went further in upholding the Scriptures, and argued for their validity as a source of faith.[29]

Answering criticisms of the book by American Friends who objected to his elevating the importance of the Scriptures, Henry wrote: 'Whilst we contend for that inferiority to the Spirit from which the Scriptures proceed, there may be a danger of depreciating them beyond their real importance. Without the Scriptures our ideas of the gift and operation of the Holy Spirit would be very vague and incorrect.'[30] But not all Quakers were critical of his book, and a letter to Henry Tuke from a Friend in New York expressed the opinion that '... there is often found an unnecessary alarm among many Friends, but [sic] the *Scriptures* should be too much *exalted*'. Although the book had caused quite a stir in Philadelphia, this Friend assured Henry Tuke that '... thou mayest infer [these] are necessarily sentiments of many Friends in Philadelphia though not the whole of them', and he suggested that alterations to the book would '... rather injure than improve it'.[31]

Despite the doubts expressed by Quaker reviewers about the doctrinal content of the book, reviews in other Christian journals were generally very favourable and encouraging. Perhaps somewhat hopefully, they expressed the opinion that, although they disputed his views on war and the Sacraments, as the reviewer for the *Christian Observer* wrote, they recognized the '... overall Evangelical tone of the book and its lack of divergence from generally accepted religious principles', adding that Henry Tuke had established his belief in, and reliance on, the Scriptures as a source of inspiration.[32] And a writer in a later edition of the same journal in 1806 made the perceptive comment that the Quakers and Henry Tuke had moved a long way from Barclay's view of the supremacy of the Inner Light.[33]

By the end of 1805 Henry Tuke had begun to formulate what was to become a radically different form of Quakerism. He has to be seen as the forerunner to the Evangelical Quakers who were to be the cause of such controversy within the Society over the next twenty years.[34] However, unlike J. J. Gurney, he had been able to formulate his tentative reordering of Quaker doctrine without any attendant controversy. His works had passed the testing scrutiny of the publications committee of the Yearly Meeting and his articles had apparently gone uncensored. His influence has to be seen as the essential force behind the revitalization of Quakerism as a whole and within York Meeting in particular. His ideological and philosophical reordering of Quaker doctrine gave York Meeting the necessary intellectual impetus to carry out policies which resulted in great works and in a leadership able to tolerate, explore and encourage new paths of co-operation between men with different doctrinal beliefs. As Rufus Jones has written, 'he raised evangelical doctrine into unprecedented prominence'.[35]

Lindley Murray's first publication in England was *The Power of Religion on the Mind in Retirement, Affliction and the approach of Death*. This consisted of extracts from the death-bed confessions of historical figures such as Socrates, the Venerable Bede, Caesar Borgia, John Donne, John Locke, John, Earl of Rochester, and others. It was not a strictly religious book, but is illustrative of the importance that Evangelicals and Quakers placed on the last utterances of the dying and was very well received by numerous journals of the period, including the *Gentleman's Magazine*, whose reviewer wrote that the book '... in the quiet hour of reflection may contribute to arrest the careless and wandering to animate the sincere and virtuous, and to convince or discountenance those who have been unhappily led to oppose the highest truths'.[36] In 1815 and 1817 he published two books which were to give support to, and further advance, the definite Evangelical influence so evident in the work of his friend Henry Tuke. In these books Lindley Murray was to take York Quakerism even further down the Evangelical track. The books, incorporated into a single volume, were *The Duty and Benefit of the Daily Perusal of the Holy Scriptures in Families* and *A Compendium of Religious Faith and Practice designed for young persons of the Society of Friends.*[37] Neither of them discussed the doctrine of the Inner Light *vis-à-vis* the Scriptures, but both upheld the importance of the Scriptures and put to the fore Murray's belief in the necessity of their complete understanding as a source of Christian belief, advising that '... a regular and devout perusal of the Holy Scriptures, morning and evening, in our families will in a high degree contribute [to] the maintenance of correct sentiments, and proper feelings with respect to what we are to believe and practise'.[38]

Although these were not ideological publications, they were of great significance, since they were specifically directed towards Quaker youth. In them, Lindley Murray placed emphasis on the importance of the Scriptures, promoting the Evangelical belief in the rational study of the Scriptures to a place of prominence never before expressed in a Quaker publication.[39] There was no mention of the pre-eminence of the Spirit and no suggestion that the Holy Scriptures proceeded from the Spirit. From his proposition flowed an interpretation which allowed the Spirit and the Scriptures simply to be complementary one to the other.

The development of doctrinal similarities between Quakers and Evangelicals was to release the former from the isolation of eighteenth-century Quietism and to result in a more or less united attitude to moral and humanitarian behaviour. As areas for co-operation and contact increased, Quakers were increasingly drawn towards an understanding and appreciation of other Protestant sects. The formation of organizations such as the British and Foreign Bible Society, the Auxiliary Bible Society, the Religious Tract Society, the Society for the Reformation of Manners and the Society for the Suppression of Vice all provided arenas within which the godly of whatever persuasion could meet in joint interest in the pursuit of a common cause, without reference to individual theological differences.

In York, Henry Tuke and Lindley Murray were among the founding members of the York Auxiliary Bible Society. Amongst its attractions was the opportunity for intellectual debate and discussion on biblical topics between theologically different, but intellectually equal, Christian citizens. As a founding member, Henry gave a speech at the first meeting in January 1812 which, in view of the mixed religious affiliations of his audience, not surprisingly reaffirmed his support for the Scriptures:

> We profess to be governed by the same laws which are contained in the Holy Scriptures: and though we may not unite in the construction of some of these laws; yet, when we consider in how large a proportion of them the professors of Christianity are agreed ... there is much cause for us to feel as Brethren and to unite as has frequently been the case, in defence of our common faith.[40]

He placed strong emphasis on his belief that knowledge of the Scriptures needed to be extended to a wider section of the population: 'the object of this Institution … is to furnish Christians of all denominations with those sacred writings which teach us our duty to God and to one another, and which open to us the way of life and salvation'.[41] Not only was there no mention in this speech of pre-eminence of the Divine Spirit as the source of revelation of the Scriptures, but he was also recommending the systematic study of the Bible as a source of faith. Although unable to attend the meeting, Lindley Murray sent a letter which was read out by Samuel Tuke. Congratulating the meeting on the establishment of the Bible Society, he added his support as a Quaker to the aims of the society : 'Divine providence has favoured us with the knowledge and comfort of the Holy Scriptures and we have long rejoiced under their beneficent influence.' [42]

Many members of York Meeting were involved in the first meeting of the Auxiliary Bible Society and their participation is indicative of the common bonds which enabled these godly citizens to associate with others who had similar aims and beliefs.[43] Their support for an organization which promoted the intellectual study of the Bible is indicative of a Quaker withdrawal from the inspirational nature of the Quietist interpretation of the Scriptures. By declaring their belief in the power of the Scriptures as a source of primary influence over man, they were giving their approval to, if not their wholehearted adherence to, the Evangelical doctrine of the supremacy of the Scriptures as the source of Christian belief. This consequent shift in doctrinal emphasis gave rise to a new rationale which would allow that, in future, Quakers and Evangelicals would have more in common than not.

Although responsibility for the Evangelicalization of Quakerism has been widely attributed to Joseph John Gurney, it was in fact Henry Tuke and Lindley Murray who laid the foundations, raising it to prominence several years before Gurney began to have any influence. Because of the firmness of these foundations, Gurney was able to build upon their work and take Quakerism further down the road to Evangelicalism and a greater integration with Christians from other denominations.

Although the intellectual influence of Henry Tuke and Lindley Murray was vital to the progress of York Meeting – which, without them, might have stagnated along with so many others – most of the articulation and dissemination of doctrinal change was the responsibility of York's female ministers.[44] They became dominant in York Meeting during these crucial years of doctrinal change, making the majority of ministerial journeys and spreading word of the new creed. It was their presence and leadership, along with the intellectual authority of Henry Tuke and Lindley Murray, that ensured the encouragement of Evangelical doctrine within York Quakerism and helped to spread their ideas throughout the Meetings of the Society of Friends.

CHAPTER 3

Quaker Women's Role
and Function in York
Monthly Meeting

Quaker women played a vital part in the organization of the Society of Friends and, as ministers, were essential as leaders and disseminators of the beliefs of Quakerism. In York Meeting it was women who were to initiate the changes in education which would lead the Meeting out of the stagnation of the early and mid-eighteenth century and revitalize its ministry, opening it up to new doctrinal influences. To reflect their importance, this chapter will concentrate on the role of women within York Monthly Meeting and on their work as ministers. Since little comparative work has been undertaken on other Quaker Meetings, evidence from Bristol Monthly Meeting will be used, particularly in relation to women and women's work within the organizational structure of the Meeting.[1] The chapter is divided into two sections: the first will look at women and the organization and the second will focus on their work as spiritual leaders and ministers.

The rise of Evangelicalism within York Meeting and, with it, the influence of ideas of perfect womanhood could have been a threat to the position of women in the Meeting and have come into direct conflict with Quaker notions of their role within the Monthly Meetings which made up the Society of Friends. The Evangelical emphasis on the supremacy of Scripture as a source of faith could have resulted in a resurrection of the Pauline argument to reject female preaching. These fears were expressed by Eliza Sturge in 1834 who, when reading a copy of Isaac Crewdson's pamphlet *The Beacon*, saw the potential threat that denial of the guidance of the Holy Spirit could be to female preaching: 'If we give up this principle [the Inner Light] how can we any longer receive the ministry of women.'[2] The position of women was challenged in some denominations, but by retaining a belief in immediate guidance, Friends marked themselves out from other groups by their retention of positive teaching about female ministry and it was this consistency which ensured that Quakers were not persuaded to change their view of the role of women within the Society. To do so would have been in conflict with the basic tenets of Quakerism and any attempt to marginalize women within the Society would have involved the refutation of the teachings of their two leading – and, by this time, almost saintly – theologians, George Fox and Robert Barclay. This would have had the effect of putting the whole of Quaker theology and organization in jeopardy.

Despite the influence of Evangelical doctrine on York Quakerism, therefore, there was a fundamental belief in the correctness of socializing and educating women and men and in the expectation that, for women, life should include something other than just the domestic role advocated by such leading non-Quaker Evangelicals as Hannah More and John Angell James.[3] Quaker women and men such as Ann and Sarah Tuke, Elizabeth Dudley, Henry Tuke and James Backhouse, born into ministering households, watched and experienced their mothers' preaching and were subjected to a conditioning which led them to accept women as essential workers within the organization of the Society. At the same time they also had the expectation that women, if they had the overwhelming emotional and spiritual experience of a calling or a conversion, could become ministers and leaders within the Meeting and the Society.

One of the most public ways in which women expressed their faith and gained equality with men in seventeenth-century Quakerism had been their testimony against tithes. Tithe testimony allowed women to demonstrate publicly the strength of their faith, and they often found themselves having to support their menfolk's positions. This was especially the case if their husbands were sent to prison for non-payment and they had actually to take over the customary male roles. Women often went to prison alongside their men, or instead of them, or sometimes even in their own right for failure to pay tithes. One, Elizabeth Wyldman, a widow of Tatham Fell in Cumberland, even died for her beliefs.[4] However, by the last decades of the eighteenth century, tithe testimony in York was no longer a cause for such punitive action and, as discussed below in chapter six, was often erratic. Nevertheless, there are cases of women having goods seized. Elizabeth Thurnam had oats valued at £15. 8s. seized in 1796; in 1809 Rachel Fowler had two lots of silver plate worth £1. 8s. and £1. 4s. 6d. taken; and Hannah Murray coal worth 17s. in 1831. As late as 1852 Elizabeth Priestman surrendered a silver soup-ladle worth £1. 9s. 10d.[5] The decline of public protest deprived women of one of their most forceful and public acts of faith and equality. But, despite the loss of this type of public testimony, they were still left with a substantial and important role within the Society.

The organization

Theoretically, all women members of the Society had the opportunity to participate in its organization and, unlike the Men's Meeting, the

Women's offered participation to a broad range of its members. However, particularly in the period before 1800, as Vann suggested for the Men's Meeting, the Women's Meeting was dominated by the wives and daughters of the more well-to-do members and the most frequent number of attendances was restricted to a narrow élite of ladies,[6] the most notable of whom were Esther Tuke and her daughters, Sarah Priestman and her daughter Ann, Katherine (Allen) Jepson (wife of George Jepson, who was a formidable presence in the Men's Meeting for twenty years), Martha Fletcher, Esther Doeg (wife of David Doeg), Sarah King, Mary Allis, Priscilla Tuke (wife of Samuel Tuke), Martha Fletcher, Martha Richardson, Hannah Waller, Sarah Rowntree and Mary Armitage (see Appendix I). Unlike the American experience described by Sonderland, York Meeting encouraged young women to take a part in the organization from an early age. Ann Tuke became involved at the age of sixteen and her sister Mabel at the age of eighteen; Rebecca Fothergill, Elizabeth Backhouse and Maria Tuke junior were eighteen; Esther Tuke junior was seventeen; Elizabeth Fothergill, fifteen; Guilielma Tuke, twenty-one; and Sarah Tuke was one of the youngest attenders at twelve.[7] This early training was essential to the continuation of the work of the Society. But women who held more lowly positions in secular society rarely took an active part in the organization of the Meeting. There may well have been practical reasons for this, such as their unavailability or inability to undertake the work, but this was an inequitable type of behaviour for an apparently equitable Society.

The system of Women's Meetings established in the Society in the seventeenth century, under the direction of George Fox, had given women an official role in their Monthly Meeting. In spite of this, Quaker women would not have considered themselves to hold any power separate from the men, and men would not have claimed an authority separate from the women. In a Society within which the family was paramount, the organizational structure of the Meeting resembled an extension to this, with many of its functions having distinctly familial overtones. Each Meeting had its own Women's Monthly Meeting, within which there was a Preparative or Business Meeting. The Women's Meeting was responsible for issuing certificates to its ministers to travel and to women wanting to move to other Meetings; reading Epistles from, and sending representatives to, Quarterly and Yearly Meetings; endorsing permissions for marriages to take place, having interviewed the prospective couple to ensure that they were free to marry, that they had their parents' approval and that there were no irregularities of relationship.[8] Each Women's Meeting appointed a clerk to the Monthly and Quarterly Meetings and appointed female overseers who worked independently from the men, checking persons coming into First Day Meetings, generally ensuring the smooth running of the sessions and overseeing the care of its women members. Although they elected their own over-seers, the appointments had to be ratified by a joint committee of men and women members. Women Friends were also allowed to discipline and judge their own, but they had to inform the Men's Meeting of any cases and, having dealt with an offender, report back to them, at which point the men could take over or join in the case, forming a committee which informed the Women's Meeting of its findings. Only such a committee could disown: 'No proceedings of the women only, are to be sufficient ground for a testimony of disownment.' [9]

The Women's Meeting was responsible, jointly with the Men's, for admissions to membership. Applications were scrutinized by two women and two men Friends who visited the applicants and reported recom-mendations as to their suitability to the Men's Meeting for approval. In 1800 Ann White applied for membership, but her entry was deferred until November 1801. In November 1803 Sarah Chivers applied for readmission having been disowned for marrying out. A year later, in October 1804, she was received back into the Meeting.[10] Applications for membership were made both by those who had been expelled from the Society and by those who underwent convincement.[11] Despite the care with which new recruits were investigated, some were admitted into membership who inevitably failed to live up to Quakerism's high standards. Rebecca Fothergill was admitted in 1806 and, despite becoming a leading member of the Women's Meeting, was subsequently disowned in 1822 for a 'change in religious belief', while Mary Lee, admitted in 1820, was disowned in 1833 for 'concealing property belonging to her late husband's creditors'.[12]

Throughout this period there was a steady flow of admissions into York Meeting.[13] York was far more successful than Bristol Meeting in attracting new converts, the majority of whom were women. In York, a significant number of these were young and single and many were servants or apprentices.[14] Some were widows and a few were reinstated having been disowned, generally for marrying contrary to the Society's regulations.[15]

A further aspect to the work of both the Men's and Women's Meetings was poor relief. The Society was rigorous in the provision of support for its poor members and offered them a considerable range of benefits, particularly to widows and widowers with children and to young, single girls.[16] When Mary Scarr applied for admission in 1826, Friends reported their concern: 'Considering the circumstances in which she is placed we are apprehensive that being united to the Society might be a protection to her.'[17] Poor relief was provided in a variety of ways and the help was often as much practical as it was financial.[18] York Meeting had two sources of funding available for poor relief: legacies left to the Meeting by Friends and a collection made by the Women's

Preparative Meeting. Although the women had access to both sources, the Legacy Fund was supervised by the men, who had to approve applications from the Women's Meeting before money could be allocated. The collection in the Women's Preparative Meeting was at its disposal, to use as it saw fit. The fund was never large, but it gave them a measure of independence and allowed them to make their own allocations. In January 1780 the collection yielded 13s. 6d. and it increased until, in March 1829, it amounted to £3. 3s.[19] The women overseers visited those in need and reported back to the Women's Meeting. Mary Oddy was visited in 1782 by Sarah Priestman and 'others' and they reported that she needed both financial and practical assistance for herself and her daughter. The women suggested that a 'suitable place' should be found for her daughter Ann, and by March she had a position and had been provided with 'necessaries'.[20] In November 1783 the Women's Meeting gave Rebecca Procter 2s. and Elizabeth Towse 2s. 6d., and in May 1800 Ann Johnson was allowed £1. 1s. because 'the prices of provisions are high'.[21]

Poor members were also given assistance from the jointly administered Legacy Fund. Significantly, women received relief much more often than men, for whom there are very few cases of assistance recorded. Joseph Hardy was helped between 1785 and 1794, both financially and practically.[22] Mary Oddy received clothing worth 19s. 10d. in 1784 and 10s. 6d. in 1786 and 1787 and a half-chaldron of coal in 1787 and 1788 along with four other women.[23] Instead of giving financial assistance, women Friends would often help poor members find employment in Quaker households, where they would be able to maintain their faith and lifestyle.[24] Besides economic assistance, children of poor Friends were educated at one of the Friend's schools at the expense of York Monthly Meeting. York Meeting regularly sent children to Ackworth School and Rawdon School, near Leeds. The Legacy Account Fund paid the school fees for all Joseph Hardy's children to go to Ackworth and did the same for Rebecca Fothergill's daughter in 1821 and for Mary Ann Bleckley in 1827.[25]

Joining or rejoining the Society could be immediately financially beneficial. Mary Cranswick was admitted into membership in 1841 and her children were sent to Rawdon School at a cost of £6 p.a. Rachel Park, who was disowned in 1845 for marrying out, was reinstated as a widow in 1851. Within weeks of her reinstatement, one of her daughters was sent to Rawdon School at the Meeting's expense. Mary Ann Bissell, a widow with four children, was admitted into membership in 1846 and over a period of nine years all her children were educated at Rawdon School.[26]

The provision of such benefits to poorer members of the Society, although humanitarian, had potentially serious implications for those who accepted relief, since it was only available so long as members abided by the rules and regulations. The acceptance of assistance tied them to the Society and they were less able to leave – as soon as they did, or if they were disowned, their means of support disappeared. This gave the Society a strong hold over its members and it was only a minority of members who were prepared to forgo the benefits. Rebecca Fothergill had a loan for the education of her child at Ackworth School in 1821 but resigned her membership the following year, having had a change in religious belief. As a result, her children had to leave Ackworth.[27] The discipline and disownment of members also came under the jurisdiction of the Women's Meeting and all cases, as with membership applications, required visits and investigations by two male and two female Friends. Discipline cases ranged from the minor faults of falling asleep in Meeting, to incest, marriage outside the Society (which, before the recognition of purely civil ceremonies, meant by a priest), bankruptcy, adultery and various moral and actual crimes. Falling asleep in Meeting or failure to attend Meeting, unless it was persistent, was usually subject to admonition rather than disownment. In the more serious cases, disownment was often an automatic penalty.

In March 1800 Mary Armitage and Mary Awmack were appointed to visit Mary Stears because she was in debt. Despite being told on their visit in April that she had almost repaid the debt and it being recognized that she was short of money, she was disowned in July of the same year.[28] In October 1807 George Knowles, a draper, married Mary Nicholson, his housekeeper. The following March the birth of their child was brought to the notice of the Meeting and it was clear that she had been pregnant before her marriage. Although the couple were disowned in May 1808, they and their two children were readmitted into membership in 1819.[29]

For a Society which cherished its reputation – a reputation upheld by regulations – there was no alternative but to deal severely with cases which brought it into disrepute. The Society in York was comparatively lenient and, in many instances, was willing to consider applications for readmission from those it had disowned.

Women were more vulnerable to disownment than men.[30] After 1820 the percentage of women disowned from York Meeting dropped, although it remained very similar in Bristol Meeting. Marriage out was still the most usual cause of disownment in York, but in Bristol the rate of marriage out fell after 1840.[31] Many of the women who were disowned in York Meeting in each period were servants or widows.

It was lower-class women, on the margins of the Society, who were especially vulnerable to disownment. Their ability to contract suitable marriages was limited by their lack of access to the wide circle of business and familial connections that were open to middle-class women of the Meeting and by their absence from the social occasions which accompanied attendance at Quarterly and Yearly Meeting.[32] Women in lower positions were less strictly watched over than those who had the security of family around them and were more likely to be persuaded to form a friendship with a person not in the Society. And some, like Sarah Hardy, were courted by young men who attended the Meetings of the Society but were not in membership.[33]

Although marriage out accounted for a large number of disownments, in some cases the visits made by the committee would result in members reconsidering their actions. Elizabeth Fothergill was reported to be intending to marry out in December 1805 but, having visited her, the Friends of York Meeting reported that the marriage might not take place.[34] Visits were often made with the aim of persuading the member to seek help for their problem or discouraging and warning in the case of proposed irregular marriages.

The number of disownments for marrying out of the Society in York began to decline in the 1850s, as the availability of civil marriage offered an alternative to Quakers. Although the Society did not sanction civil marriage, there is evidence that members were not disowned if they could show that they would have married within the Meeting had the option been available. Jane Hood (*née* Casson), a long-time member of York Meeting, was married in a Registrar's Office in 1852. The report filed by the committee pointed out that she was attached:

> to the principles and practices of Friends and of the satisfaction it would have afforded herself and her husband, could their union have taken place in accordance with the rules of the Society ... The Committee may say in conclusion that they have felt much interested in Jane Hood's case and that after a careful review of it, they apprehend that she has strong claims upon the sympathy and kind consideration of Friends.

She was the first member of York Meeting not to be disowned for marriage outside the Society.[35] Before the rules were amended by the Society in 1860, there were three more similar cases in which the Society took a lenient attitude.[36]

Male and female servants were particularly vulnerable to charges of immoral conduct and Ann Baker, daughter-in-law of James Hessay, was disowned in April 1789 for 'several years imprudent and unguarded familiarity of conduct with her father's servant given occasion to scandalous reports, to the reproach of herself and our religious society and even after she knew such reports were spread, was not any more cautious or circumspect'.[37] Ann Penny, John Sanderson's servant, was disowned for immoral conduct with a fellow servant in 1820.[38]

Disownment from the Society, particularly for lower-class members, meant a total dislocation of social contact and often loss of employment as well as the loss of religious practice. Mary Wright Sewell of Suffolk expressed what many who had to leave the Society must have felt: 'Oh I was lonely – almost all my friends and acquaintances were Friends.'[39]

Although the Women's Meeting was not officially involved in the investigation of cases of business failure and disownment, they were deeply affected if this happened to their husbands, feeling themselves partly responsible. Mary Stears, wife of Samuel Stears, who was disowned in 1787 for insolvency, wrote to the Men's Monthly Meeting:

> Being informed that you expect some acknowledgement from me on account of my husband's failure, I am ready to acknowledge that I might have been more prudent in the management of that part of our concerns which lay more particularly under my direction and consider myself as blameable on that account.[40]

For Mary Armitage, a leading member of the Women's Meeting between 1800 and 1808, the experience was particularly painful. In a letter to the committee she suggested that it was her indulgent husband who kept her in ignorance of his situation and that she would '… most assuredly have acted in many respects very differently to what I did …'; she hoped that they would not disown her as well as her husband: 'these mournful particulars I hope will excite your pity, so far as not to add to my affliction by depriving me of the privileges I have enjoyed in the Society …'.[41]

As women became less involved in business, attitudes changed and when William Richardson, a tanner, was disowned in 1832, his wife rejected any implication that she might have been involved in his failure in business: '… I do not feel myself as a woman answerable for trans-actions in business …'. But she did express her support for him: 'yet I do feel myself implicated in the close connexion and love I hold my dear W. R. in and I believe I shall never feel differently or act differently – than as if I had been included in the decision of Friends towards him …'.[42] Although Martha Richardson's husband had been disowned, it did not mean that she had to resign her position as an overseer.

Quaker women had a specific and recognized role within their Society, but it was restricted in its actual devolution of power and in the reality of its function. Almost every activity undertaken by the Women's Meeting had to be ratified and sanctioned by the Men's, a member of which accompanied them on every visit made. Women ministers and elders had no separate Meeting in which to conduct their business. In York, although women had their own Preparative Meeting, the funds that they handled were insignificant and, despite the fact that the women contributed through their own collections to the Men's Preparative Meeting, the men did not reciprocate, keeping both collections under their jurisdiction. Women could investigate the needs of the poor but, for all but the smallest sums, had to apply to the men for permission to grant relief.[43] Certificates of Removal for women moving from one Meeting to another were prepared in the Men's Meeting, while the women had the task of making enquiries and reporting back. Visits to new members or to reinstated members were initiated by the men, who also judged the outcome before informing the women of their decisions. In many respects, the Women's Meeting lacked any real power to regulate its own affairs or to represent the needs and cares of its own members without the sanction of the Men's Meeting.

As Nancy Cott has argued, although the role of Quaker women within the Meeting might lack power, by working together they '... nourished the formation of a female community that served ... as both a resource and resort outside the family'.[44] Working in the organization helped newly arrived women to become assimilated into York's Quaker society. When Hannah Murray arrived in York in 1785 from New York, she was elected a representative at Monthly Meeting within three months of her arrival. Compared to women in Wesleyan Methodism, Primitive Methodism and the Bible Christian Connexion, where women had a limited organizational role, Quaker women had a forceful presence.[45] Although the Women's Meeting largely operated under the guidance of the Men's, the role available to the women had sufficient acknowledgement and recognition to give them a considerable degree of status, a status that was unavailable to women more generally, both within other denominations and the Established Church.

Spiritual and ministering roles

The most powerful and influential public expression of the status of women within Quakerism was derived from their role as ministers. Their ministry arose from George Fox's rejection of the Pauline argument against women preaching and the reciprocal nature of the spiritual doctrine of the Inner Light. This doctrine emphasized the spiritual relationship of women and men with God, and allowed a reinterpretation of the biblical arguments against women's preaching. Scripture was to be used as a guide and a source of illustration in argument, not as a basis for Quaker belief. Everybody, whether man, woman or child, could receive the Light. George Fox, in setting the case for women's ministry, said that they 'were Priests as much as Men', and Barclay's *Apology* pointed to the 'manifest experience' of the usefulness of women's ministry, which 'puts the thing beyond all controversie'.[46] He reinforced this, suggesting that 'seeing male and female are one in Christ Jesus and that he gives his Spirit no less to one than to the other, when God moveth by his Spirit in a woman, we judge it no ways unlawful for her to preach in the assemblies of God's people';[47] he completed his argument by pointing out that: '... the same Paul who had reproved talkative women' speaks of a woman that laboured with him in the work of the Gospel, 'and it is written that Philip had four daughters that Prophesied'.[48]

Like the Evangelicals, Quakers experienced highly emotional conversion experiences, but, unlike the Evangelicals, most of them were not moving from a totally different creed but were experiencing a stronger reinforcement and affirmation of their existing beliefs and conversion to a plainer, more dedicated type of Quakerism, which led to the conviction that they had received a direct call to do God's work. Conversion was usually experienced at an age when young men and women were particularly receptive to powerful emotions, from adolescence to their early twenties, and often followed an illness or the death of a close family member. The desire for conversion was usually expressed in terms of sinfulness, depression, morbid introspective self-examination and a heightened awareness of death, together with the prospect of entry into the next world, leading to a growing realization of a change in life's direction.

Most of the evidence for the conversion experiences of men and women Quakers has been taken from journals published posthumously.[49] These journals have inherent problems if taken as evidence, not least because they have been edited so as to produce convincing material directed at bonding the writer to the reader as well as guiding, reinforcing and introducing devout Quakerism to a pre-selected readership.[50] In the majority of cases, editors were male and may well have selected material to suit their own purposes. Consequently, the description of female conversion, in particular, may have lost something of its spontaneity in the retelling. Added to these external influences on conversion narrative are the inherent perceptions contained within the writer's own imagination of what he or she thinks conversion should be, and this also intrudes into the description – though not necessarily rendering it any the less sincere – as the writer delivers his life up '... to a pre-established sanctified model, allowing the genre, as much as anything, to communicate the meaning of life'.[51] J. J. Gurney's conversion unconsciously reflects the prevailing fear of sudden, dramatic conversion as expressed by leading Evangelicals such as Charles Simeon.[52] As Carol Edkins comments, it is noticeable that all the journals have a 'recognizable formula of religious experience' which was followed in the journals kept by Methodists, Baptists, Bible Christians and Independents.[53] The conversion experience was narrated in very similar patterns and there were really only two variations on the theme: the sudden, dramatic (road to Damascus) conversion, and the gradual, step-by-step (road to Emmaus) awakening to conversion. Edkins has identified six steps which had to be experienced in any conversion, although not all are necessarily described in every journal.[54]

A further problem with such records is that they under-represent lower-class Quakers; indeed, there is only one lower-class spiritual tract extant for York Meeting.[55] Sarah Tuke Grubb's experience displays all the features of gradual conversion. Recuperating from an illness in 1773, when she was seventeen, she wrote that she did not know where her life was to lead her and, fighting against the idea of subjecting her will to God, she was aware that '… if this be rightly performed, no mundane enjoyment would be adequate to the foretaste of that consummate felicity, which I believe is the result of so desirable a work'.[56] Two years later, still struggling with her conscience and writing about the adversities to be undertaken by believers, she admits that she does not like the 'trials and conflicts' which have to be undertaken by the faithful and hopes to find an easier solution: 'I, and such-like, instead of being benefited by these baptisms, find them unpleasing and contrary to our natural propensities; and so shun them, for a more easy way to peace.'[57] She had appeared in the ministry at the age of twenty-three, but this had not resolved her inner conflicts and she was still trying to balance her worldly life against her religious life: '… now in this time of deep poverty, the world has indeed occupied much room, and what may be called the enjoyments of it, are as clay, fettering that part appointed for immortality'.[58]

Other Quaker women experienced the sudden, dramatic type of conversion. It happened to Mary Alexander while she was lying in bed in 1789, when she '… heard a voice intelligibly say: Thou art appointed to preach the Gospel.'[59] For others, conversion entailed discarding un-Quakerly amusements, such as dancing, painting and the theatre, or adhering more strictly to Quaker manners and dress.[60] Not all the Quaker women who experienced these intense conversions were middle-class. Ann Scott, a servant in a Quaker household in York, began to attend Meeting in 1825 at the instigation of her Quaker employers. She was admitted into membership in 1830 and in her journal she describes the depth of her faith: 'O, how my soul feels to be watered when I act in obedience to the will of God.'[61] The constant conflict between the demands of the world and the demands of God made the experience of conversion a time of soul-searching as well as a time of direct experience of God.

Male Quaker experiences show many similarities to women's but tend to be expressed in a different language. There was less emotion and a generally lower level of self-abasement as they dwelt on real rather than imaginary sins. Not surprisingly, women had a noticeably higher awareness of, and fear of, death, an ever-present fear which accompanied childbirth and child-rearing.[62] Despite these differences of expression, Quaker men, like Evangelicals, displayed the two styles of conversion. John Banks of London related his experience with Pauline overtones: '... I was smitten to the ground' on the road to Meeting '... with the weight of God's judgment for sin and iniquity that fell heavy upon me ...'.[63] J. J. Gurney wrote of how he '... lay in bed one night, a light from above beamed in upon me and pointed out in a very explicit manner, the duty of submitting to decided Quakerism, more particularly to the humbling sacrifice of plainness of speech, behaviour and apparel'.[64] But, unlike Banks, he refused to emphasize the dramatic nature of his conversion, stressing instead the gradual, self-sacrificing tests of his decided Quakerism. William Savery, like Elizabeth Fry, records his abandonment of a lifestyle which included the un-Quakerly amusements of 'taverns and places of diversion' and, like all Evangelicals, castigates himself for 'mis-spending our precious time'.[65]

The conversion experiences of Quaker men and women were echoed by other denominations and described in similar language. Methodist women almost all record their decision to rid themselves of the worldly pastimes and gay clothes that went with their previous lifestyle. Some, particularly early Methodists, had dramatic conversions, while others record a growing need to dedicate themselves and their lives to the work of God. Ann Mason came from Devon and became a convinced Methodist sometime in 1814, when she and her sister Mary joined Northcott Methodist Society, giving up 'ungodliness and the ungodly as companions'.[66] Hester Ann Roe Rodgers went through a religious crisis after an illness when she was thirteen years old. She came under the influence of an Evangelical Anglican minister and slowly began to accept his views on frivolous pastimes, which she feared would 'shut God out of her life'.[67] In 1773/4 she destroyed her fine clothes and cut her hair short so that she could not style it in a fashionable manner and vowed never to dance again.[68] Despite family disapproval, she became a committed Methodist and was one of their most active preachers and band leaders.

Women of the West Country-based Bible Christian Connexion experienced similar conversions. Jane Bear Bird, a minister, began her conversion in 1819, having attended a Bible Christian Meeting at Burrington in Devon. She too stopped going to places of amusement, 'her former companions [were] given up for Gods people', and she gave up her gay clothes for those 'that which becomes women professing Godliness'.[69]

Conversion brought Quaker men and women into closer contact with God, giving them validity as ministers, but it also gave them authority and, through that, power. This was of particular importance to female ministers who, in following what they interpreted as God's will over and above all other considerations, were able to use their inner authority as a defence against the ungodly with whom they had to mix and against whom they had to justify their actions, just as their dress declared to the unconverted the type of women they were. Conversion had set them apart and above these others and they found themselves able to use their skills as ministers to influence and control non-believers. The implications for women were immense, since many of the unconverted were men; through the use of explicit signals of conversion, women not only had authority and control over their own destiny but also over that of the men and women to whom they preached. Conversion allowed them to enter a male world with a validity and equality which men could not deny.

The ministry of Quaker Women

'The Lord has marvellously raised the position of women at the end, by thus giving to the world through Her, His prophecies of things to come.'[70] By the end of the eighteenth century, the number of women ministers in York Monthly Meeting exceeded men for the first time since the 1720s. The Meeting for Ministers and Elders had degenerated between 1726 and 1768 under the stewardship of Nathaniel Bell and Daniel Peacock and had ceased to send female representatives to the Quarterly Meeting in about 1718. It was not until 1783 that women once more began to feature strongly in the Meeting of Ministers and Elders and appointments were again made to the positions of both elder and minister.[71] From 1706 to 1775, York Meeting had seven male ministers, of whom four were itinerant, and five female ministers, of whom three made more than one journey. From 1775 to 1860 there were ten male ministers, two being itinerant, and twenty-one female ministers, of whom eleven made regular journeys (see Appendix II).[72]

At the same time as the Society of Friends experienced a rise in the number of female ministers, the newly emergent Primitive Methodists and the breakaway West Country-based Bible Christian Connexion were also encouraging women itinerant preachers. But, for Wesleyan Methodist women preachers, it was a period of decline. Whilst they had been prominent in the early years of Wesleyan Methodism, by the 1820s, as membership of the denomination became increasingly middle-class, women's ministry had almost been prohibited, although they were still working as class leaders.[73]

Generally, women preachers in Wesleyanism and Primitive Methodism were as working-class as their audiences, who added their own verbal and vigorous participation to the meetings. These sects drew both ministers and supporters from amongst the labourers and poor cottagers in agricultural areas and the poor workers of the newly industrializing towns.[74] Ann Carr of Leeds was just one example of the type of woman who was able to appeal to the labouring poor, dispossessed by industrial upheaval and the failure of the Established Church to meet their needs.[75]

In contrast, Quaker women ministers were increasingly drawn from the growing numbers of middle-class merchant families and, by the last two decades of the eighteenth century, the ranting and prophecy element of the seventeenth-century ministry had given way to a seemly and quiet style of preaching.[76] The truly spontaneous, participatory style of street-corner preaching of women such as Ann Mercy Bell, who could collect large, emotional crowds to hear her in London in 1753, had given way to organized, often pre-arranged, indoor meetings, where quietness was desirable if not always obtainable.[77] Quaker Meetings were of two distinct types: firstly, those held in their own Meeting Houses for the consumption of their own members and, sometimes, a few interested followers who were non-members and conducted in the usual Quaker silent manner; and, secondly, those held in public places for a public audience.

The opportunity to minister was open to all female members, regardless of social position within their own Meeting, but by the end of the eighteenth century in York they were all drawn from the leading families of the Meeting. Having been recorded as ministers, they sat in a separate gallery, creating an invisible but symbolic barrier between themselves and the rest of the Meeting. Of the twenty women ministers in York between 1790 and 1860, all were connected to leading families within the Meeting. They included: Esther, William Tuke's wife, and his daughters Sarah, Anne and Elizabeth; Isabel Richardson, the cousin of William and Samuel Richardson; Sarah Priestman, wife of Thomas Priestman, and their daughter Ann; Ann Awmack; Ellen Abraham; Sarah Baker; Celia Wilcoxs; Deborah Backhouse; Sarah Backhouse, daughter of James Backhouse; and Sarah Rowntree, wife of Joseph Rowntree. Not all were itinerant ministers. Neither Ann Awmack, Ellen Abraham, Mary Hustler, Elizabeth Janson or Sarah Rowntree made trips outside the jurisdiction of the York Monthly Meeting.[78] Although they did not travel, they did carry out pastoral work in the city. In 1845 Celia Wilcoxs and Jemima Spence visited 281 public houses and other dealers in intoxicating drinks, distributing tracts on the evils of drink.

Public Quaker Meetings were held by itinerant ministers in all kinds of venues from town halls to barns, sometimes even in Methodist rooms and meeting-houses, indicating a degree of co-operation between the two sects. They often attracted large audiences drawn from all classes. Those attending the Meetings ranged from tin miners in Cornwall to 'some of the higher class' in Windsor.[79] The form that these Meetings took can be found in a description of a Meeting held by Mary and Elizabeth Dudley in Windsor Town Hall in December 1812, at which there were a thousand people and 'several hundreds turned away'.

Firstly, the beliefs of the Society of Friends were stated and then Mary Dudley spoke on 'the eternal, unceasing, unchanging love of God. Can there, she said ... be a heart so hard, so insensible as not to love such a Saviour? ... She then addressed the audience with much affection calling them her dear brethren and sisters ...'.[80] In 1817 the Dudleys, with Priscilla Gurney and Elizabeth Fry, preached at the Argyle Rooms, Westminster, to those 'chiefly of the description wished for, mostly titled, and some very high personages'.[81] However, not all Meetings were held in such auspicious circumstances or with such august audiences. More often they were in barns or a room at the local inn to which the people of the neighbourhood would be invited.[82] Ann Alexander held a Meeting in a barn in Daventry about which she made the comment that it was 'greatly disturbed by the number being more than could be accommodated in a barn without almost any seats except a cart in the middle which only contained our two selves who were the principal and no doubt striking objects of not less I should think than 300 spectators'.[83]

Under whatever circumstances the Meetings were held, audiences were expected to maintain a degree of decorum and in fact, if possible, silence. Preaching in Douglas, Isle of Man in 1805, Mary Alexander comments that the Meeting was large and, to begin with, noisy, suspecting that this was partly caused by the novelty of a woman preacher but that 'in a short time they became much quieter and more attentive ...'.[84]

In some respects, the style of these meetings was not exclusive to Quakerism. In Shrewsbury in June 1822, the Primitive Methodist minister Sarah Spittle 'preached three times to very large congregations' and on 1 July she spoke at a coal-pit bank 'to a large company, all in tears. It was a good time.'[85] Elizabeth Smith had to make her own decision as to whether to preach at Ramsbury, because of the possibility of a hostile audience, but she carried on and: 'The preaching had been out of doors, but a man offered her a barn; and while she was preaching, there came a number of young men with eggs, stones etc. to throw at her [but] ... as soon as they saw her, one of the ringleaders turned and said, "None of you shall touch that woman".'[86] The women ministers of the Bible Christian Connexion express similar thoughts and concerns to their Primitive Methodist sisters. Jane Bear Bird, who travelled throughout the South-West of England ministering, described her work on 8 July 1823:

Last Sunday I was at Crediton. Before Meeting, I felt much tried: it appeared to me I had told the people all I knew. I went into the Meeting House with fear and trembling and attempted to speak from Jer. IX.1, 2. I felt much for the souls of the people and could scarcely speak for weeping and Mary wept with me.[87]

In July 1825 she 'spoke at Dick in Clovelly to a very large congregation and had a truly melting season, the power of God was felt among us'.[88]

The quietness required at public Quaker Meetings was also hoped for by the itinerant preachers of these other sects, but was rarely obtained. The preaching of these women was largely inspirational, but it is probable that there was more interjection, general excitement and conversional vigour about Primitive Methodist or Bible Christian preaching than would have been the case in a public Quaker Meeting. Quakers were not actively seeking converts, but they were looking for approval and understanding of their beliefs.[89] The style of Wesleyan Methodist, Primitive Methodist and Bible Christian preaching was similar to that of the Quakers, but it lacked the seemliness and respectability of a woman Friend's ministry. At the same time, Friends had to adapt their own style to suit the nature of a non-denominational public; the long silences that were normally a feature of Quaker Meetings were dropped, and Gospel preaching was adopted to maintain the attention of a non-Quaker audience.

York Meeting had three particularly active itinerant women ministers. Esther Tuke came to York in 1765 when she was thirty-eight, was appointed a minister in 1771 and became a powerful and eloquent speaker. In 1775 she made a journey to Tadcaster, where she held a public Meeting in the Methodists' rooms 'which was attended by many of the towns people', and then went on to Bradford.[90] Three years later, in 1778, she was ministering in Durham Shields and Newcastle. But Esther's travels were minor compared with those of her stepdaughter, Sarah Tuke. Sarah was born in 1756, second child of William and Elizabeth Tuke. In 1782 she married Robert Grubb of Clonmel in Southern Ireland, who was resident in York at the time of their marriage. By then she was already known as one of the Society's most successful women preachers, a reputation which was to grow throughout her lifetime.

Sarah Tuke Grubb first stood up in the ministry in York Meeting sometime in 1778 and, as she described it to her cousin Tabbitha Hoyland, it appears to have been a profound, even frightening experience:

> After such a conflict as I have cause ever to remember I ventured onto my knees and in a manner I believe scarcely intelligible poured out a few petitions that appeared and now I feel in such a state of humiliation and fear as I never before experienced and my strength, both natural and spiritual, so low that without making stability my labour to attain, the [sic] are ready to come upon me again.[91]

In April 1780, she was given her first certificate to travel in the ministry to the Meetings of Cumberland and Westmorland with her stepmother

Esther Tuke and, later in the same year, she visited the Meetings and families in Cheshire with her cousin Tabbitha.

Throughout her life Sarah Tuke Grubb pursued her work as a minister, visiting Friends throughout England, Wales, Ireland and Scotland. In 1788 she applied to the Yearly Meeting of Ministers and Elders in London for a certificate to accompany George Dillwyn (from New Jersey), his wife and Mary Dudley of Clonmel Monthly Meeting to visit France, Holland and Germany. They held public Meetings in Rotterdam, Amsterdam, Leyden and Harlem. She records that the Meeting at Amsterdam is very small and that the Friends here are 'despised amongst the worldly minded'.[92] They travelled on through Holland and into Germany and Switzerland, covering 2,500 miles across the Continent in four months. She set out on her last European journey in June 1790, returning in October. However, her health had suffered and she died in December of the same year, aged thirty-four.

Sarah's stepsister, Anne Tuke, also became a leading minister in York Meeting. Ann was Esther and William Tuke's eldest daughter. In 1796, aged twenty-nine, she married William Alexander of Needham Market in Suffolk, with whom she had two children, one of which died aged nine. William's sister, Mary Alexander, was already a celebrated minister.[93] Ann started travelling in the ministry with her mother in 1789. In August 1793 she went to Southern Ireland for seven months and in 1794 she visited families and Meetings in London and Croydon before going on to Hampshire, Wiltshire, Devon, Cornwall and Bristol. Throughout the next few years she was almost continually on the move, often joining up with her future sister-in-law, Mary Alexander. Her two sons were born in 1799 and 1801, but these babies do not appear greatly to have curtailed her activities, for as soon as she had weaned them and before they were a year old, she was once again travelling in the ministry, leaving them to the care of her husband and their nurse. In 1803, when her youngest child was two and the eldest four, she went to America, travelling as far south as South Carolina and not returning until July 1805.[94] In 1808 the Alexanders moved back to York and between 1818 and 1841 she was given certificates to travel on fifteen separate occasions, to places as far-flung as Edinburgh and Suffolk; to Europe, including Pyrmont in Germany; and to Dublin.[95]

For these women ministers, as for those in other sects, these journeys were undertaken under the guidance of divine inspiration. Sarah Tuke Grubb wrote in her journal: 'There is still a secret belief that the growth and cultivation of my views respecting a northern journey were by that hand from which I have apprehended my most important engagements have proceeded.'[96] The inspirational nature of their work and the authority that conversion had given them cloaked them with a respectability that allowed them to undertake the public exposure necessary to stand up in front of large, mixed-sex crowds of both Friends and non-Friends and, generally, not to meet with disapproval. As with female preachers in Primitive Methodism, who faced a barrage of eggs and stones, there were undoubtedly occasions when Quaker women were not protected and there was obvious prejudice against them.[97] From comments in Sarah Tuke Grubb's journal, the reception that she and her friends had received in Germany and Switzerland was not always favourable: 'There was also in this place [Basle] and in most others where we stopped, a prejudice against women's preaching, which increased the difficulty our minds often felt in obtaining relief amongst a people of a strange language.'[98] Henry Tuke, when visiting Oban in Scotland in 1797, noted prejudice against women preachers there:

> there is such a strong prepossession in the minds of the people in this country against women's preaching it makes it additionally difficult to my dear companions, who I apprehend are the first women Friends that have travelled in these parts in this line and in most places it seems necessary to obviate this difficulty.[99]

There was only a small number of Scottish Friends, so it is likely that people in remote areas had never encountered women's preaching before.[100] Whilst both these particular examples are from outside England, there is evidence from the writings of women from other groups to suggest that women preachers of any sect were a novelty and, as such, faced the possibility of a hostile reception.

In fact, Quakers themselves only considered women's preaching to be acceptable so long as it was under divine inspiration. Elizabeth Fry felt that she could only speak when 'much covered with love and power', and J. J. Gurney could only approve of women speaking in public when 'under the immediate influences of the Holy Spirit. Then and then only, all is safe.'[101] To begin with, Wesley was very sceptical as to whether women's preaching was acceptable, and in a letter to Sarah Crosby in 1761 he accepted women preaching so long as it was done 'calmly and steadily'; but by 1771 he was writing to Sarah in a more positive manner, assuring her that he thought '… the strength of the cause rests there: on your having an extraordinary call'.[102]

Women preachers in Primitive Methodism and the Bible Christian Connexion only served for a comparatively short period of their lives and, for most of them, marriage meant that they had to give up preaching. The only circumstance in which they were allowed to carry on was if they married another preacher. And there were always a few who had to give up preaching because of ill-health.[103] Unlike these other sects, Quaker women ministers saw no reduction in their numbers in the nineteenth century. Indeed, compared with the first eighty years of the eighteenth century, the next eighty saw a growth in their numbers. For

Quaker women, marriage and ministering could be and were combined and neither wedlock nor child-rearing was an obstacle to the continuation of their work.[104] Unlike Methodism, the increasingly middle-class nature of the Society did not result in a restriction or a reduction in either the importance of their contribution or in their activities.

Quaker women ministers were powerful disseminators of their faith and beliefs to a wide and diverse audience. Their powers of persuasion and the unconscious image that they projected of women who had a role to play other than that of simply motherhood and marriage challenged the social and sexual organization of the society within which they preached and lived.[105] Although they did not directly question prevailing sex roles, their very presence – and the acceptance of it – signalled to other women what they too might achieve. It was a limited, subliminal challenge which, although potentially subversive to male authority, was only made when under the influence of divine inspiration. It was in this way that Quaker women publicly flouted existing sex roles, achieving a degree of equality which spilled over into the private sphere, removing or limiting their subservience to men.

The factor that made Quaker women different from those in other denominations was that they and Quaker men were socialized and educated to expect women to take up a position within the Society that allowed them to function with the approbation and encouragement of their fellow members, fathers, husbands, and brothers and sisters in a sphere far removed from the domestic. These expectations, which began within the home, were reinforced by the growing number of Quaker girls' schools. By the 1780s, institutions such as Esther Tuke's in York had been founded to ensure that Quaker girls received an education which, although separate and different from that of the boys, was none the less sufficiently broad to ensure that they acquired the skills which would be necessary to them as the future leaders of the Women's Meetings and as ministers.

Although their sisters in Primitive Methodism and the Bible Christian Connexion undertook similar work as well as being class leaders, they were not given an official role within the organizational structure of their sects. Quaker women were, however, and their influence extended beyond that of being a preacher to being disciplinarians, organizers, overseers of morals, charity workers, etc., giving them a separate sphere within which to operate and creating a network of self-supporting and self-fulfilling relationships. Rather than hindering the development of women's role within the Society, it is likely that the influence of Evangelicalism, which was well entrenched within the doctrine of York Quakerism by the beginning of the nineteenth century, reinforced the position of women within the organization of the Society of Friends and in their role as ministers.

CHAPTER 4

The Structure and Pattern of Family Life

The rise of Evangelicalism placed emphasis on the importance of the home as the centre of nineteenth-century family life and this, combined with the growth of identifiable middle-class values, developed an ideal of perfect womanhood. As a result, a powerful new domestic ideology was created. The work of Leonore Davidoff and Catherine Hall has shown how closely, despite differing religious and geographic backgrounds, the families of the middle classes during this period developed their own unified culture and set of values which were to give them legitimacy and a separate identity.[1] As the most Evangelical of poets, Cowper wrote: 'Domestic happiness ... [is the] only bliss of paradise that has survived the fall.'[2] An essential element of this ideology of domesticity was the gradual exclusion of middle-class women from most areas of production. Middle-class men were increasingly advised by writers such as Hannah More and Evangelical preachers like John Angell James that a married woman's place was '... in the centre of domestic cares', and that 'What is gained by her in the shop is oftentimes lost in the house, for want of the judicious superintendence of a mother and a mistress.'[3] In general, these powerful exhortations slowly led to the perception that the correct sphere for women was the home. As a result, middle-class family life became increasingly gender-differentiated, split into two distinctly separate male and female spheres – the public and the private.

But it was not only women who became more home-centred. According to Davidoff and Hall, men could not have operated in the harsh, public world of business and manufacturing without the new values attached to the family. Whereas in previous centuries the home and family had been a source of labour and production, by the beginning of the nineteenth century, as production became increasingly separated from the home, family life became a retreat from the harsh realities of the outside world and a reflection of the success of the male as provider.[4]

York was slow to industrialize and, as a consequence, slow to move away from traditional, family-run artisanal and shop-based businesses. Since Quakers were predominantly involved in these types of business, their families were late in moving towards suburban lifestyles. Not until 1847 did Joseph and Sarah Rowntree and their family cease to live over the shop.[5] But, despite these factors, by the beginning of the nineteenth century York's Quakers were becoming increasingly bourgeois and were influenced by the developing ideas of what constituted middle-class family life. However, as with the households studied by Patricia Branca and Deborah Gorham, they varied in status and in income,[6] which had implications for the lifestyle of the family. Branca has shown that, because of the differing status and employment of the head of the family, incomes could vary from as little as £100 p.a. to as much as £500 p.a. or more.[7] Women trying to run a household on £100–300 p.a. would, of necessity, have been hard-working, taking on a wide range of domestic chores with the help, in the majority of cases, of only one servant girl. In an age when housework entailed a large amount of manual labour, middle-class women were increasingly faced with conflicting ideals. On the one hand, they were expected to maintain an air of genteel woman-hood and correct social appearances, whilst, on the other, struggling to keep a home with very limited help and often increasingly large numbers of children on a restricted budget. As Deborah Gorham per-ceptively noted, the 'ideal of womanhood' was probably only realized by a very few middle-class women, and then only by those who could afford more than one servant.[8] It was the pressure of social aspiration which ensured that women were continuously juggling the family's resources to meet their social expectations. Quaker incomes in York varied widely and are very difficult to assess, but a study of Quaker wills between 1791 and 1857 has shown that, in general, York Friends were reasonably affluent, with a few very wealthy members (see Appendix III).[9]

In an attempt to make an estimate of household incomes, the employ-ment of servants has been used to determine socio-economic status.[10] An analysis for York Meeting shows that the majority of Quakers employed at least one servant and that there was a marked rise in their ability to afford a more expensive type of servant in the later period. Out of a household budget for 1791–2 which included £61 p.a. for household expenses and yearly school fees of 8 guineas, William Richardson, a tanner, was also able to afford a maid, whom he paid £8. 8s. p.a.[11] This would suggest that his income was probably at the lower end of Branca's estimate for the middle classes. On the other hand, Lindley Murray, who had retired to York in 1785 already a wealthy man, was able to employ several servants. At no time did he have fewer than two maids and sometimes he had three; he also employed a coachman and a gardener.[12] Although Samuel and Priscilla Tuke employed two maids, a nanny and an 'assistant' in 1813, they still only had the same number of servants in 1827, when she had thirteen children.[13] Since Branca has estimated that the cost of the most lowly servant maid would have been up to £14 p.a. by the middle of the nineteenth century, Lindley Murray's maids were comparatively well paid for their work. The growth in the numbers of servants, the rise in their wages, and the increasingly expensive type of servant employed over this period (several households employed a governess, which would have cost up to £45 p.a.) appear to be indicative of a rise in the standard of living experienced by York's Quakers and place the majority of them firmly within the middle-class income band.[14]

Davidoff and Hall have used evidence from Quaker families to support their discussion on the middle classes, but they have not considered the differences which might arise from Quaker doctrinal emphasis on egalitarianism and the role prescribed to women within the Meeting. These influences were of particular importance to women in their intra-marital relationships and for their expectations for independent action, and were largely created through the different socialization and education that they received. Education was particularly influential in creating differing expectations. By the late eighteenth century, educationalists and writers such as Hannah More were beginning to place emphasis on the mother as the educator and socializer of the next generation.[15] Quaker mothers were influential in teaching both their sons and daughters to adopt a specific set of aspirations for themselves. By the 1780s, many of these women were becoming increasingly concerned with the education of girls, and in 1798 Priscilla Wakefield, the Quaker writer on education, scathingly remarked that most girls were being taught inadequately, acquiring 'A smattering of the French language, and skill in the ornamental works which are in vogue ...'.[16] In York, Esther Tuke approached the subject from a different direction. She recognized the importance of not only a sound education for girls but also the fact that, as the next generation of Quaker women, they were to be leaders of what she hoped would be a revived and revitalized Society of Friends.

The establishment of Trinity Lane School in 1784 was a conscious decision to create a separate class of educated Quaker women. This school offered a higher standard of education to girls whose parents could afford the fourteen-guinea annual fee.[17] Emphasis was laid on a curriculum which prepared girls not only for their role within the domestic sphere but also for their work as members of the organization of the Society. The school reinforced the socialization that Quaker girls had received at home and helped them to develop expectations of self-fulfilment which were arguably higher than those created by traditional female education. In an age when women were increasingly being socialized to be self-denying and self-abasing, Quaker girls were educated to believe in their importance to the organization of the Society. This emphasis on self-esteem and self-worth was to create a subtle, but essentially different, attitude to women's role within the Quaker family and helped to maintain Quaker traditions as the influence of middle-class ideals began to infiltrate family life.

Quakers were inevitably responsive to the growth of an identifiable middle-class culture, including its emphasis on the centrality of the home. Like other middle-class Evangelicals, members of the Society of Friends shunned participation in the external amusements of society – or, indeed, any unnecessary contact with the contaminating outside world. This ensured that, for Quakers, the home was the dominant source of entertainment and relaxation.[18] But Quaker women were able to retain a greater hold on the public world than their middle-class sisters. They had their work in the schools and the Meeting which, unlike the philanthropic organizations, did not reduce the importance of their contribution. Quaker men, like all men, had access to the institutions which constituted the public sphere – their businesses, phil-anthropy and the work of the Meeting.

Like all middle-class males, Quaker men were the providers of the finances which established their homes. But the letters of Quaker court-ing couples in York show that, although both sexes were preoccupied with the acquisition and decoration of the future home before marriage, it was the women who ensured that the home became a sanctuary and a source of harmony and regeneration for their men.[19] Increasingly, women were seen as protecting their menfolk from the sins of the outside world, with which they had contact through the daily conduct of their businesses. It was argued by Evangelicals such as John Angell James that since women raised and nurtured children, their purity was essential, for it was they who were largely in charge of young children in their early formative years. Home was the source of a child's knowledge of God, and it was to God that parents were responsible for their children's upbringing. For Quaker women, added to this responsibility was that of ensuring that children were educated in the ways of the Society; at the same time they were also expected to ensure that men upheld the practices and functions of a good member of the Society. The Quaker home was the dominating source of the strengthening, upholding and regeneration of Quaker idealism.

At the heart of Quaker idealism was the family, within which the women played an essential part. The structures of the Meeting, the schools and the Retreat were all strongly influenced by the self-disciplining, self-regulating and caring characteristics of the Quaker family. As a result, the women's role extended beyond the realm of the private family to the public family of the Meeting, giving them a radically different set of expectations from those of other Evangelical women.[20] Although domesticity was central to the lives of most middle-class wives and mothers, Quaker women had another very clear and specific role which took them outside the home and away from the domestic sphere. By tradition and training, they were expected to be fully involved in the running of the Meeting and were responsible for the organization, education and social welfare of the women of the Meeting. For a few, the most demanding role was to be called to the ministry. The female ministers of York Meeting, eight of whom made regular journeys in the ministry during this period, often left their homes and children in the care of husbands, servants and family members for several months. These journeys, besides being a divine calling, were made with the approval and approbation of fellow members, the Meeting, husbands and the family.[21]

We find, therefore, that middle-class Quaker women were also working women, with formal and recognized functions outside the home. These accepted and sanctioned roles introduce conflicts and contradictions into a comparison with work on the middle class as a whole. This is particularly so in relation to the concept of a growing ideology of perfect womanhood and its implications for the family and the level of integration and response that it found within the Quaker middle class. For although Evangelicalism was a liberating doctrine for women of all denominations, including Quakers, in relation to philanthropy and politics, it could also have become a restricting doctrine for Quaker women.

Marriage and courtship

Quaker marriage was defined by George Fox in the seventeenth century as not simply a matter of love or lust or monetary consideration. Fox and Margaret Fell elevated it onto a spiritual plane. Proposals of marriage brought before the Meeting were greeted by a succession of inquiries into suitability, religious purity and motive and required the approval of both parents and the elders of the Meeting. To achieve a suitable state of spirituality, sexual relations between engaged couples were forbidden. If any such behaviour was discovered, couples could be summarily disowned as being unworthy representatives of the Quaker faith. Barry Levy found that, among North-West English Quakers in the seventeenth century, this spiritualization was so advanced that in some cases marriages were not consummated for several years.[22]

By the end of the eighteenth century, Quaker marriage, although retaining much of its spiritual nature, has increasingly acquired more earthly attributes. Social position and monetary considerations were becoming as important as spiritual and moral purity. For a middle-class

Quaker man, marriage was the ultimate expression of his spiritual growth, his independence and his financial success; for a woman, it meant rescue from a potentially depressing existence on the fringes of society, acting as unpaid companion, nursemaid or housekeeper to a succession of relatives.[23] Even for those who had acquired a certain independence through work in the ministry, marriage was the key to their future social and economic status, bringing added purpose and enhanced respectability to their lives as they automatically adopted the social position of their husbands. In Quaker terms, this meant their social standing within the Society of Friends, calculated according to the prestige and successes achieved by their husbands in business.

Even though marriage might be an important goal in a Quaker woman's life, the age at which this was achieved was comparatively high: the average for all Quaker women in York between 1776 and 1820 was 29.3 years. This fell slightly over the next forty-year period, to 27.4 years (Appendix IV, tables 1 and 2).[24] An analysis of non-Quaker marriages within the York parish of St Mary's, Castlegate, in which the Meeting House stood, further emphasizes the late age of Quaker marriage. From 1800 to 1830, the average marrying age for females was 25.1 years, falling to 22.8 years from 1830 to 1860.[25] Davidoff and Hall's sample for the middle class in general gives an average age of 26.5.[26] This compares with an estimated national average between 1800 and 1849 of 23.4 years. Clearly, compared with the local population and the middle class as a whole, Quaker women in York were marrying late, which had the effect of reducing potential fertility rates within the Meeting.[27] Add to this the restrictions on the choice of marriage partners, and it could also be an explanation for the overall restricted growth of the Society,[28] although it should be noted that 39% of women were married by their twenty-fifth birthday.

However, although this high average age for marriage might have dramatic effects on the reproductive capacity of the Society, it could also be seen as an indication of the lack of pressure on Quaker women to rush into wedlock, with the Society providing other outlets for their energies and talents. This attitude had particularly important implications for single women, who, rather than being limited to a domestic role, also had the activities and interest of the Meeting. Ministering women were particularly fortunate, for although they were not allowed to travel alone when unmarried, they did have this added important dimension to their lives. Marriage and ministering were never mutually exclusive: they could be, and were, combined. All Esther Tuke's journeys in the ministry were undertaken after her marriage in 1765, as were the majority of those by her daughters Ann and Sarah. Within two weeks of Sarah Tuke's and Robert Grubb's wedding in 1782, Sarah left for a religious visit to Friends in Scotland which lasted over three months.[29]

Quaker men also married late. Their average age at marriage for the period 1776–1820 was 32.6 years, and for the following forty-year period it was 31.2.[30] This compares with 27.6 years in the period 1800–30 for non-Quakers in St Mary's parish, and 25 years in the period 1830–60.[31] Davidoff and Hall's sample for the years 1780–1850 gives an average age of marriage for men of 29 years, while nationally it was 25.4 years for the period 1800–49 (Appendix IV, tables 1 and 2).[32] These figures show that Quakers in general were marrying at an older age than those either in St Mary's parish or in the Davidoff and Hall sample. This also reflects the emergence of an identifiable middle-class culture which believed that early marriage was fast becoming the height of folly and should be deferred until such time as a man was sufficiently established in business to afford a wife, a home and the children that often followed so quickly.[33]

The Society of Friends regulated marriages strictly and did not allow alliances between first cousins or between members and non-members. Members would be disowned if they married out or were married by a priest.[34] Widows and widowers had to wait one year between bereavement and remarriage, to prevent any disputes over paternity. In York Meeting there were very few second marriages in comparison with the parish of St Mary's, where 10.8% of all marriages involved a widow and 21.6% a widower (Appendix IV, table 3).[35] In the sample of Quaker marriages, only six widowers found second wives and only two widows remarried. Although the Society did not dictate any specific regulations on age differences, it is apparent from studying records from York Meeting that large age discrepancies were not encouraged and any over ten years are very rare.[36] Over the whole period, there were only two marriages with an age difference of over ten years, one being between John King and Sarah Awmack in October 1810, when she was twenty-five and he was forty-four (Appendix IV, table 5).[37]

Francis Basch has suggested that, in general, the idea of romance in marriage was not a middle-class expectation, but there is evidence that Quaker marriage did hold the hope of a certain level of love and companionship.[38] Many of the letters exchanged by the courting couples and husbands and wives of York Meeting express sincere and deep levels of affection for each other. Mary Maria Tuke wrote long impassioned letters to 'My dear Henry and most dear husband'.[39] But despite these expectations, many Quakers, including Elizabeth Fry, struggled with the conflicts between their faith and the need to do God's will and the realities of marriage and its temporal pleasures and employments.

Since Quakers did not recognize the validity of the Fall and its emphasis on females as weaker vessels, women were accorded a spiritual equality with men. Accordingly, the Quaker marriage service does not place emphasis on wedlock for the procreation of children or as a remedy against sin and plainly expresses their egalitarian ideals. Friends promised simply to 'take this my Friend [name] to be my husband/ wife, promising through divine assistance, to be unto [him/her] a loving, faithful [wife/husband], until it shall please the Lord by death to separate us'. Spiritual equality is implicit in the simplicity of the wording and in the lack of distinction between the male and female form, as it is in Fox's interpretation of the equality bestowed upon them as equal receptors of the Inner Light and the word of God.[40] Furthermore, women who were not spiritually weaker were not to be denied social equality within the marriage relationship. Jacques Tual has suggested that women's level of equality within the organization of the Society inevitably spilled over into familial structures.[41]

Nevertheless, whilst Quakers emphasized spiritual equality and found the concept of one partner being singled out to be obedient to the other quite in conflict with their beliefs, this did not alter the basic male/ female relationship: women were still expected to be submissive, an expectation which, despite the egalitarian ideals, some Quaker men continued to express. Frederick Smith's tract *On the Duty of a Wife*, written in 1810, was clear on a wife's duties. She should '... sooth him by every little kind of attention, tho' at the expense of her own natural will and inclination', and should be prepared to submit to his every whim.[42] Although many Quakers believed in a traditional marital relationship, there was also a strong streak of radicalism within the Society, and women such as Ann Knight, Elizabeth Heyrick and Priscilla Wakefield would have been unlikely to subscribe to Fredrick Smith's description of wifely duties.[43] In her tract on education, Priscilla Wakefield suggested a more liberal interpretation, pointing out that improved learning would prevent women giving men '... a servile, unqualified obedience as can only be observed by slaves'.[44] Unlike Smith, who wished to enforce the existing status quo, her impassioned plea was aimed at raising still further Quaker women's expectations within the domestic sphere. However, it was, as she acknowledged, a fact that any equality that a Quaker woman gained within marriage was still likely to be bestowed at the discretion of her husband, to be given or removed at his whim, with no recognition beyond the purely spiritual or in the eyes of the law. It was these insubstantial notions of equality which were most vulnerable when faced with the rise of a middle-class ideology incorporating the idea of perfect womanhood.

Despite the law and a somewhat whimsical type of egalitarianism, a study of the wills of Quaker men shows that their women were frequently given the responsibility of executorship; money which had formed a dowry was often returned to them under the terms of their husband's will. Nathaniel Bell, who died in 1778, left his wife's dowry of nine acres of land in trust for her during her lifetime. David Priestman died in 1851; his wife, who was an executrix of his will, had her dowry of £2,420 returned to her. More interestingly, he also left her his work premises, including the tanning yards and pits in Marygate, to enable her to carry on the business. When Lindley Murray died, his will, dated March 1826, shows that his wife Hannah was executrix of his English estate, valued at £14,000, and of his New York estate, valued at $42,000. Robert Waller, who died in 1848, left his wife some land in Holdgate and Lombard Street, London in a trust fund to be administered by her and Joseph Rowntree.[45]

The only extant document that could be described as a marriage contract was as a result of the will of Nathaniel Bell. He left instructions that his daughter Rachel's inheritance of ten acres of land should, upon her marriage, remain her own property. Thus, when Rachel Bell married Thomas Fowler, she had an instrument made previous to her marriage 'to prevent her husband having the disposal of her property'.[46]

By the end of the eighteenth century, as they became increasingly prosperous and worldly, Quaker marriages were very similar in many respects to those of other middle-class groups. As Davidoff and Hall noted, marriage was not a 'free choice' but a result of family and business considerations.[47] As Quakers became affected by middle-class beliefs, their alliances were increasingly contrived for the mutual benefit of the two families.[48] Although they stressed the need for love, if not physical attraction, as the basis for marriage, the emphasis in the case of second marriages, such as that between William Tuke and Esther Maud, was more likely to be on mutual support, as she indicated when she wrote to him in 1764 suggesting that she be a '… true helpmeet, as willing to bear a share with thee in suffering, as in rejoicing and that [we] might harmoniously labour, for one anothers [sic] growth'.[49]

Although '… finances were in theory of secondary importance, [in the arrangement of Quaker marriages] they were in fact frequently a prime consideration', particularly when linked to social status.[50] The emphasis on carefully arranged dowries and land settlements indicates the importance of considerations of the financial side of marriage. And this equality of social and financial standing was reinforced when the expression 'equally yoked' was devised to explain this concept of marriage. This meant that even unions between lower middle-class members display the same care in the choice of suitable partners as do those of their social superiors. John Briggs married Caroline Jackson in 1840; her father was a butcher and John Briggs and his father were grocers. Jane Ventress, whose father had been a gardener, married John Johnson, a cabinet-maker, the son of an innkeeper. John Richardson married Hannah Procter; both their fathers were yeoman farmers with adjoining lands. Amongst the upper middle-class members of the Meeting, the emphasis on suitable economic and social marriages was even stronger.

Henry Tuke married Mary Maria Scott, whose father, a banker, had died, leaving her and her sister a considerable fortune which was no doubt of use in building up the Tuke tea and coffee business. Elizabeth Tuke, whose father Samuel had married a banker's daughter, married George Gibson of Saffron Walden, who, like his father, was also a banker.[51] All these families, regardless of social background, were not only opting for partners who were equally yoked, but were also choosing to make alliances which reinforced relationships of mutual business and economic benefit. Although the close-knit social organization of the Society encouraged and helped in the establishment of suitable friendships and in the development and cementing of inter-familial relationships, the late age of marriage of some of the members also indicates how difficult it was to find partners who were suitable in a small Society.

Naturally, many Quaker courtships had their roots in family acquaintanceship, the inter-connecting web of relationships within the Society and the apprenticeships which founded many Quaker businessmen's careers. By the 1820s the Society of Friends was beginning to reflect the changes in social and financial status of its membership which had begun in the last decades of the eighteenth century. The marriages of many Quakers in York, including those of Elizabeth Tuke with George Gibson and Samuel Tuke with Priscilla Hack, were increasingly typical of the majority of middle-class Friends, coming from old, long-standing Quaker families and representative of the growing number of enriched merchants and bankers within the Society. Strictly, Quakers expected that parental approval should be obtained before any courting was begun. However, it appears that the couple had usually agreed in principle to develop a relationship before the formal, parental approaches were made. Samuel Tuke asked James Hack for permission to court Priscilla, but only told his parents that he had proposed to her after the event.[52] There was evident parental approval and pleasure in a good match and, as the daughter of a wealthy and influential banker, Priscilla was an eminently suitable wife for an increasingly prosperous tea merchant. Samuel Tuke received a letter from his father expressing his pleasure in the engagement and feigned surprise: '... as the subject was not quite new to us, we are the more prepared to say, that thy prospects and attachment toward Priscilla Hack meet with our hearty concurrence. From what I know and from what we have heard, of the young woman, we cannot but approve of thy choice ...'.[53]

Once agreement to courtship had been given, parents were extremely unlikely to withhold their approval of the marriage; nor would they wish to do so, for courtship implied a period when a couple could get to know each other better, and a time during which a certain level of physical intimacy was expected. This growth in confidence and intimacy was evident between Samuel and Priscilla, as he wrote of the time when he would be able to 'clasp thee, my dear, once and forever in my arms'.[54] They became less formal in their terms of address; he created a pet name for her, 'Celia', and she wrote to him as 'My dear Friend' rather than the more formal 'dear Friend Samuel Tuke'.[55] In general, Quaker engagements were not long. Samuel and Priscilla were engaged for just over a year before marriage, having met when she attended the Quaker girls' school in York; their friendship developed when Samuel made frequent visits to the Hacks' family home in Chichester, after business trips to London. The marriage of Samuel's parents, Mary Maria Scott and Henry Tuke, was approved by their respective parents in 1780, when Barbara Scott met with William and Esther Tuke, writing to her daughter that she was '… as easy and composed as their request [for Maria to marry Henry] could admit … [it was] their great love to you My Dear that gave me more resolution … I hope his love [Henry's] is as sincere as I believe his excellent father's is …'.[56]

Friends and family were often essential go-betweens for courting couples and were of particular value when relationships were faltering or experiencing difficulties. The courtship of Esther Tuke relied heavily on the helpful friendship of Martha Smith. Esther was the eldest daughter of Maria and Henry Tuke and had a long-standing friendship with Thomas Priestman, a yeoman farmer from Hull. Their courtship was a long and difficult one, not least because there was general family disapproval; Priscilla Tuke's mother in particular felt that he was not good enough for Esther, making the acerbic comment to her daughter that 'Esther is of more importance as Esther Tuke than she would be as Thomas Priestman's wife.'[57] After five years, in 1818, Esther's friend Martha Smith had to act as an intermediary between the couple and they were finally married in 1819, when she was thirty-seven, after a courtship lasting six years.

By the 1850s the Society's marriage rules were beginning to be relaxed in York, with the introduction of civil ceremonies, and several members of York Meeting were not disowned for being married in a Registrar's Office. However, marriage by a priest could still result in disownment.[58] Despite this relaxation of the rules, Quakers still considered religious differences, the beliefs of the Society of Friends and the threat of disownment and dishonour to be important reasons for refusing a marriage proposal. Sarah Richardson, daughter of William and Martha Richardson of York, was courted by an Anglican clergyman, Robert Coates, from Northampton. He proposed sometime in September 1850 but, despite several long letters from him, she refused his proposal in October, saying that she could not go against the Society and the beliefs it upheld and she felt, particularly in view of his position, that they would have '… too important a difference of religious feeling to find happiness'.[59]

Parents and children

Children appeared within the first two years of most Quaker marriages and often within the first fifteen months. Generally, there is little evidence to suggest that Quaker women either used or had any knowledge of the rudimentary types of artificial birth-control available, but it is interesting to note that the pregnancies of the wife of Caleb Williams, a surgeon in general practice at the Retreat and eventually for the York Penitentiary, were well spaced. Her babies were born with a six- and a four-year gap.[60] However, for most women, babies arrived more frequently. Quaker births studied in York show that, like so many of their counterparts, women Friends spent most of their fertile years involved in pregnancy, giving birth and nursing babies (Appendix V, tables 1 and 2).[61]

Mary Maria and Henry Tuke had six children in as many years; three were to die as infants. Their son Samuel and his wife Priscilla had thirteen children (one set of twins), born within a period of sixteen years, and Sarah and Joseph Rowntree had five, four of them in six years. Generally, these were healthy, active women, who enjoyed walking, riding and even swimming.[62] Whilst they occasionally suffered, particularly in the case of Maria Tuke, from a variety of unnamed illnesses, there were only a few known deaths in childbirth or as a result of childbirth and generally they appear to have had little trouble in pregnancy.[63] There is no direct evidence to suggest that their physical relationships with their husbands were not pleasurable and, judging by the regularity of new babies and the love expressed for each other in their letters, there is no reason to suppose that Quaker women did not enjoy their sexual relationships or that they were sexually repressed.[64]

Although Quaker mothers had responsibilities which took them out of the home, they were still relied upon to provide emotional and caring support. The middle classes scorned the aristocratic habit of handing children over to nursemaids and believed that domestic life should be centred around mothers. Priscilla Wakefield wrote one of the many pamphlets advising women that they, not servants, should be the ones to care for their children, or they risked '… the destruction, or at least the diminution, of that sympathy between the mother and the child'.[65] Nevertheless, some York Quaker women did employ nursemaids and nannies, but none of them was wealthy enough to have sufficient domestic help to remove herself entirely from the chores of childcare.

The development of full-time motherhood for women was slow to materialize and, early in the period, was only available to those whose time was not required in the family business. For many such as Sarah Rowntree, who in the first years of her marriage lived over the shop, where she gave birth to five children, infant care had to be conducted in between serving customers and preparing meals for the apprentices and family.[66]

Breast-feeding, which appears to have been a Quaker norm, reinforced a mother's relationship with her child. Several of York's Quaker mothers breast-fed their infants, including Maria Tuke, her daughter-in-law Priscilla Tuke, Caroline Briggs and Sarah Rowntree. The correspondence between Maria and Priscilla Tuke would indicate that they both weaned their babies at six months.[67] Weaning was completed by removing the child from the mother for several days and placing it in the care of a servant. Maria Tuke's description of the weaning process would suggest that both baby and mother suffered from the deprivation:

> Mary [Weatherald – servant] weans him [William] ... This is the 6th day he has been deprived of it – we thought he had forgot the breast – and as he evidenced a strong remembrance of me by many little actions – I thought I might comfort him with a sight of me, which he seemed to long for – therefore had him brought to me, I can't express his joy – first looking at me then hiding his face in my breast by way of embrace and congratulation, for sometime – at last he recalled his former enjoyment – and requested it in a language so helpless, so importunate that it was hard refusing him – but as it was better so to do – sent him from me – I hear him now very uneasy cannot be pacified for long, ever since we parted this day – which is many hours since.[68]

With weaning, any natural contraceptive effect of breast-feeding came to an end; by plotting the intervals between weaning and births and between births and deaths of infants, it might be possible to see whether it was at all effective. Assuming that weaning took place at six months, it is possible to recognize a pattern for births. Mary Maria Tuke had six pregnancies; after the death of her baby Henry at six months, she gave birth to Henry II within a year, the contraceptive effect ceasing upon the death; her daughter Esther was born fourteen months later. Priscilla Tuke was pregnant twelve times in sixteen years; on two occasions, she was pregnant for three years in succession. Caroline Briggs, who gave birth to twelve children over a period of eighteen years, also breast-fed; she gave birth to her fourth child nine months after her third had died at nine weeks. If babies were breast-fed for six months, breast-feeding as a form of contraception would appear to have been very unreliable, since many of these pregnancies began within this period. There is no clear evidence that wet-nurses were ever used, but it does seem likely that some mothers may have employed them.[69]

Children played an important role in Quaker households and reinforced the centrality of the home and the family in their lives. Quaker parents were heavily involved within these large families. For mothers whose children's ages could span a generation, there was a huge variety of continuous worries and concerns associated with motherhood, ranging from the feeding of babies, the education of older children and the search for apprenticeships, and often, for the eldest child, the arrangement of a marriage. Esther Tuke's youngest daughter was only thirteen when her first step-grandchild was born in 1784. All these concerns came on top of late pregnancies, which were often accompanied by declining health. It was not unknown for mothers to be grandmothers to babies the same age as their own.

Full-time motherhood became an essential feature of middle-class notions of gentility and this, combined with the low level of domestic help, ensured that Quaker children spent a lot of time with their parents, building up strong ties of mutual affection and respect. Maria Tuke wrote to her mother in 1787, when her eldest daughter, Esther, was five:

> ... thou canst think how little trouble she is, her disposition is very sweet – and never needs reproof, instruction is sufficient, indeed I often think when I look back to the trouble I have seen many parents have, that I hardly know what it is to be a mother, for my little creatures are miserable if they think they shall displease me.[70]

This close contact with their children meant that Quaker parents developed a good relationship with them. Both Henry and Maria Tuke and William Richardson wrote long letters full of advice and affection to their children when they were away at school, and Joseph Rowntree took his sons on regular trips in the school holidays.[71] As Davidoff and Hall point out, relationships between fathers and daughters could be particularly intense and Maria Tuke writes of this closeness with regard to her daughter Esther and her husband: 'Thou knowest a man and wife have two heads and two hearts, so much more a man and his daughter and do not let the above hint exclude free communications ...'.[72]

Although fathers were not generally involved in daily childcare, they were often left in charge of very small children, albeit usually with the help of a nursemaid and various female relatives. This was particularly true in the case of the families of female ministers. For a select few, this was the only legitimate escape from household pressures and the continual round of pregnancies and childbirth.[73] In the 1770s, Esther Tuke travelled all over the British Isles, leaving her two young daughters to her husband's care. Her daughter, Ann Alexander, also travelled extensively throughout Britain and Europe in the ministry, and she left her small sons, aged two and four, in her husband's care for over two years in the early 1800s while she was away preaching in America.[74]

Quaker women often made pastoral journeys to families within the Meeting, which included visits to Tadcaster, Selby and Thirsk, and two representatives from each Meeting were elected to make annual trips to London for the Yearly Meeting. When Sarah Rowntree left her one-year-old son with his father whilst she attended Yearly Meeting in 1835, Joseph wrote to her that 'he is pretty good [but] ... his greatest joy is to get into the yard or shop. The nursery is out of favour. It is too quiet.'[75] Priscilla Tuke often left her increasingly large family with Samuel while she visited her parents in Chichester. These absences ensured that fathers were not remote disciplinarians, but active, caring partners and companions for their sons and daughters, playing games with them and teaching them. The young Joseph Rowntree remembered his father as 'a comforting presence'.[76] However, this freedom to travel was available only to middle-class Quakers, those who had servants to help with childcare, and it is noticeable that few of the poorer members of the Women's Meeting were able either to attend Yearly Meeting or become ministers.

In a period of high infant mortality, it was inevitable that many Quaker children died. Three of Maria and Henry Tuke's children died as infants, and of Caroline and John Briggs' twelve children, seven died as infants. For both Quakers and Evangelicals, the greatest fear of children dying came from their unconverted state. Dire warnings from such sources as the *Methodist Magazine*, that unconverted children could not '... enter the Kingdom of Heaven', resulted in anxious parents seeking reassurance from dying children that they show some sign of response to religious exhortations.[77] Maria Tuke described the state of her nine-year-old son's mind on his death-bed as: '... constantly in a state of gravity and recollection and I have no doubt was preparing for a state of purity ...'.[78] The death of a child was often accompanied by expressions of guilt and pain and was even considered to be punishment for a mother's sins. Faith Gray, the Evangelical Anglican, wrote in her diary after the death of her eleven-month-old daughter: 'Lord grant that I may accept the punishment and see and submit to thy righteous hand in it', and when her son died fourteen months later, she believed it to be God's punishment for the '... great grief for the loss of my dear Frances'.[79]

Despite the frequency, and even the expectation, of losing children, their illness and death were devastating events for both parents. Four weeks after the death of her son in 1799, Maria Tuke could still not write in detail to her sister about it: 'I find it is yet a subject I cannot fully enter upon so must cease for present to describe the most affecting scene I ever was witness to ...'.[80] And it was not only Maria who cared for her son, but also his father Henry Tuke, who shared the nursing and bedside vigils, praying for and comforting his child.[81]

Conclusion

The increasing influence of Evangelicalism and the rise of a distinctive middle-class culture which embodied specific ideas about social behaviour throughout the early decades of the nineteenth century could have had wide-reaching implications for traditional Quaker lifestyles, in particular for the role of women. But, in spite of these influences, many aspects of Quaker family life and rituals, including marriage, still retained the sect's original ideas and traditions. A spiritual egalitarianism was particularly evident in Quaker marriages, and in part these traditions were protected by a social conditioning which, whilst allowing the existence of some Evangelical writers such as Hannah More and Cowper, did not include the reading of novels or attending plays. This, combined with a highly developed sense of individuality and adherence to the Faith, was influential in the retention of many of the traditional Quaker views of a woman's role. Nevertheless, Evangelicalism was beginning to infiltrate Quaker family life and, furthermore, Friends were not immune to the general changes taking place in middle-class culture. The growth of the belief in the public expression of family religion, and its perceived ability to raise the social and moral nature of women, was evident in the homes of Samuel and Priscilla Tuke, Sarah and Joseph Rowntree, J. J. Gurney and Elizabeth Fry. The development of the middle-class ideal of domesticity and rising incomes, along with the transformation of domestic production, had slowly forced Quaker women out of the workplace as they acquired suburban homes. These forces could have required Friends to reinterpret the role of women within the Society and threatened older Quaker traditions which had given women a role outside the home.

However, if Evangelicalism was responsible for restricting women's role, it also did much to expand their opportunities. Evangelical emphasis on the battle against sin and its ascription to women of the qualities of purity, selflessness and nurturing led to the perception that they were the natural purifiers of a sinful world. These perceptions offered women the opportunity to take part in the numerous philanthropic and social enterprises which were founded towards the end of the eighteenth century. In the same way, Evangelicalism offered women in other sects and denominations the chance to perform within the structure of the chapel, although there was nothing to equal the opportunities available within Quakerism.

In order to retain their traditional roles, Quaker women had to find a route through these conflicting ideologies. This was particularly well achieved by ministers, who could reinforce their independence by referring to the spiritual nature of their work. But because of the strong traditions and collective belief in women's inherited role within the organization of the Society, even ordinary Quaker women were able to maintain their non-domestic role. They never lost their responsibilities within the organization and retained the freedom to partake in Meeting, ministering if they felt moved to do so. The influence of Evangelicalism also reinforced and added to Quaker women's independence by expanding their sphere of operation to include philanthropic works. One result of this expansion was that Quaker women were able to encourage and help their menfolk to develop in their political, social and philanthropic endeavours, socializing them to believe in their role as good and godly humanitarians. Quakerism had succeeded in adapting rather than adopting the Evangelical ideology of perfect womanhood by assimilating only what was acceptable and appropriate and rejecting that which either conflicted with its own inherited ideals or restricted the role of its women.

CHAPTER 5

Quakerism and
Philanthropy in York

The aim of this chapter is not to catalogue all the social and philanthropic activities of York Quakers, although they will be used to illustrate
the range and diversity of their interests and the level of integration with
both Evangelical Anglicans and other denominations (see Appendix VI).
Because of the diverse nature of Quaker philanthropic work, the chapter
will be divided into two sections. In the first, I will show how existing
Quaker humanitarianism, when overlaid with the growing influence
of the doctrine of Evangelicalism and a rising socio-economic status,
drew Quakers into social work, and how Evangelicalism influenced
their choice of activities and moulded their attitude to those they were
helping. In the second, I will concentrate on their contribution to non-
denominational education in York. A considerable amount of work has
already been done by historians on several of the city's philanthropic
enterprises and discussion of these will therefore be touched upon only
in so far as they are of interest to this book.[1]

The espousal of Evangelical doctrine by York Quakers acted as a
catalyst, drawing them into humanitarian and philanthropic activities
and, as David Swift has suggested, '… into organisational and personal
association with many non-Friends'.[2] The fact that there was '… a clear
nexus between philanthropy and evangelicalism', as Elizabeth Isichei has
noted, has been discussed by many historians, but the influence of Evangelicalism on Quaker philanthropy has been subjected to less attention.[3]

The establishment of the Retreat in 1797, as a result of the suspected
ill-treatment of a Quaker girl in York Lunatic Asylum, acted as a public
demonstration of Quaker humanitarianism and can be used to pin-point
the beginning of Evangelical influence over their actions.[4] It also signalled a willingness to experiment with unorthodox and untried forms
of treatment. No longer could Quakers take a back seat in philanthropic
endeavour. They had effectively signalled to the rest of York's socially
aware élite that they too were available for service in the growing
number of societies and organizations concerned with the care and
treatment of the less fortunate and with their religious and moral
welfare. Quakers such as William Tuke, the founder of the Retreat,

found themselves in demand to join and add weight to a variety of medical and social endeavours.

A vital part of Evangelical doctrine was directed towards sinners and the biblical injunction that 'All have sinned and fall short of the glory of God.'[5] Evangelical leaders such as Wilberforce thought that they recognized an innate sinfulness in man which led him to be '... an apostate creature, fallen from his high origin, degraded in his nature and depraved in his faculties, indisposed to good and disposed to evil ... that he is tainted with sin, not slightly and superficially, but radically and to the very core'.[6] It was this emphasis on the basic sinfulness of man which, combined with the doctrine of the Atonement, was to become a powerful mix, dictating that the rescue of man should be a priority for the Evangelical. Man was '... created in Christ Jesus to do good works' and God had created the subjects for the good works '... in advance for us to do'.[7] Therefore, the true Evangelical was told that caring had to become a feature of his lifestyle. Leading Evangelicals believed that life should be a striving to do all things '... for the glory of God',[8] and this became the motivation behind their philanthropic philosophy. But, besides the perceived sanctifying benefit that good works gave to the worker, Evangelicals also emphasized the absolute necessity of bringing the cared-for to a knowledge of God through Christ crucified. Wesley had urged his followers that, by assisting the poor, they might '... inherit the ever lasting Kingdom'.[9] It was the emphasis on the rescue of the human soul from its innate sinfulness – particularly by those who, by definition, believed that they had reached a state of grace – which gave Evangelicalism its other, less caring dimension: an overtone of condemnation. Thus it became an essential feature of Evangelical philanthropy to reach as many souls as possible and to strive to show them the way to personal salvation through the redemption of their sins.[10]

Much of the Evangelical philosophy for everyday life had a ready response within the Society. The absolute necessity for a daily observance of an individual's Quakerism was reflected by Evangelicals, whose duty it was to demonstrate their Evangelicalism through hard work and clean living. Like Quakers, Evangelicals had to fill with great diligence the hours which God, in his infinite mercy, had given them, so that, on the dreadful Day of Reckoning, they could face their Maker with a clear conscience that they had not wasted God's given time.[11] And because this life was merely an anti-chamber to the next, Evangelical Quakers such as J. J. Gurney endeavoured to use their time to best advantage and to God's approved formula, so that they might gain entrance to the next world.[12] But it was not only time that Evangelicals and Quakers considered God to have entreated them to use with good purpose.

It has been suggested that Quakers became involved in philanthropy as a sop to their consciences and as a 'psychological assuaging of guilt' as they observed the gulf between rich and poor.[13] This suggestion relies for its validity on a sense of guilt; guilt brought about by the acquisition of wealth. It seems improbable that either Quakers or Evangelicals would have perceived the making of money as wrong in itself. It was a duty: a duty in the first instance to provide for a family; in the second to God; and in the third to relieve the suffering of the less fortunate. Wealth, as Joseph Sturge wrote, brought a responsibility to those who had it and, in his eyes, it should not be accumulated on the pretext of providing for the future comfort of children or relatives, since that '... is not a justification in the sight of God for the *present* neglect of anything that duty appears to require'.[14] What was to be accompanied by guilt was the accumulation of wealth for its own sake, in excess of an individual's immediate needs.

York's Evangelical Quakers shared many of the common mores of their fellow Anglican Evangelicals. Humanitarianism was at the centre of their concern for the suffering that they saw around them.[15] Stephen Grellet, the nineteenth-century American Quaker, wrote: 'I shall pass through this world but once. Any good thing, therefore, that I can do or any kindness that I can show any human being, let me do it now. Let me not defer nor neglect it, for I shall not pass this way again', a precept underlying most Quaker philanthropy. But their response, like that of Evangelical Anglicans, was emotional rather than ideological, and it would not occur to a nineteenth-century Quaker that the social order was responsible for the human suffering that they observed; they could only treat the disease, not the cause of the disease, and dispense charity with a strong dose of faith in God.[16] But there were some differences of emphasis in Quaker attitudes, particularly in relation to the war on vice. Quakers, unlike other Evangelicals, did not limit their criticisms to the leisure activities of the poor. They also castigated the rich for their love of vain sports such as fox-hunting and shooting.[17]

Evangelical Quaker social work fell into two distinct categories: organizations which were founded to correct the morals and lifestyle of society, both rich and poor, and to protect the good and godly; and those founded to help, in the broadest sense, the poor. There were few charitable organizations between 1780 and 1850 which did not involve Quakers and Evangelical Anglicans working together.[18] During the 1780s the latter became a dominant force within York philanthropy and several enterprises were taken over and run by these industrious Evangelicals, amongst whom women were particularly prominent. These included the Blue Coat and Grey Coat Schools, the Dispensary and the Female Friendly Society.[19]

Evangelicalism was a religion of duty and it has been argued that philanthropic work appealed particularly to women because it provided a service and became an extension of their domestic duties – caring for the sick, the nurturing of children, etc. Organizations such as the Society for the Prevention of Vice therefore found a ready echo in their hearts.[20] The demands of philanthropic work gave women an outlet beyond the confines of the home, but it was one that could be sanctioned by men such as John Angell James because it embodied the same type of caring, nurturing work that they undertook within the confines of the home.[21] For Quaker women, who already had a wider sphere of operation than their Evangelical sisters, philanthropy brought an added dimension to their lives. Often excluded by beliefs and manners from many areas of social activity, it formed an important opportunity to expand their experiences, and their journals give the reader a profound sense of the importance of this aspect of their lives.[22] However, the range of activities was nevertheless limited to those that were considered suitable. Catherine Cappe (the wife of the Unitarian minister in York) and Elizabeth Fry both accepted that different spheres of operation existed for men and women and that this limited them to work with their own sex.[23]

In York, women's involvement in philanthropic work until the early nineteenth century was left to the Evangelical coterie which surrounded Faith Gray (wife of William Gray, a prominent York Evangelical Anglican) and Catherine Cappe; Quaker women were not prominent until the foundation of the British School in 1812, an exclusively Quaker concern. But although they were not active in early philanthropic concerns in the city, they did advise and encourage the activities of their men. It was not until the foundation of the York Society for the Encouragement of Faithful Female Servants in 1820 and the formation of a ladies' committee which included several Quakers that they stepped outside the sphere of the activities of their own Meeting.[24] This more public activity came about forty years later than that of the Evangelical Anglican women. It is probable that the considerable opportunities for them to work within the organization of the Society, especially the Quaker schools, delayed their participation. Also, their behavioural beliefs may have excluded them from the drawing-rooms of Faith Gray and her friends. Quaker women's participation in philanthropy developed from their own interest in education and from the influence of their men's increasing involvement in philanthropic work.

The York Dispensary was a joint Quaker–Evangelical Anglican venture. Founded at the instigation of Dr Thomas Withers in 1788, it also drew on the support of the leading medical Quakers William Tuke and Dr John Fothergill as well as a broad selection of men and women from other denominations, including the Evangelical Anglican minister, William Richardson, the wife of the Unitarian minister, Catherine Cappe, Oswald Allen, a Methodist chemist, and the city recorder, Peter Johnson. By 1802 William Tuke had become a director, and by 1808 support had expanded to include fifteen Quakers as well as the Unitarian minister, Charles Wellbeloved, and both William and Jonathan Gray (Evangelical Anglicans).[25] The strength of Quaker support in financial terms was demonstrated when twelve of them, including Joseph Awmack, David Doeg, Lindley Murray, John Mason, David Priestman, Samuel Richardson, William Richardson, Henry Tuke, and John Tuke, gave large donations and legacies of between £10. 10s. and £21.[26]

The increased level of Quaker participation in these organizations is indicative of the integration and support which York's Quakers were beginning to give to philanthropic enterprises in the city. As leaders of the Evangelical movement within York Quakerism, both Lindley Murray and Henry Tuke were supporters of these and other Evangelical charities.[27] As early recruits to the work of the Clapham-based Evangelicals, including the anti-slavery campaign, York's Quakers were drawn into their other endeavours as they expanded, and helped to develop local offshoots of the national organizations which they had founded. The Clapham Sect's influence over the type and direction of Evangelical philanthropy which had begun with the Anti-Slavery Society was successful in recruiting supporters from all denominations from far and wide.[28]

However, the work of William Wilberforce and the Evangelicals was not limited to the abolition of slavery. Its members were also dedicated to a reordering of the moral behaviour of society, which they saw as a necessary defence against the dangerous influence of the radicalism of the French Revolution and its sympathizers. In pursuit of these ends, their war against vice was as relentless as their war against slavery. The powers of persuasion available to the 'Saints' had been amply demonstrated in 1787, when they persuaded George III to issue a proclamation against vice, acquiring a royal seal of approval on their actions. The Society for the Suppression of Vice quickly established many local counterparts. In York, the Society for the Prevention and Discouragement of Vice and Profaneness (SPDVP) was established in February 1808. Echoing its national counterpart, its stated aim was to stamp out lewdness, drunkenness, profane swearing and Sabbath-breaking. Its first committee was a true mix of representatives from various denominations and included William Gray, Jonathan Gray, Edward Prest, the Revd William Richardson (Evangelical Anglicans); the Revd Charles Wellbeloved (Unitarian minister); and the Quakers William and Henry Tuke.[29] Sabbath-breaking was one of the prime targets of the organization and the First Annual Report of 1809 reported that barbers, hairdressers, some small shopkeepers and ale-house keepers were particularly guilty of this crime. Aware of the lack of local support for its activities, particularly from those whose livelihood was threatened, the SPDVP was sufficiently concerned to moderate its demands, directing that shops need only be shut by 10 a.m. on Sunday morning, the time that Divine Service commenced.[30]

By 1809, the SPDVP had become mainly concerned with the campaign against prostitution, reporting, to its obvious horror, that 'The lamented prevalence of this vice amongst us in its various modifications ... has been found on nearer enquiry to extend itself through the different orders of society to a degree and in instances which would scarcely have been credited.'[31] The diligence with which the SPDVP pursued brothel-keepers and prostitutes, albeit with limited success, was influenced by the fact that several of the committee members had their homes and businesses in Castlegate, where the Quakers also had their Meeting House.[32] This street was adjacent to the Water Lanes and Friargate, one of the main areas frequented by prostitutes and the site of many brothels. In an attempt to control the flow of lawless people, including prosti-tutes, into the city, a Vagrancy Office was founded in 1822 under the chairmanship of the Quaker Samuel Tuke.[33] The problem of prostitu-tion in the city had become so great by the 1820s that a Penitentiary Society was established in 1822. In the first instance it was known as the York Female Penitentiary Society, but it changed its name in 1842 to the York Penitentiary Society.[34] Its formation had evolved out of the work of the SPDVP and the realization that prostitution was not to be cured by policing, but by rescuing the girls and attempting to help them regain their respectability, training them to become useful citizens.[35] In 1844 it purchased a house but, because the Penitentiary Society could not force girls to enter this refuge, its work always had a limited effect. The only realistic hope that the committee could have had was that it might contribute to a decrease in the number of prostitutes. From the outset, it was a combined Quaker and Evangelical Anglican organiza-tion, dominated by the Evangelical belief in an ability to convert sinners by convincing them of their desire to return to the path of virtue and redemption. Led by its president, the Evangelical Anglican William Gray, and with a committee which included his son Jonathan and the Quaker Samuel Tuke, it also attracted the subscriptions of many other Quakers, including William Alexander, Benjamin Horner, Lindley Murray, John Tuke, Hannah Mennell and Ann Alexander.[36] In 1846 a Quaker doctor, Caleb Williams, was appointed surgeon to the Refuge, and in 1845 a ladies' committee was established which was dominated by Quakers, including Sarah Rowntree, Jemima Spence, Maria Tuke, and Elizabeth and Sarah Backhouse.

Frances Finnegan has argued that, under combined Evangelical Anglican and Quaker rule, the Penitentiary Society had a less condem-natory tone to its proceedings than it did later in the nineteenth century, when the committees came under the influence of Anglicans.[37] This was a matter of degree, however, for, from the outset, the reports were not lacking in censure, the first commenting that prostitutes were '... prowl-ing the streets for their prey'.[38] All rescue work was dominated by an expectation of contrition; when the Refuge was first opened, it aimed to provide '... a place of permanent refuge for such miserable young females as may seem in the spirit of true penitence ...'.[39] This emphasis on penitence and repentance was as much a feature of the York Penitentiary Society when there was a strong Quaker presence as it was later. Evangelicalism demanded an expression of true repentance from sinners and it was inevitable that many of the women seeking admission were insensible to notions of guilt, so the quality of remorse displayed was often questionable. The middle-class composition of the committee, with its religious and moral overtones, meant that it was often unreceptive to the illiterate and superficial expressions of contrition that were offered and, not surprisingly, there were many instances when the committee expressed disbelief at the level of repentance. When two girls were admitted in 1855, it reported that '... they each expressed their desire to be admitted but no distinct expression of penitence was elicited'.[40] Girls often escaped from the Refuge and, when they were brought back, confessions of guilt were extracted.[41]

An Evangelical emphasis on a fear of God was an essential part of the reformation process and was instilled through a continual stress on a true sense of personal sin. This was often imposed upon the girls, as, for instance, in May 1856, when two girls were sent to the workhouse '... as a test of their desire to turn from sin'.[42] Such tests were reinforced with a harsh discipline, effective incarceration and detention, and a limited, poor-quality and often inappropriate training. The Evangelicals and Quakers on the committee had a shared expectation and philosophy with regard to their role as rescuers and, although the Refuge's regime was harsh and condemnatory, it represented current notions of humanitarianism. These intensely religious people, with a heightened sense of their own sinfulness and salvation, believed that they were doing God's work by reforming sinners and saving souls. The chance to save just one soul was sufficient encouragement to further striving; added to which, the possibility of heavenly rewards for earthly duty and the opportunity to protect themselves and their families from a perceived vicious, criminal element created a powerful set of incentives to become involved in such unrewarding work.

By the 1830s, the crusade against vice was also encompassing a crusade against drink. Drink, it was acknowledged, was the source of much violence, poverty and disease and led to prostitution, gambling and debauchery. But it was recognized by Evangelical leaders such as Hannah More that it was insufficient simply to attack the vices of the poor; those of the rich and powerful should also be reformed. It was from the rising mercantile middle classes that the temperance movements gathered their most active supporters – those who had pressing, economic reasons for trying to instil the habit of sobriety in the working classes. They saw a reliable, sober workforce as essential to the prosperity of their businesses and families. It was in their personal interest to support organizations which would, it was hoped, achieve these ends.

The Society for the Prevention and Discouragement of Vice and Profaneness had included the prevention of drunkenness as one of its original aims. The Beer Act of 1830 had increased the number of beer-houses in York to almost one per hundred head of population and, whilst beer was a valuable source of nutriment to the poor, when com-bined with spirits, it was also perceived to be a source of the destitution and immorality that temperance workers observed around them.

Temperance movements attracted the same type of supporters as other humanitarian movements – '... women, Quakers and Evangel-icals'.[43] Among those recruited to the temperance movement nationally were J. J. Gurney, Joseph Sturge and Richard Cadbury, the same men who had been supporters of the anti-slavery campaign.[44] In York, the list of subscribers and committee members included the familiar names of Gray, Tuke, Rowntree and Backhouse. The founding of temperance organizations began in Yorkshire in the 1830s and led to the establish-ment of a society in York in 1836. Although the York Temperance Society lectures were held initially at the Protestant Methodist chapel in Lady Peckitt Yard, they were dominated by Wesleyan Methodists.[45] The movement gradually became more inter-denominational and Quakers, who, from the start, had been amongst the subscribers to the Temper-ance Society, grew in influence and, with the Evangelical Anglicans, became dominant.[46] By 1850, the president, James Backhouse, the vice-president, Joseph Spence, and the secretary, James Mason, were all Quakers, and the Evangelical Anglican Henry Gray was on the com-mittee.[47] There were many Quaker subscribers and workers, including James Backhouse, junior, David Priestman, Hannah Scarr, Joseph Rown-tree, Sarah Rowntree, Samuel Tuke, James Hack Tuke, Esther Tuke, Jemima Spence, Celia Wilcoxs, Henry Richardson and Henry Tuke, along with members of other denominations, including William Gray, junior, James Meek (Wesleyan Methodist) and Alderman George Leeman (Independent).[48] A number of Quaker women, including Jemima Spence, Hannah Scarr and Celia Wilcoxs, were involved in distributing leaflets in public houses. James Backhouse and Joseph Spence became lifelong supporters of teetotalism and took it up as a personal belief.[49] Several of the Quakers and Evangelicals who were involved in the York Tem-perance Society were also members of the York Temperance Band of Hope, including James Backhouse, Joseph Rowntree, Henry Richardson and George Mennell.[50] Although many Quakers, including J. J. Gurney, were proud of their efforts to give up drink, teetotalism was never espoused by the Society of Friends as a rule.[51]

Both temperance work and prostitute-reform were inextricably linked to a belief in moral weakness, which, it was argued, could be overcome by an encouragement of self-discipline. The existence of a link between sexual weakness and alcohol and the fact that both drink and prostitution could be bought in the male preserve of the public house were seen by respectable women to be a threat to the family and home, central to both Quaker and Evangelical beliefs. It was this perceived threat which helped to encourage women from all denominations into the work of reforming drunks and prostitutes.[52] They were united by the vision of saving and converting their fellow beings: religion, reform and temperance became totally interrelated.

Non-denominational education

All the work undertaken by York's Quakers and Evangelical Anglicans which has been looked at so far has concentrated on the correction of the fallen. It was recognized that education was a key to the hearts and minds of the young and that, only through literacy, could the Evangelical emphasis on Bible study be nurtured. Education played a fundamental role in introducing the young to religion and, when it was combined with an opportunity to save young souls, sinful but not yet hardened in sin, it became too great a chance to be ignored.

The first educational reformers in York was the group of Evangelical ladies that included Faith Gray and Catherine Cappe. The Blue Coat and Grey Coat Schools had been founded at the beginning of the eighteenth century and were amongst the earliest attempts to provide education for the poor in the city, but both offered a very limited curriculum and training.[53] Both these schools underwent a reorganization programme in 1785 led by Faith Gray, Cordelia Withers (wife of Dr William Withers, the founder of the York Dispensary) and Catherine Cappe. Until 1784 the committee of the Blue Coat School for Boys had included Dr William White, a leading member of the Society of Friends.[54] However, he was voted off the committee with the rise in power of these Evangelicals and, as a result, Quaker support for the school declined. It was not revived until 1810, when Lindley and Hannah Murray became regular subscribers to its funds. Their involvement was to lead to a Quaker take-over, and by 1828 ten Quakers served on the school's management committee, outnumbering those from other denominations.[55]

Despite the existence of a variety of schools in the city, consisting largely of dame-schools, Sunday schools, of both the Established and Dissenting Churches, the Quaker day school and the Wesleyan school, education for the poor in York was still largely disorganized and hap-hazard.[56] In 1812 York Quakers began what was to become one of their greatest contributions to the welfare of the poor. They already had experience in providing education for their own poor at Ackworth School, and this, together with the work of Esther Tuke and her daughters at the more middle-class Trinity Lane School, had given them a basic interest in, and a knowledge of, the educational needs of children.

When York Quakers turned their attention to the education of other denominations, their first concern was for the girls. The British School was founded in 1812 for the education of non-Quaker girls and was organized on the Lancasterian School Society system.[57] This was entirely run, funded and organized by members of York Meeting. From the beginning, the school was supported by most of York's Quakers, including William Tuke, William Richardson, William Alexander, Henry Tuke, David Doeg, Martha White (sister of Dr William White), Priscilla Tuke, Martha Fletcher (who had taught for many years at Trinity Lane School), Mary Mildred and Elizabeth Fothergill. At the time of its foundation, there were fifty-eight Quaker annual subscribers and donations were received from fifty-four Friends. The pupils were to be taught reading, writing, arithmetic and needlework.[58] In the first instance the school appears to have been known as the Quaker School for Poor Girls, but it came under the auspices of the British and Foreign School Society in 1815. It opened in Newgate Street in July 1813 with 109 pupils and using the monitor system of teaching, under the guidance of Hannah Wilkinson, a mistress who had been trained in Leeds.[59]

The school had a general committee of men, but was in effect run and organized by a ladies' committee which was responsible to the men. The elected Ladies' Committee of the Quarterly Meeting of female subscribers consisted of most of the leading women of York Meeting. Martha Richardson was the treasurer, Elizabeth Fothergill and Martha Fletcher were secretaries, and Mary Mildred, Sarah King, Hannah Galilee, Rebecca Tuke and Ann Priestman were all committee members. A group of women visitors was appointed, including Martha White, Esther Tuke, junior, Ann Tuke and Favilla Copsie, who visited the school to supervise the work of the mistress and to ensure that the school was run on the lines laid down by the general committee.[60] Several of the committee members were personally involved in the running of the school; Priscilla Tuke was a 'good deal engaged' with its affairs in July 1813 and was one of those who trained the monitors: '... have[ing] two of the monitors at a time ... at out houses to bring them forward in the different branches of learning'.[61]

In 1816 the school moved to St Saviourgate and in 1827 a purpose-built school was erected next to the Bishophill Friends' burial ground.[62] By 1856, the Annual Report shows 150 pupils, split into six classes of 25.[63] In 1857 the government took over the funding of the school and finally, in 1896, under the provisions of the 1870 Education Act, it was closed down.

Although this school attempted to alleviate the lack of educational facilities in the city, in general they were still woefully inadequate. It was in recognition of this that in 1826 a group of Nonconformist 'friends of education' was formed, led by Quakers William Alexander and Joseph Rowntree and an Independent, the Revd James Parsons. They conducted a survey of educational facilities in the city which revealed the inadequacy of provision. It showed that only 44.9% of the children in the parishes within the age range 6–12 years attended a day school,[64] an appalling statistic which spurred Friends into joining the British and Foreign School Society and resulted in the opening of a boys' school in Hope Street in 1827. This was the equivalent of the British Girls' School and was run by Samuel Tuke and Joseph Rowntree, under the auspices of the British and Foreign School Society. Although the school had 200 pupils by 1833, it failed to flourish and the number of pupils declined over the next twenty years until a new headmaster from Albion Street Wesleyan School came to Hope Street, bringing with him many of his former pupils.[65]

Despite the work of these men, however, when a House of Commons Committee commissioned a report from the Manchester Statistical Society in 1846 on the provision of education for the poorer classes in the city, it was still found that only 4,749 scholars attended dame-schools and day schools and that one-third (or 2,300) of children between the ages of 5 and 15 received no instruction at all. At the 160 existing day and evening schools, there were 4,037 boys and 3,409 girls – a total of 7,446 pupils – 14 of the schools were entirely free; 20 were partly fee-paying and 126 were entirely fee-paying. Reading was taught in 78.8% of the schools, writing in 47.5%, arithmetic in 48.4% and needlework in 52.5%. Other subjects included geography, history, languages, drawing and, of course, religion, which was taught in 50% of the schools. Although most of the teachers were untrained, 104 of them had no other occupation and the report noted that a majority of them had been teaching for over seven years; 68 of the teachers were from the Established Church and 47 were Dissenters.[66] By 1836 there were 24 Sunday schools of all denominations in the city and these were attended by 3,363 pupils. Reading was the most widely taught subject, but writing was only taught in one school.[67]

Most of the educational provision discussed so far was available to children of parents who could afford to pay the 1d. or 3d. fees, but was not available to the destitute. The York Ragged School was opened in February 1848 by the Wesleyans[68] and, although dominated by them, it was projected as an inter-denominational venture. Several Quakers subscribed to the school and Maria Tuke, Ann Alexander and Mrs Priestman contributed children's clothing. In general, the school did little more than provide shelter and meals for the children, but for some it was the source of a rudimentary training.[69]

Adult education

It is generally recognized by historians of Quakerism that the greatest contribution that they made to education was in the field of basic adult education. Again, it was Evangelical Quakers who were in the forefront of the adult school movement, many of whom, such as Joseph Rowntree, Joseph Fry and George Cadbury, had been leaders in the temperance movement.[70]

Until 1848, the only further education available to young men in the city was provided by the Mechanics Institute. Unfortunately, the institute had set out with the inappropriately high ideals of promoting '... the mental cultivation of and to instruct the working-class in useful knowledge'. Founded by the Unitarian minister the Revd Charles Wellbeloved, it was dominated by the middle-class businessmen of the city, including the Quakers Joseph Awmack, Joseph Spence, Joseph Rowntree and Samuel Tuke, but the Evangelical Anglicans were highly sceptical of it and had little involvement in its activities. The failure of the organization lay in its inability to understand the type of classes needed by its potential pupils and in its adoption of values and ideals which were totally out of touch with the reality of the lives of its students. Much of its curriculum was beyond the comprehension and ability of most of its pupils, and the useful subjects of reading and writing were relegated to being an afterthought, available only once a week. As a consequence, it failed to attract many pupils and in time became little more than a middle-class literary society.[71]

The failure of the Mechanics Institute proved useful experience for York's Quakers and in 1848 York Meeting opened the doors of Hope Street Boys' School to boys and men from the ages of 15 to 20 and began to call it the First Day Sabbath School.[72] First Day schools, as they became called, were primarily for the education of illiterate adults and were organized and staffed entirely by members of the Society of Friends. In 1849 the York First Day School had two classes divided by age: 8–16 years and 16–20/25 years. Some Bible reading was carried out, but the 'committing of hymns or portions of Scripture to memory is not insisted upon, as the teachers do not think the effects good, as it discourages those who come to read and have not time for learning passages'.[73]

At the First Day Conference in 1852, Thomas Pumphrey from York reported that the average length of attendance at the school was 2 years 8 months and that it was now '... more definitely an Adult School'.[74] Most of the men and boys who attended were in employment or had a trade.[75] Robert Taylor, Caleb Fletcher and James Harrison King were in charge of the school, with several assistant teachers, including James Backhouse, junior, Morris Baker, Thomas Conning, Richard Cadbury Barrow, Daniel Tuke, George Sedgwick, John Inchcliffe and Robert Dunning.[76] The religious principles underlying their work were reinforced through a system of prizes for good work, which consisted mainly of booklets from the Religious Tract Society.[77]

In 1849 the Hope Street Friends Day School Saving Fund was formed 'to promote habits of care and forethought amongst scholars'.[78] Middle-class values and habits, reinforced by strong Evangelical religion, were instilled in the pupils in an attempt to turn them into thrifty and worthwhile citizens. The philosophy behind the school differed little from that of schools run by their fellow philanthropists, but what was different was that it catered for a section of the poor who had no access to education of any kind. The type of young men and boys being taught were generally semi-skilled artisans, amongst whose given trades were those of shoemaker, tinner, cabinet-maker, plane-maker, etc.[79] The Register for 1856 shows how effectively it cut across denominational lines; of the 184 entries whose religious denomination is listed, there were ten Methodists, three Independents, five Church of England, seven Wesleyans, one Catholic, one 'The Brethren' and one Primitive Methodist; there were also three who attended the Meeting but were not Quakers, two who claimed they attended both the Methodist chapel and the Quaker Meeting, as well as a few Quakers.[80] Since most pupils claimed some religious affiliation to a particular denomination, it is unlikely that Quakers gathered many recruits from the school. As Joseph Rowntree said: '[we] did not want to proselytise Quakerism but that the example of teachers might lead their scholars to it'.[81] He also recognized that Quakerism was difficult to understand and unattractive when compared with the 'enthusiastic' style of religion practised in the Methodist or Wesleyan chapels.[82] Elizabeth Isichei has suggested that Quaker recruits also suffered the indignity of being 'second-class citizens' within their adopted Meeting and many who attended Meeting noted this treatment.[83]

In 1856 a Sabbath School for Girls was opened by the Friends, but it failed to attract consistent attenders, although the library was a successful part of the school, with 922 borrowings in 1859. Although the school was run by female Friends, with Elizabeth Ransome acting as secretary, it was in reality an offshoot of the boys' school.

Conclusion

Elizabeth Isichei has suggested that because Friends were predominantly middle-class, they shied away from becoming involved in the Sunday school movement and the teaching of poor children. This, she argued, was partly because they did not see their schools as centres of recruitment for their Church, as did other denominations, and because they had to decide whether or not to teach Quaker doctrine to people whom they felt would have little taste for it.[84] But whilst York Quakers were late in establishing a Sunday school, they did have an early involvement in the teaching of poor children.[85] The Blue Coat and Grey Coat Schools, the British Girls' School and Hope Street School were all involved in the education of the poor and when they did establish their First Day schools, although many of their pupils were skilled, most of the recruitment was undertaken in areas of great poverty, particularly the areas around Walmgate and the Water Lanes, off Castlegate. The unique feature of the Quaker First Day schools was that they were specifically targeted at older children and young men and women, i.e. those above normal Sunday school age.

Besides their activities in establishing schools, it was the Quakers in York who were responsible for initiating an important investigation into educational facilities in the city in 1826, and it was as a result of this that schooling in the city gradually improved. The experience that Quaker women had gained from involvement in the establishment of their own schools for girls encouraged them to become involved in the founding of new institutions. Quaker men were encouraged in their pursuit of a better education for all children by the example set by their womenfolk and by their Evangelical friends. The move towards providing an education for the poor in establishments run and organized by themselves was a logical further step in this pursuit.

Quaker philanthropy in York had a necessary and enduring connection to its theology. Once Evangelicalism had become established within the creed of the Meeting and the Bible had become central to their beliefs, the doctrine of Atonement became a key to Quaker involvement in philanthropic pursuits. The early date of this Evangelical influence is crucial to an understanding of the high level of Quaker participation in the various charitable activities of the city, as inter-denominational connections ensured that they became inexorably drawn into local social work.

York's Quakers and Evangelicals were part of the national Evangelical crusade to raise the level of public morality and protect good and moral citizens from immorality and lawlessness. Most of the organizations in which they were involved reflected their common interests and, as leading members of the business community, as parish officials, as representatives of the middle class and the godly élite in the city, they had a shared concern to control those elements of the populace that they perceived to be a threat to the existing social and moral order. These joint concerns ensured that York's Quakers became increasingly integrated into the social and political affairs of the city.

CHAPTER 6

Quakerism and Politics
in York

In 1777 Bishop Porteous of Chester wrote of the threat which towns posed to good and godly men and of their:

> Intemperance and licentiousness of manners; a wanton and foolish extravagance of dress, in equipage, in houses, in furniture, in entertainment; a passion for luxurious indulgences and frivolous amusements, a gay thoughtless indifference about a future life ... a neglect of divine worship, a profanation of the day peculiarly set apart for it; and perhaps, to crown all, a disbelief and contempt of the Gospel.[1]

Added to their fears for men's souls were worries about the criminality, immorality and potential for revolution inherent in town life. If bishops such as Porteous were alarmed, so were other members of the godly community. Only by becoming involved in town life could God-fearing groups such as the Quakers hope to influence local government and local organizations in their efforts to make their societies less dangerous, more moral and, as all traders hoped, more prosperous. But while Friends were primarily members of a religious sect, wishing to maintain their individualism and uphold their position as members of the godly community, they were at the same time facing increasing pressure to become more integrated into the wider community. It was this conflict that challenged York's Quakers, as they began to recognize their potential influence as citizens and as their levels of political awareness, activity and integration grew.

The increased success and wealth of York's Quakers, which was becoming manifest by the last two decades of the eighteenth century, was accompanied by a rise in social status and resulted in an increased inability to retain their separateness. As John Seed says: '... separation off into the closed world of the sect was increasingly incompatible with the complex and differentiated social life of the bourgeoisie'. And as trade expanded, 'successful merchants and tradesmen were required to move into the world and to deal with strangers and thus could not hold themselves apart as "the elect". Simple opposition between "saints" and "sinners" was increasingly at variance with the complexities of social interaction.'[2]

Interaction with the world was not a new phenomenon for York's Quakers. In David Scott's view, they had already found by the end of the seventeenth century that '... involvement in the local community life, as businessmen, voters, tax-payers and as municipal, guild or parish officers, vitiated their testimony against the world'.[3] For Friends, parish and civic obligations came as much from a sense of loyal and neighbourly duty as from economic or social self-interest. In Lancaster, Nicholas Morgan found that Quakers were '... anxious to carry out the fiscal obligations expected from prosperous members of the community ...'.[4] In fact, the lower offices of the corporation and those in the parish were more onerous and economically draining than they were socially advantageous. The challenge for Quakerism in York was that growing wealth and social prominence brought increased levels of pressure for interaction with the world – and thus conflict with any remnants of Quietist idealism.

Although there might be increasing pressures to adopt new areas of social and political action, there were also strong forces within Quakerism which held the Society together and reinforced group beliefs. These intra-Societal forces were enhanced by external pressure of identity. As Max Weber argued, to be a member of a recognized, socially and economically prestigious group brought an individual public recognition of personal respectability and financial stability.[5] Recognition of Quakers as humanitarians ensured that they became important contributors to the philanthropic organizations of the city, which, at the same time, increased public awareness of their worthiness as citizens. As a result, Friends became increasingly integrated into the political structure of York, although this could only be achieved with the consensus of the majority of Quakers, who wished to enlarge their spheres of operation and influence.

Within York Meeting, the idealism of Quietism had been stretched to a point where it was merely doctrinal and, by the 1780s, was beginning to show signs of strain. Despite strong bonds of cohesion, there were signs of growing divisions of interest and activity within the Meeting. York's Quakers were dividing into two harmonious but distinct groups: those who were publicly active in the political, social and humanitarian life of the city; and those who maintained and supported the more Quietist style of Quakerism. Esther Tuke addressed York Quarterly Meeting in 1792, warning Quakers against the pursuit of worldly riches: '... many having gone into the Spirit of the World in an inordinate pursuit of riches and a multiplicity of business far beyond divine limitations', and against '... uniting in any of the various political association which have been, or may be formed amongst the people ...'.[6]

This address encapsulates the apparently unresolvable problem and tension of late eighteenth-century Quakerism – the desire to retain a godly identity and to maintain the sect's principles, while at the same time facing increasing pressure to become ever more outward-looking.

The divisions of interest which began to exist within York Meeting by the beginning of the nineteenth century are most noticeable in the list of attenders at the Monthly Preparative Meeting (Appendix VII, table 1). Vann's description of the membership of the Monthly Meeting in the seventeenth century as generally comprising men who had the most experience in business and were, therefore, the most 'business-like' was still applicable to York Monthly Meeting in 1780.[7] Inevitably, Meetings became dominated by the wealthier and more bourgeois members. But this did not mean that they degenerated into an oligarchy or that John Stephenson Rowntree's contention that the Monthly Meeting was the preserve of '… two or three true and faithful Friends from each particular meeting' was necessarily the result.[8] As Appendix VII shows, there was a wide range of attenders, although it should be noted that many of the weightiest public members were the least frequent attenders.

By the end of the eighteenth century, York Monthly Meeting had become less and less diverse in its social composition and, consequently, represented more exactly the views and composition of a greater proportion of the membership; few of the poorer members ever attended Monthly Meeting. Because attendance was by appointment, accredited members were able to limit those delegated to be present and to regulate the Meeting so that its financial affairs, discipline and organization fell into the hands of a minority of diligent, well-to-do members. It seems likely that the work of the internal organization of the Meeting was deliberately delegated to those who did not have heavy external responsibilities. Although these arrangements are indicative of a conscious strategy, there was also some doctrinal basis for the division of labour. There was a group of members who wished to retain a Quietist lifestyle, for whom their businesses and the Meeting comprised their entire world and who were more willing or able to run the Meeting, leaving those who sought to further their humanitarian and political interests free to contribute to society at large.

The parish

The parish formed the base of a political pyramid which relied on oligarchic rule and vertical ties of patronage for its structure and maintenance. Since many offices within the parish were held by the friends and relatives of corporation members, it became a highly politicized forum for local activism. For the wealthy and ambitious Dissenter or Quaker, it was often the only arena in which to pitch a political tent, and for many it was the starting place of a political career.[9] As Frazer comments, the vestry was one arena in which the *nouveau riche* merchant, often a Dissenter, could 'legitimize his role as a social leader'.[10] Within this arena, there was a range of offices which, should Quakers wish to serve, gave them an opportunity to exercise their influence and, as godly, peaceable, upright citizens, to confirm their reputation as sober and moderate people. These attributes, combined with their financial and social standing and their reputation as good and honest businessmen, made Quakers desirable recruits to parish government and they became natural candidates for positions as collectors of the various taxes, auditors of the parish accounts, constables and even churchwardens.

The main structure for parish government was the select vestry. As W. E. Tate noted, it was recognized from earliest times that members of the vestry were the 'most substantial', 'the principal', the 'most discrete' inhabitants of the parish, or '... the aristocracy, plutocracy or oligarchy ...' who formed the base of parochial administration.[11] Between 1740 and 1780, five Quakers had served as constables, including William Tuke, two as land-tax surveyors and eight as assessors and collectors of the window tax, including Nathaniel Bell, Thomas Priestman and Jonathan Storr. However, in spite of their prominence, the level of Quaker participation in York's parishes was very varied. In some it was very high, whilst in others it was almost non-existent (Appendix VII, tables 5 and 6).

Relationships between individual clergy and Quakers could be both harmonious and acrimonious.[12] In York, despite doctrinal conflicts over church rates, relations between parish and Quakers were generally the former. It is difficult to assess how many Quakers actually refused to pay church rates and how much those who did suffered for their refusal. Quaker refusal, although still seen as a threat to social order and property rights, was also established and tolerated behaviour, not least because of their social status within the parish. David Scott found that in seventeenth-century York, whilst Quakers remained strong in their testimony against tithes, '... the sums involved were usually so modest it would seem that most of the city's parish clergy could not be bothered to go to the trouble of dragging Friends through the church courts just for the sake of a few shillings'.[13] This was not true in late eighteenth-century York, when the sums often involved more than a few shillings and Quakers recorded substantial sufferings (Appendix VII, table 7). Although they had goods and cash taken in lieu of church rates on a regular basis and, as table 7 shows, although social position and parochial service were no protection against the seizure of goods (William and Henry Tuke, who were conscientious parish officials in St Mary's,

Castlegate, had goods valued at £21. 19s. 8½d. taken between 1780 and 1810), the actual levels of distraint, when compared with the levels of church rate demanded, show that they were generally treated leniently. When goods were seized, the amounts raised bore little resemblance to the amount chargeable and, if it was any comfort to the Quakers, the parish was making a loss on their collection. Thomas Priestman's recorded suffering for the period 1800–10 of £2. 3s. 9½d. was considerably lower than the actual church rates payable over the same period of £8. 7s. 8d., as were Caleb Williams', whose rate was £7 but whose suffering was only £2.[14]

However, this was only true for the city. Rural Quakers suffered particularly from rapacious parsons. There were few cases in the city of warrants being issued or constables searching for goods or cash and, if they did, the constable sent to collect the rate, being a neighbour, often did not charge for his trouble.[15] In fact, according to the Book of Sufferings, only five warrants were issued between the years 1780–1855. In most cases, as the parish records show, distraint of goods was a last resort, only used when church rates remained unpaid for many years. And despite the continuous affirmative answers to the Query on Tithes and Church Rates, Quakers in many parishes were either paying their rates or having them paid for them, although there is not a single instance of disciplinary action being taken by the Monthly Meeting.[16] Although there are very few recorded instances of refusal to pay, James and Thomas Backhouse, who lived in the parish of Holy Trinity, Micklegate, were continuous non-payers and between 1830 and 1852 they were backed up by several other Quakers, including Joseph Rowntree. This had all the characteristics of an organized campaign of disobedience, mounted to coincide with Joseph Rowntree's leadership of the York campaign for the abolition of church rates.[17]

Although inter-parochial relationships might be muddied by the church rates issue, this did not stop Quakers from being actively involved in their parish organizations. Within parish structures there was a range of offices open to ordinary parishioners and generally filled by the most substantial of them. These included overseers of the poor, auditors of the various accounts – both posts which Quakers were most likely to fill – and churchwardens. The overseers attended select vestry meetings and dealt with the administration of the poor rate. The humanitarian aspects of this post appealed to the Quaker sense of caring for those worse off than themselves (Appendix VII, tables 5 and 6).

The most prestigious post and, for Quakers, potentially the one most likely to cause conflict of action and conscience, was that of church-warden. This involved the setting and collection of church rates and the presenting of persons for non-attendance at church, and it was these duties which were most likely to cause problems for Quakers and could bring them up against the Society's regulations. Although there was only one instance of a Quaker serving as a churchwarden in a York parish, it happened in several London parishes.[18] The Quaker watchmaker Jonathan Storr began his civic career with the parish of St Michael le Belfrey in 1770, when he was selected to audit the churchwarden's accounts.[19] In 1776 he was elected churchwarden in the parish. Like most select vestries, St Michael's was a self-perpetuating oligarchy, and churchwardens were re-elected for three one-year terms of office. Jonathan Storr was re-elected over three successive years until, in 1779, he had reached the position of senior churchwarden. Over the next twenty years he served the parish continually, attending vestry meetings, auditing the lamp accounts and the poor rate accounts from 1792 to 1799, laying the lamp and poor rates as well as auditing the church-warden's accounts. Finally, in 1800 he was re-elected, again serving for three years. The last time his name appeared on the vestry minutes was in 1805.[20] Despite potential conflicts between doctrine and practice, they were generally negated by pressure for community solidarity. Jonathan Storr never refused to pay his church rate or entered a suffering for refusal. But neither was there any disciplinary proceeding against him in the records of the Monthly Meeting.

Jonathan Storr's level of involvement in parish affairs had no parallel in any other York parish records until the 1830s, when Quakers who had always served in a variety of offices in the parish of St Mary's, Castlegate, became attenders at select vestry meetings (Appendix VII, table 6). The minutes of vestry meetings for St Mary's are extant from 1831 to 1856. From the first entry in August 1831, it is clear that the Quaker businessmen Henry Ransome (linen-draper of Castlegate), Thomas Mason (tea-dealer of Castlegate) and William Alexander (bookseller/printer) were, and probably had been for several years, members of the select vestry. Because of the widely divergent social mix within the local population, which was more renowned for its prostitutes and brothels than for its upright citizens, there was a sufficiently high level of fundamental agreement on the issues facing the good and godly men of the district for Quakers, as honest moral citizens, to become integrated into the government of the parish. Their Meeting House, William Alexander's School and several of their homes and businesses, including Samuel Tuke's, were located in Castlegate, in the midst of a potentially lawless neighbourhood.

Of foremost importance to these men was the regulation, for the comfort of decent parish citizens, of the brothels and bawdy houses which were situated in the Far Water Lanes and Friargate, and several vestry meetings were dominated by concern over law and order. In October 1831 a special vestry meeting decided to proceed against Samuel Dean and his wife for causing a riot.[21] There were continual problems with prostitutes, and the parish frequently prosecuted houses of ill-fame.[22] Besides dealing with the criminal elements in the district, the select vestry also cared for the poor, appointed constables, set the poor rates and distributed a number of charities under its control, including Alderman Myers' coals, which had been left for the paupers of the parish.

The Quakers who became involved served in a variety of posts. In 1833 Thomas Mason was elected chairman of the select vestry, a post he was to hold until 1856, when the minutes cease. In October 1834 he was also appointed parish visitor to the workhouse, and in November both he and Henry Ransome were elected members of a select vestry for the management of the poor.[23] The good relationship which existed between Quakers and their fellow Anglican parishioners was shown in 1843, when the vestry gave a vote of thanks to Thomas Mason for '... the ability zeal and perseverance with which he has discharged the onerous duties of the Office of Guardian in this parish from the first formation of the Union, to the present time ...'.[24]

The distinction between Quakers and Anglicans became blurred within the close-knit environment of parish life. General agreement over problems of security and morality ensured co-operation and involvement, which diluted the doctrinal differences between good and godly men who were also wealthy and socially prominent citizens. And at the same time their work as parish officers served as an apprenticeship for corporate politics in the wider arena, in which several Quakers were to become involved.

The corporation

Dissenters who wished to enter the corporate government of the city of York were limited in the offices open to them by the sacramental requirements of the Test and Corporation Acts. Occasional conformity was the only back-door route by which, if their consciences would allow, they might circumvent these restrictions and enter the higher offices of the corporation.[25] However, for Quakers in general, occasional conformity was not an option and there is no evidence to suggest that, in York, ambitions for personal and political advancement or integration ever overcame their testimony against the Sacraments.[26] But this did not mean that they were excluded from those spheres of local government which were open to them, or from parliamentary politics. The Affirmation Act of 1722 had removed one impediment to their participation in a whole range of civic positions, including the corporate office of chamberlain.[27] Although generally excluded from the corporation of York, a body which was not only paternalistic but, from the mid-1750s, dominated by the moderate Whiggism of Rockingham, it was probable that Nonconformists in general, and Quakers in particular, did not oppose but supported the Whig corporation. Appendix VII, table 2, shows that the Quakers who voted in the 1774 election were all Whig supporters.

Quakers appear to have had a good relationship with the corporation in the period from 1780. The one office that was open to them because there was no sacramental test was that of chamberlain. The chamberlains kept and audited the corporation accounts, but they had no say in the conduct of corporate business and no control over corporate expenditure. A guide to the city published in 1828 described the office of chamberlain as 'an office which was formerly considered honourable, is now shunned and despised and is generally conferred on those with whom the Corporation are not on friendly terms'.[28] However, despite this condemnation, Quakers served as chamberlains on many occasions, their reputation for sobriety and business-like attitudes recommending them to the corporation (Appendix VII, table 4). In some years, three of the six chamberlains were Quakers.

Exclusion from the corporation ensured that Quakers had no entrée into the world of corporate hegemony or to the lucrative or prestigious corporate posts. They could not tender for corporation work, such as the rebuilding and refurbishment work carried out on the Mansion House in 1780, nor for supplying goods and services to the corporation and Mansion House. The chamberlains' accounts show that no Quaker trader or merchant supplied the corporation during this period or was appointed to such lucrative posts as city surgeon, which carried a salary of £15 p.a.[29] Although Quakers were not appointed searchers for the guilds, the guilds did appoint Quaker masters. Three, Stephen Priestman, William Bleckley and George Knowles, were appointed master of the Worshipful Company of Merchant Tailors between 1798 and 1811.[30]

Not only did Quakers miss out financially, but they also had no redress to the government of the city to defend their rights, or to an arena in which they might object to matters which contravened their Testimonies, such as the recruitment of men under the bounty schemes to defend the country during the French Wars.[31] They could only approve or disapprove of the corporation and its activities from the sidelines. Despite this, they still relied on the corporation and magistrates for protection. In March 1789 Friends petitioned the magistrates and inhabitants of York on the occasion of the celebration of George III's recovery from his first period of illness. They were aware that such celebrations might involve damage to Quaker property from those who objected to the Quaker refusal to show celebratory lights. The petition, besides pointing out the '... too common consequences, rioting and excess ...' of such 'illuminations and feasting ...', also sought '... protection from the magistrates who by their offices are ordained and ought on all occasions to be, a terror to evil doers and a praise to them that do well'.[32] Any influence that Quakers had over the magistracy relied on the goodwill of the corporation and the individuals who formed it, a goodwill which owed more to economic and social interaction than to political influence.[33]

Economic ties with the corporation as a whole might have been loose but, on an individual basis, Quaker business acumen ensured that they were on sufficiently good terms for it to look favourably on their requests for help in business affairs. In May 1782 the House Book made special note of the high regard of the corporation for Charles Forbes and John Fothergill, horn- and comb-makers, resolving that they had '... introduced several very extensive branches of business into this city, shall have liberty to erect a chimney in the moat between the City walls and their workshops at Toft Green'.[34] Quaker masters regularly took non-Quaker apprentices, some from high-ranking local families, and were awarded corporate charity money for taking on poor boys from the parishes. George Peacock took on John Bowland, a poor boy from St Crux parish in 1786; William Richardson, a tanner, took on Mathew Turner from the Blue Coat School in 1811; and William Alexander was awarded £4 from Alderman Tireman's gift for giving George Hope an apprenticeship in 1826.[35] The Quaker farmer Francis Flower leased a farm owned by the corporation at Fordington.

Personal relationships between individual members of the corporation and Quakers ensured a high level of corporate co-operation. Jonathan Gray (Evangelical Anglican) was Lindley Murray's (Quaker) solicitor, and Samuel Tuke (Quaker) and Jonathan Gray worked together on many philanthropic concerns, including the re-drafting of the 1825 Police Act.[36] James Meek (Methodist), a common councilman, Joseph Spence and Thomas Backhouse (Quakers) were the owners of the York Glass Works. These economic and business ties flowed both ways; York Quakers intermittently helped to finance the corporation. From the early years of the nineteenth century the corporation had suffered continual financial embarrassment. A long-established system of annuities existed to alleviate its problems. These annuities could be purchased by wealthy local businessmen and in January 1807 amounted to £3,260 in new borrowings. Amongst the annuitants in 1807 was Lindley Murray, who invested £400, which earned an annual dividend of £50. And in September 1814 Anne Oddie, wife of William Oddie, both Quakers, purchased an annuity of £100.[37]

Political contacts were of vital importance both to individual Quakers and to the Society as a whole. Those made by William Tuke when serving on the committee to protest against the building of a bridge at Selby in 1797, were invaluable to York's Quakers when agitating for help in securing the release of the Lothersdale prisoners.[38] William Tuke used his friendship with members of the arbitration committee, Bacon Frank, Lord Hawk, Fairfax Fearnley and the York MPs, to give him access to those who could lobby for, and finally secure, their release in 1798.[39] In May 1808 William and Henry Tuke used their friendship and support for William Wilberforce during the anti-slavery campaign to secure an audience with the Chancellor of the Exchequer to plead for a reduction in duties on coffee.[40] Business and the politics of conscience were mutually supportive.

If Quakers had maintained harmonious but distant relations with the corporation in the years before 1825, when the local Police Act was passed, this was to change over the next ten years. The Police Act was the first step towards the modernization of local government and provided for the appointment of 'Improvement Commissioners'. The Act was to give Quakers their first opportunity to become active participants in local politics.[41] It was the first draft of the Bill in 1824 that brought out the radicals and reformers amongst the town's middle-class merchants and professionals. It was an ill-disguised attempt by the Whigs to retain their existing powers. Tories, whom the corporation had been effective in excluding from local government, and Dissenters joined together to put up an effective, vociferous opposition to the Corporation Bill.[42] It received a hostile reaction at a public meeting in January 1825, and amongst its detractors were the Quakers Samuel and Daniel Tuke and the Tories Jonathan Gray and Robert Cattle. Daniel Tuke reputedly cried: 'send no Corporation man – send no Orange man'. The meeting resulted in the formation of the United Committee, which worked to undermine corporation proposals and to insert a clause allowing Quakers to act as commissioners.[43]

Quakers now found themselves involved in a reformist, anti-corporation movement, opposed to the rule of the 'old aristocratical Aldermen', determined to redefine local government and legitimize their claims for participation.[44] The parties were clearly aligned: Tories and the general populace of York on one side, and Whigs and the corporation on the other. As the *Gazette*, *Herald* and *Courant* all reported during February 1825, even previously reticent Quakers such as Samuel Tuke were sufficiently roused to comment that he hoped the corporation would '… lay aside aristocratical pretensions', and Daniel Tuke complained that '… they [the corporation] are about 100 individuals, not elected by the city, but a self-elected body, who, instead of being the natural guardians of the city, retard and keep back its improvements'.[45] The Friends' first venture into political lobbying was highly successful. The Bill was redrafted to include the provisions proposed by the United Committee and resulted in a complete capitulation by the corporation, a capitulation which laid the foundation for a long series of acrimonious disputes between the corporation and the commissioners appointed under the revised Bill.

The Tories triumphed in the elections which followed, gaining a majority, and the Quakers were rewarded with the election of two commissioners, James Backhouse and William Alexander, who were appointed to a range of committees.[46] Corporate antagonism quickly became apparent and, within weeks of the establishment of the Improvement Commission, it was in dispute with the corporation.[47]

In the midst of these disputes, Quaker members of the commission were rising to prominence. William Alexander was chairman of their meetings, alternating with John Pemberton throughout the first years of their existence. On 1 May 1828 a new set of commissioners was elected and the Whigs made a few gains. Although neither Robert Cattle nor John Pemberton, both Tories, were re-elected, both William Alexander and James Backhouse (Whigs) were and, despite continuing disputes with the corporation, Quakers continued to serve over subsequent years. Relations between the commissioners and the corporation eventually improved and an uneasy truce was declared.

The Quakers' first venture into local pressure-group politics had been a resounding success and, as Improvement Commissioners, they had come comparatively unscathed through the first turbulent years of trying to work with an uncooperative and resentful corporation. They were now in a position to take up the opportunities presented to them by the repeal of the Corporation Act in 1828, bringing to an end the sacramental test and opening up corporate office to Dissenters.[48] However, strict Quakers were still not happy with the declaration required by the new Act, which read: 'I ... having been elected Mayor (Alderman, Councillor, Auditor or assessor) for the Borough of ... do hereby declare that I take the said Office upon myself and will duly and faithfully fulfil the duties thereof according to the best of my judgment and ability.'

York Quakers were quick to take advantage of their newly gained freedom and in 1830 the city had its first Quaker sheriff, Benjamin Horner. At the swearing-in ceremony, he affirmed and 'made and subscribed the declaration required to be made in lieu of the Sacramental Test', but, as the corporation minutes note, he made the symbolic and public gesture of his Quakerism by refusing to wear '... a gown according to the custom of members of this house'.[49] In this same year, York also had its first Roman Catholic lord mayor, Edward Petre.[50] Although the panoply of corporate ceremonial processions, the robes and the bands may have caused some disquiet to Quaker officials such as Benjamin Horner, the Friends were now part of a reform movement, working to push forward the political claims of the Dissenting middle class. It was these pressures, combined with his social and business standing, which ensured that Horner accepted the office of alderman later in the same year.[51]

The final phase of Quaker integration into local politics came in 1835 with the passing of the Municipal Corporation Act, which established local town councils. The old-style, self-elected Whig corporation was abolished and, at the same time, the magistracy became a Crown appointment, reducing the power and influence of the local authority. Candidates for councillors had to be property owners of £1,000 value or pay a poor rate of not less than £30. Six new wards were created, each with six councillors who were elected annually in November. Although several councillors were members of the old corporation, it was the first chance for Nonconformists and Tories to enter the previously exclusive world of local government and work together to achieve their own political aspirations. Amongst the Tory reformers were Jonathan Gray (Evangelical Anglican) William Gray, junior (Evangelical Anglican) and Robert Cattle (Anglican) – all of whom had been a party to the redrafting of the Police Bill – George Hudson and William Oldfield; Liberal Dissenting councillors included Joseph Rowntree and Thomas Backhouse (Quakers), as well as Police Bill activists James Meek (Methodist, former member of the 24), and Seth Agar (Roman Catholic, ex-sheriff and former member of the 24). Among the new Justices recommended were Jonathan Gray, James Meek and William Hotham, the latter two being Dissenters.[52]

The first meetings of the new council were taken up with the practicalities of reorganizing the old corporation into a city council. The Quaker councillors were elected to a wide range of committees: Joseph Rowntree was appointed to the committee to look at bye-laws, the Ouse Navigation Committee and the Watch Committee; and Thomas Backhouse found himself on the Finance Committee and the Watch Committee.[53] In 1836, new charity trustees were appointed, including Jonathan Gray, Robert Cattle, Samuel Tuke (Quaker), Seth Agar and William Oldfield.[54] These new committees often found that there had been widespread abuses of trust by the old corporation, such as the charitable gift intended for use for poor boys' apprenticeships which had been used to apprentice sons of freemen to their parents, and the corruption that was found to have been rife within the Ouse Navigation Committee.[55] But the new council was not to be above reproach or beyond helping its own members. The investment opportunities in the railway companies proved too attractive for even the most scrupulous of men, and brought together those who otherwise would have been politically and morally totally opposed. In 1836 the York and North Midland Railway was given council approval for its line. George Hudson (Tory) was not only chairman of the committee looking into the matter, but also of the railway company. Amongst other directors who were also on the council were James Meek (Methodist Whig), Thomas Backhouse and Benjamin Horner (Quaker Whigs). Other directors included the Quakers Samuel Tuke and Thomas Mason.[56]

George Hudson and the Tories were to dominate council politics for ten years from 1835. Backed by the vociferous Tory press, any efforts by Hudson's opponents to temper his excesses were continually thwarted. George Leeman, Joseph Rowntree and Robert Henry Anderson, Hudson's detractors, were constantly on the receiving end of their vitriolic attacks. In 1838 Hudson was elected to a second term as lord mayor, but Rowntree and Leeman (Liberal councillors) objected because he was not qualified and '... voting papers not being in the form required by the Bye-Law of the Council'. Regardless of their protests, Hudson had sufficient power to force through his re-election.[57] At the same election, Joseph Rowntree was nominated an alderman but, not surprisingly in view of the machinations of Hudson and his cohorts, was defeated.[58] George Hudson had consolidated his power base within the council to such an extent that any decisions regarding his railway businesses went unchallenged and many Liberal councillors who had financial investments in his railway companies were persuaded to support him. Even the Quaker Thomas Backhouse fell prey to his power, voting with the Tories when the Liberals opposed a vote of thanks to George Hudson for his work as lord mayor in 1839. Finally, in 1846, when Hudson's fraudulent business dealings began to come to light, George Leeman, James Meek and Joseph Rowntree were able to expose him and speak effectively against his excesses.[59] The decline of Hudson coincided with the decline of Tory domination of York local politics. In 1849 a Liberal alderman replaced a Tory and in the elections of 1850 the Liberals came to power. In Castlegate, Robert H. Anderson, Leeman's long-time *bête noire*, paid five shillings for votes and defeated Joseph Rowntree, who, scrupulous as ever, had not bribed voters.[60] In 1852 Rowntree was re-elected a councillor and in 1853 he became an alderman. Finally, in 1858, he was elected lord mayor but declined to serve, paying the £100 exoneration fee. He died the following year.

The opening-up of local government to Nonconformists had immediate financial benefits. Within a year, Quakers began to pick up council contracts. The new police force was equipped with uniforms in February 1837 and the Quaker boot-maker, John Clemesha, supplied the council with thirteen pairs of boots at a cost of £9. 18s. per pair. George Knowles, woollen-draper, won a contract to provide day coats for the police in August 1838 and from 1840 regularly supplied all that was required.[61]

By 1853 York Quakers were fully integrated into the city's local government structures. As members of the rising middle class, they had proved themselves not only to be worthy and responsible citizens, but also radical and reforming political allies, prepared to take an active part in agitation for the reorganization of local politics. Alongside this growth in local political activism was a corresponding expansion of their involvement in parliamentary politics.

Parliamentary politics

From the 1750s, York's parliamentary politics had been dominated by the moderate Whiggism of the Marquis of Rockingham and his candidates.[62] His death in 1782 brought this to a temporary end. His nephew, Earl Fitzwilliam, who succeeded to his title, massive wealth and lands, had neither the political acumen and experience nor the personal following to be able to retain the loyalty of the increasingly fickle voters of York, and the election of 1783 brought about the first challenge to the Rockingham cabal.[63] Besides blundering in their choice of a candidate, they also found themselves up against a new force in York politics, the Revd Christopher Wyvill and the Yorkshire Committee of Association.[64] This committee, formed in 1779, added a new dimension to York and Yorkshire politics.

At the centre of Rockingham's political campaign organization in York was the Rockingham Club, which encouraged his agents in their work for his candidates, promoting and presenting his interests and their attributes to the voters. In July 1782 representatives of the club were included in the funeral ceremonies accorded to the Marquis. Among those attending were the Quaker doctor William White, a long-standing member of the club, alongside Peter Johnson, the city recorder, Aldermen Stabler, Bacon and Myers, and Peregrine Wentworth, Lord Rockingham's staunch supporter and chief party organizer.[65] William White was one of the committee members who wrote to Earl Fitzwilliam in August 1782, after the death of his uncle, informing him of his election as president of the Rockingham Club. Membership of the club was to lead White into a sphere of operation which, as Elizabeth Isichei has noted, the majority of Quakers generally shunned.[66] Although York was a Rockinghamite corporation, it and several of its members also supported the claims of Christopher Wyvill.[67] William White was one of these admirers and he attended a Yorkshire Committee of Association Meeting in the Assembly Rooms in December 1782, commenting in his diary that 'The Rev. Mr Wyvill, Mr. H. Duncombe, Mr Stanhope, the Earl of Surrey etc. spoke excellently … and the greatest unanimity appeared upon the occasion.'[68]

Despite the increasingly sterile and restrictive exhortations issued by Yearly Meeting during the 1780s and '90s, York Monthly Meeting did not condemn William White's political activities and appears to have been able to tolerate its more idiosyncratic members and their activities.[69] After 1790, these directives were specifically aimed at trying to ensure that Quakers were not accused of radical or revolutionary activities during the French Revolution and subsequent wars with France. To try to counteract any such accusations, the Yearly Meeting of 1792 advised: 'Let us not suffer our minds to be drawn after that in which it is not our duty to be engaged; much less let us attach ourselves to any party.'[70] The many Epistles urging Friends not to converse about the war or to enter into any business which might help the war or be involved in war-like trade show that it was becoming increasingly difficult for the Society to keep its flock on a straight and narrow path.

Fears caused by the ferment surrounding the French Revolution, accompanied by a perceived breakdown in the control of the Established Church as manifested in the rise of Methodism, ensured that Quakers, as Dissenters, were often accused of radicalism. In 1791 a Lincoln Quaker wrote that when Thomas Paine's pamphlet *Rights of Man* was published, he was '... one of those charged with disaffection from Government and I am branded with the infamous names of republicans and Painites'.[71] Anti-war and, as a result, perceived to be anti-Pitt, anti-slavery and opposed to Pitt's Two Acts of 1795, York's Quakers were well aware of the ease with which such accusations could be levelled and Lindley Murray warned Henry Tuke not to publish an anti-war article in the *Christian Observer* for fear it might '... raise or increase a spirit of resentment against us', and he added: '... a controversy of such a nature, at this time, is not calculated either to produce conviction in the minds of others or to disarm their resentment against ourselves'.[72] In these troubled times, William Richardson, the Evangelical Anglican vicar of St Michael le Belfrey parish, York, 'suffered great distress and anxiety of mind, on account of the spirit of revolt and blasphemy which extended over Europe' and wrote an article in the *Christian Observer*, suggesting that: 'They who have learnt to despise their ecclesiastical superiors, and the established religion of their country, are easily led a step further – to murmur against their rulers in the state, and to despise the government under which the providence of God has placed them.'[73] Connections between radicalism and nonconformity – and, by implication, Quakerism – may have been, as Roy Porter has suggested, over-stressed, but in the minds even of learned men like William Richardson, William Wilberforce and Edmund Burke, it was only too easy in a period of political sensitivity to interpret the Quaker refusal to pay church rates and tithes as quasi-revolutionary behaviour.[74]

Despite Yearly Meeting's attempts to restrict political argument within the Quaker community, there was a debate in 1796 between two of York Meeting's most intellectual members, Henry Tuke and Lindley Murray, on the subject of the Society's attitudes and reactions to political involvement. At the Yearly Meeting of that year, Henry Tuke raised the subject of whether Friends should vote. He prepared a speech suggesting that it was inconsistent with Quaker principles to be involved in party politics and that they should '... wholly decline voting for members of Parliament'. He objected on the basis that they ran the risk of electing 'men ... who generally support the forced maintenance of a hiring ministry, and perhaps, in some instances, for those who promote the continuance of an unjust and unmerciful traffic in the persons of men'.[75] He felt that, by voting, Friends might give their implied approval to things which were against their principles, because they were unable to limit the actions of the elected representative. Lindley Murray responded, pointing out that if Quakers did not vote, they restricted their sphere of influence, giving themselves no chance to repeal, change or influence parliamentary affairs or to choose the type of men elected:

> ... from a sense of the benefits of a free Government with respect both to religion and morality, and the importance of promoting the wiser and better sort of rulers to the Legislature, we come forward on our own behalf and that of our fellow citizens, to procure as much good, and prevent as much evil, as we can to the community ...[76]

Henry Tuke was running against a gathering tide. His father, who in 1784 had put aside his scruples and spoken out for voting in that election, wrote to Henry in 1804 acknowledging that Quakers had gained certain rights and that this was not inconsistent with Quakerism:

> ... [I] wish that Friends who incline to give their vote may do so quietly without endeavouring to influence others but I think it is not yet a time for Friends to make a general stand against voting at all. Our situation both in a Society capacity and as members of the Community make it necessary for us at times to apply to Members of Parliament for their aid and as legislators and therefore we cannot I think reasonably refuse our votes to such as we deem most suitable for that important station.[77]

Anti-slavery campaign

The increased need for political pressure necessitated by the anti-slavery campaign forced many Quakers to reassess their views with regard to voting. By the last decades of the eighteenth century the anti-slavery movement had become a Quaker *cause célèbre*. As early as 1671, George Fox had recommended that Friends should set their slaves free. By 1758, Quakers had prohibited the importation of slaves and by 1761 they had excluded from the Society anybody who had any trade in slaves or dealings with slave-produced goods. In 1787 Quakers were amongst those who formed the Committee for the Abolition of the Slave Trade. The original committee consisted of nine Friends and three others who were members of the Evangelical wing of the Established Church, including Granville Sharp, and their agent, the industrious Thomas Clarkson.[78] The movement gained further impetus when John Wesley put the numerical strength of Methodism behind the abolitionist cause, but their most resounding coup was the recruitment of the young William Wilberforce.[79] Contact between the powerful London Quakers behind the Abolition Committee and the provinces soon caused information about their work to spread throughout all the Quarterly and Monthly Meetings.[80] Epistles from Yearly Meeting and instructions to investigate the activities of members who might be involved in the slave trade grew more frequent and more urgent and hardly a year passed between 1772 and 1844 without encouragement. Inexorably, provincial Quakers were drawn into an expanding national concern.

York Quakers were early recruits to the cause. In 1772 John Woolman, the American Quaker abolitionist, toured the Quarterly Meetings of England, arriving in York in July 1772. He stayed with Thomas Priestman, who wrote that he would eat '... no sugar nor anything that came through the hands of the negro slaves'.[81] Tragically, Woolman contracted smallpox and died a few days after his arrival in York. William Tuke noted the great encouragement that he had given to Quakers involved in the anti-slavery campaign and '[h]is last testimony ... was on the subject of the slave trade ... [he advised Friends to] remonstrate their [slaves'] hardships and sufferings to those in authority, especially the legislative power in this Kingdom'.[82]

In 1784 York Meeting received 10,500 copies of a paper entitled 'The Case of our fellow creatures, the oppressed Africans', one of the numerous pamphlets against the slave trade issued by the Meeting of Sufferings which were to be distributed to people of influence in the city to '... invite them to afford all opportunities to discourage the traffic'; William Tuke was amongst those involved in the distribution.[83] In 1788 York Corporation decided officially to back the campaign and sent a petition to the House of Commons, suggesting that the slave trade was '... wholly inconsistent with the dictates of morality and true religion'.[84]

The first political test for the loyalty of York Quakers to the Abolition Committee was the election of 1790. Wilberforce, who had abandoned his friendship with Pitt in the name of abolition, was to find out if his change in political allegiance was to lose him his Hull parliamentary seat. The poll book for Yorkshire for the 1790 election is not extant, so it is impossible to know how the York Quakers voted, but it would be unlikely that they did not support Wilberforce. The Yearly

Meeting Epistle of that year had urged that '... Friends may continue united in a fervent concern, that the reproach of a traffic so iniquitous, may be done away from the Christian name ...'.[85]

Although the cause of abolition was so strongly supported by a growing number of Quakers, Methodists and an increasingly powerful lobby of humanitarian activists in York, it was not until the election of 1807 that York Friends became involved in Wilberforce's election campaign. By then, Wilberforce's name had become synonymous with the anti-slavery cause. The first practical help that Friends gave him was in October 1806, when three of the most prominent members of the Meeting, Lindley Murray, William Tuke and Thomas Priestman, put their names to his electioneering pamphlet. But this was only a beginning of what became a wholehearted effort by a group of York Quakers to ensure that Wilberforce was elected. For Henry Tuke, it entailed an ideological volte-face when he suggested in 1807 that his son Samuel put a notice in the press, suggesting that Quakers help defray Wilberforce's election expenses.[86] This suggested financial support led the young Samuel to become more involved in electioneering than his father had anticipated, raising the disapproval of both his father and his grandfather. But Lindley Murray's support, combined with the nature of the cause, ultimately succeeded in reducing their objections. Murray wrote reassuringly to Henry Tuke on 23 May 1807: '... I think he [Samuel] conducts himself with great judgment and prudence'.[87] On 24 May, Murray wrote to Samuel congratulating him on his work for Wilberforce:

> The prudence and well timed zeal with which my Friend Samuel Tuke has conducted himself in the cause of William Wilberforce during the present contested election, have appeared to me to be so proper, so suited to the feelings of a mind, desirous at the same time to support the interests of virtue and honesty, and to avoid every infraction of our humble and peaceable principles ...[88]

Although Henry Tuke did not approve of Samuel's electioneering, he began finally to appreciate that Quaker assistance could not be limited to financial contributions, and wrote to Lindley Murray from Yearly Meeting on 25 May:

> ... the spirit of electioneering is so apt to hurry the mind out of due bounds, that it was no small satisfaction to find that Samuel had conducted himself with so much propriety and prudence. ... I should have been glad that Friends could have avoided taking so active a part on this occasion but William Wilberforce and the cause of Abolition are so intimately united, that it seems almost impossible to separate them.[89]

Only a few York Friends held Yorkshire freeholds, but those that did voted for Wilberforce (see Appendix VII, table 2). The efforts of York Quakers, Wilberforce, Thomas Clarkson and all abolitionists were rewarded in the next session of Parliament, when the Bill to abolish the slave trade was passed on 24 February 1807.

The anti-slavery campaign brought to the fore the conflict between Quakerism's needs and its idealized vision of political activity. If the Society was to become more public and support such causes, it needed access to the political system, but it was a system of which it could not approve. The exchanges between Henry Tuke and Lindley Murray and the actions of Samuel Tuke highlight the paradoxical situation that existed for Quakers when they came face to face with their own conflicting ideals. Their dilemma was reflected within the membership of individual Meetings as Quietist principles came up against the more worldly outlook of a growing proportion of Quakers.

Despite these conflicts of conscience, York's Quakers continued along a politicized path and, having achieved the abolition of the trade in slaves, they turned their efforts towards the abolition of slavery itself. Leading Quakers in the city, including Samuel and Daniel Tuke, William Alexander, Benjamin Horner, Lindley Murray, David Priestman and James Backhouse, and the Anglicans William and Jonathan Gray, the Revd John Graham and Robert Cattle were members of the Anti-Slavery Society, many of whose York branch meetings were held in the Friends Meeting House. On 1 August 1823 a newly formed committee of the Anti-Slavery Society petitioned the Lord Mayor to call a meeting of the inhabitants of York to petition Parliament to adopt measures for '... ameliorating the condition of slaves and carrying into effect the gradual abolition of slavery'. York's Anti-Slavery Society did not adopt the more radical call for immediate abolition and the Revd John Graham spoke in favour of a gradual approach. At a meeting on 4 August, when Thomas Clarkson was present, a committee was formed which included Samuel Tuke (treasurer), Jonathan Gray (secretary) and Daniel Tuke.[90] Throughout the next twelve months, the committee continued to collect money and hold anti-slavery meetings. In 1828, a pamphlet was published by the Quaker printer William Alexander to '... enable every man to judge whether religion and patriotism do not alike call for a renewed effort ... [to remove] this stain upon the moral and religious character of our country'.[91] But progress was slow, and in 1830 Joseph Sturge suggested that this was because Quakers had taken gradual rather than immediate abolition as their motto, which had '... not only in some degree retarded the great object but have allowed a subject ... to merge into a question of expedience'.[92] This lack of commitment to a more radical campaign was reflected in a petition to Parliament from the York Anti-Slavery Society in 1830 pointing out that the 'British

Colonies have done nothing to alleviate the plight of the slaves and Parliament has done little to insist they do'.[93]

However, by the time of the 1832 election, Quakers and Wesleyan Methodists had joined in a pledge not to support any candidate who '... would not pledge himself to supporting the total abolition of colonial slavery'.[94] The Anti-Slavery Society and the abolitionist cause generally did much to bring together many of the leading members of York's godly community: Evangelical Anglicans such as Jonathan and William Gray, William Richardson and Dean Fontayne and many members of the corporation, including the lord mayor, were in full support.[95] The movement brought Quakers like William and Henry Tuke into contact with members of the Clapham Sect and with leading York Evangelicals such as Faith and William Gray, all of which was influential in introducing Evangelicalism into York Meeting.

Although there is no evidence that there was a ladies' Anti-Slavery Society in York, Quaker women, including Priscilla Tuke, Maria and Esther Tuke, Hannah Murray, Ann Alexander and Alice Horner, and the Anglicans Mary and Faith Gray all contributed to the cause, helping their husbands and fathers behind the scenes and attending the huge anti-slavery meetings held in York between 1823 and the 1840s.[96] Quaker women were natural recruits to the abolition campaign, being amongst the few women in nineteenth-century England with a training in committee work and public speaking. When James Cropper (the Liverpool Quaker abolitionist) and his daughter Eliza visited York in 1825, Priscilla Tuke described a dinner at William Richardson's house at which Cropper had spoken passionately to his audience on abolition.[97] Quaker women who were involved in the movement were often more radical than the men. Elizabeth Heyrick believed that the campaigners were too soft and that slavery should be 'crushed at once'.[98] Although women abolitionists such as Lucretia Mott found her an inspiration, the men generally ignored this radical female approach.

Parliamentary elections

Although the cause of slavery brought the first public response to electioneering from the Quaker community in York, Quakers had always voted in elections (Appendix VII, table 2). The poll books are not extant for the elections between 1774 and 1807, but the majority of Friends were Whigs. In 1774 there was no dissension in their ranks, but in the first election of the nineteenth century the Tories were able to claim three split votes and two whole votes from the Quakers. In 1818 the Tories gained as many Quaker votes as the Whigs did, but the next election in 1820 saw a revival in Quaker support for the Whigs.

After the election of 1807, it was not until 1826 that a Quaker once again became involved in the election campaign for a parliamentary candidate in York. Francis Carbutt was a member of the campaign committee of Lord Milton and John Marshall.[99] Radical Quaker support for the 1832 Reform Bill was confirmed in York in the election of that year, when not only did the previously enfranchised members of the Society vote Whig, but so did many of the newly enfranchised Quakers; the Tories registered only seven Quaker votes.[100]

Although the Reform Bill was a disappointment to many, it did open up Parliament to a wider section of the middle classes and in 1833 two to three hundred of the city's leading citizens proposed to Samuel Tuke that he stand for election as a Whig candidate in the forthcoming parliamentary elections. He refused, giving as his reason: '... my unfitness for the high and important trust, which you are willing to repose in me'. His memoirs note that his refusal was based on his belief that his involvement in local affairs would clash with his parliamentary duties, and it is probable that the expense of a campaign was also a consideration.[101] Although he declined to stand, he gave his support to Lord Dundas, who had declared that he was for 'purity of election' and '... stood [against] the torrent of corruption in our city'. Having deplored the tactics of the Tories, he readily admitted that the Whig campaign was not uncorrupt.[102]

The election of 1835 was particularly controversial in York. The corporation gave their support to Charles Barkley, a Whig who stood for advanced radical reform. Amongst his demands were the commutation of tithes, broader access to, and provision of, education, an extension of the franchise and abolition of sinecure offices. Barkley had the support of the Dissenting deputies in London as well as some Quakers, including William Allen, a leading member of the anti-slavery movement, who nevertheless failed to persuade York Quakers that they should vote for Barkley. As Joseph Rowntree noted: 'We [Quakers] are accustomed to think for ourselves.'[103] The vice-chairman of Barkley's election committee was John Clemesha, a Quaker shoemaker.[104] In a somewhat over-confident statement, Barkley predicted that he had the support of all the York Friends, but in fact the voting figures show otherwise (Appendix VII, table 2h).[105] Once again the city elected a Tory (Lowther) and a Whig (Dundas).

The campaign had been particularly bloody and Lowther demanded an inquiry, suggesting wide-scale bribery of voters. Two petitions to Parliament were raised accusing Lowther of election fraud. One was organized by Barkley and his followers, in particular the Tory radical solicitor Robert Henry Anderson, and one by Joseph Rowntree, whom the *Courant* (a Tory newspaper) accused of being '... the radical Quaker whose fastidious stomach could not digest the allegations in Mr.

Anderson's Petition'.[106] Rowntree's petition dealt with the widespread bribery, accusing Lowther of sending sovereigns through the post to voters and suggesting that '... to such an extent does the practice of bribery prevail in elections in the city of York, that the representation of the City may be said to be offered to the highest bidder'.[107] The Select Committee set up by the House of Commons showed that in fact it was Samuel Tuke who was behind the organization of the petition and in effect it was the Whigs who were damned, although the Tories were not totally exonerated.[108]

Throughout the 1840s there was a growth in Quaker radicalism. Respected Quakers such as Joseph Sturge, who had learned their political art during the anti-slavery campaign, were increasingly willing to take up causes which appealed to social improvers.[109] Although Chartism was a predominantly working-class movement, many Nonconformists sympathized with the moderate Chartist artisans. Parliamentary reform and the repeal of the Corn Laws neatly dovetailed with radical Nonconformist interests. York Quakers were active supporters of the Anti-Corn Law League and when Cobden, Bright and Perronet Thompson visited the city to rally provincial support in 1844, many Friends attended their meeting. A subscription amounting to £115 was raised and donations were received from many prominent local Liberals, including the Revd Charles Wellbeloved (Unitarian), George Leeman (Independent), Joseph Rowntree (Quaker) and Caleb Williams (Quaker).[110] As the League became increasingly radical, many of the more moderate Liberals withdrew their support, including George Leeman, Joseph Rowntree and the York Member of Parliament, Henry Yorke.

Quaker radicalism did not die with the Anti-Corn Law League. In 1848 Henry Vincent, the quasi-Quaker radical, came to York to build support for his bid for parliamentary election. He was a known supporter of the Chartists, and the local press claimed that he was the 'candidate of the Quakers' in a thinly veiled attempt to link, incorrectly, the Quakers with the Chartists.[111] But his views on temperance, church reform, peace and parliamentary reform did match those of the Quakers. In January 1850 Vincent was in York to form a branch of the Reform Association. Again, this was supported by several Quakers, including John and William Briggs, James Backhouse and Joseph Rowntree, each of whom had become a vociferous protester against church rates.[112] Many members of the York Reform Association were also members of the Anti-State Church Association and had also been abolitionists. Vincent, despite support from the Friends, failed to be elected in 1849, but he tried again in 1852, when the Quaker James Baker was his campaign secretary. Once more he failed, polling only 887 votes.

Quaker radicalism did not disappear with the defeat of Vincent and Quakers continued to be involved in election campaigns. William Coning, a working-class Quaker grocer, supported the radical Liberal candidate Malcolm Lewin (a Methodist) in the 1857 election.[113] Lewin, a supporter of the Sunday Reform Movement, aimed to relax the regulations against Sunday band concerts, the opening of museums, etc., suggestions which, once again, Rowntree and Leeman joined together to oppose.[114]

In the 1780s York Friends were quietly active politically, voting in elections, objecting to the corruption and bribery which attended them, but taking little further part. The needs of the anti-slavery campaign had forced them to take a more vigorous and public role in politics, but their increased involvement also came from an astute awareness of their own self-interests – as increasingly prominent and wealthy members of a rising middle class, Quakers wanted recognition for the humanitarian concerns of the Society. However, although their participation was high by Quaker standards, in numerical terms it was low, particularly in a city which was so highly politicized.[115] It was a minority, albeit an increasingly radical one, of Friends who actually took an active part in politics and they were led by those already most active in the wider arena.

Levels of integration of York's Quakers were directly linked to a range of common mores and godly principles held by a section of the urban middle class in the city. As Jonathan Barry correctly noted: 'The real distinction in religion was between the children of God and those of the Devil not between churches.'[116] The great common enemy of the Quakers and their fellow citizens was ungodliness, unbelief and lawlessness. Religion was such an integral part of civic life that distinctions of forms of worship became blurred in the common pursuit of evil. As restrictions were eased and Quakers grew in wealth, status and influence, pressure to become active in the pursuit of a more egalitarian and humanitarian social order increased and distinctions of difference diffused even further. As a consequence, York's Quakers moved more forcefully and positively into the political arena.

CHAPTER 7

Demographic and Socio-Economic Profiles of York Monthly Meeting

Socio-economic profile

In the years 1780–1860, York Monthly Meeting underwent a gradual socio-economic revolution. During the early and mid-eighteenth century, it had become a largely urban, *petit bourgeois* Meeting, with the majority of its members involved in artisan trades and shopkeeping. This trend continued throughout the eighty years being studied and, as table 1 shows, by 1820 it had become predominantly middle-class, with an increasingly large upper-class element.[1] Appendix X is a breakdown into five social classes of the trades present in the Meeting between 1780 and 1860.

Table 1   YMM: analysis by socio-economic status

	Class I %	Class II %	Class III %	Class IV %	Class V %
1780–1820	10.0	36.4	38.6	10.4	4.6
1821–1860	17.1	45.7	25.7	8.6	2.9

Table 2   BMM: analysis by socio-economic status[2]

	Class I %	Class II %	Class III %	Class IV %	Class V %
1780–1794	6.8	22.7	63.6	4.6	2.3
1810–1824	8.5	19.2	63.8	6.4	2.1

Tables 1 and 2 show that whereas York Meeting changed structurally to develop a large upper middle-class element in its membership, Bristol Meeting did not do so. It is significant that there was no parallel increase in Bristol Meeting in class I membership, the numbers remaining almost static for this period. Furthermore, the membership continued to be dominated by a large class III majority. This failure to develop an economically powerful and intellectually stimulating upper class, from which a strong leadership could have developed and under whose guidance doctrinal change could have been introduced, could be one of the factors which led to the decline of the Meeting in the 1830s and '40s. However, without further detailed study of Bristol Meeting, this can only be supposition, but it may be significant.

These analyses of two Meetings, different within themselves, support the general consensus among historians of Quakerism that the Society of Friends had become predominantly middle-class by the beginning of the nineteenth century.[3] To put the analysis of York Meeting into context with the socio-economic structure of the city of York, a similar analysis of two York parishes, St Mary's, Castlegate, and St Michael le Belfrey, was undertaken.[4] These two parishes have been chosen because no single York parish could provide a satisfactory comparison. St Mary's was the site of the Quaker Meeting House and several Quakers lived in the area, while St Michael's was the centre of Evangelicalism in the city and, of all parishes, was probably the most middle-class.[5]

Tables 3 and 4 show that, even at the beginning of the period, York's Quakers belonged more to socio-economic class II than the inhabitants of either of the two parishes did. Both parishes had a significantly greater percentage of inhabitants in class IV and V occupations than either YMM or BMM. By the end of the eighteenth and the beginning of the nineteenth century, the Society was becoming dominated by the middle classes: a membership consisting of shopkeepers and craftsmen, headed by a skilled and increasingly well-educated élite. By the 1820s the

Table 3   The parish of St Mary's, Castlegate: analysis by socio-economic status

	Class I %	Class II %	Class III %	Class IV %	Class V %
1773–1813	5.4	18.1	56.4	18.1	1.8
1814–1820	12.2	12.2	51.2	17.0	7.3
1821–1830	13.0	17.4	47.8	17.4	4.3
1831–1857	6.0	30.3	45.5	12.2	6.0

Source: Baptismal registers

Table 4   The parish of St Michael le Belfrey: analysis by socio-
economic status

	Class I %	Class II %	Class III %	Class IV %	Class V %
1779–1804	10.1	19.1	50.6	15.7	4.5
1805–1820	9.5	25.7	50.0	10.8	4.0
1821–1840	8.0	21.8	48.3	16.1	5.7
1841–1860	11.0	30.0	39.0	15.0	5.0

Source: Baptismal registers

Quakers in York had become even more middle-class, with nearly twice as many members in class I occupations and fewer belonging to classes III and IV.

Two other indicators of socio-economic status can be used to confirm these findings. Servants have been used by a variety of historians as an indicator of social class;[6] a considerable and increasing proportion of York's Quakers employed servants.

Table 5   Employment of servants by York's Quakers

	No servants %	One servant %	Up to three servants %	More than three servants %
1780–1820	37.0	33.0	30.0	0
1821–1860	4.0	70.0	19.0	7.0

A further indicator of the wealth, social status and education of York's Quakers was their level of literacy. Marriage registers can be used as a source for the study of literacy rates. Those of YMM show that even the humblest Friend was able to sign the register. There are no cases during the whole eighty-year period of a Quaker simply making a mark on a marriage certificate. This compares with the literacy rates shown below for St Mary's and St Michael le Belfrey, although it should be noted that signing a register does not necessarily indicate literacy; some might have been able to sign their name, but could not write anything else.

Table 6   Literacy rates shown as a percentage of all marriages
celebrated at St Mary's, Castlegate

	Bride signs	Groom signs	Bride marks	Groom marks
1799–1812	45	63	55	37
1813–1837	59	76	41	24
1838–1859	66	81	34	19

Source: Marriage registers of St Mary's, Castlegate

Table 7   Literacy rates shown as a percentage of all marriages
celebrated at St Michel le Belfrey

	Bride signs	Groom signs	Bride marks	Groom marks
1780–1812	72	89	28	11
1813–1837	77	79	23	21
1838–1853	79	87	21	13

Source: Marriage registers of St Michael le Belfrey

The rate for St Mary's is very close to Alan Armstrong's figure for York between 1851 and 1853 of 21.3% of grooms and 32.9% of brides making a mark rather than signing, but the figures for St Michael's show a higher level of literacy.[7] This would suggest a better level of education amongst the parish population of St Michael le Belfrey, reflecting its higher socio-economic profile, although it is still lower than the level achieved by the York Friends.

Demographic profile

John Stephenson Rowntree's prize-winning essay of 1859 on the decline in membership of the Society showed that, whilst the majority of Monthly Meetings and the Society as a whole had declining numbers over the period from 1780, York Monthly Meeting not only maintained its figures, but progressively, if slowly, increased in size.[8] The fundamental question to be addressed in this section is whether demographic explanations alone were responsible for this growth, or whether there were other contributory factors which helped to retain or attract members.

By 1780, York Monthly Meeting encompassed the towns and villages of York, Selby, Clifford and Cottingwith (see Appendix VIIIa). All these towns and villages had their own Meeting, but the scope of this research is limited to the environs of York Meeting, which includes outlying suburbs such as Fulford, Askham Bryan and Naburn. In 1827 the township of Thirsk and the village of Huby were amalgamated with York Meeting because of the decline in their Meetings' memberships (see Appendix VIIIb).

Table 8   YMM membership statistics, by decade[9]

	1780	1790	1800	1810	1820	1830	1840	1850	1859
	125	130	108	125	155	157 (243)*	210	210	234
Change		+5	-22	+17	+30	+2	+53	0	+24

* With the amalgamation of the Thirsk and Huby Meetings into York Meeting in 1827, membership increased by 70. However, in 1828 York reverted to counting its membership exclusive of Thirsk and Huby, reducing the membership by 86. This gives a corrected figure of 157 for the year 1828.

The general trend of an increased membership is clear, but a detailed analysis has been made in three stages to establish the underlying causes. The first considers whether it was natural causes which were responsible for the rise in membership. An analysis of deaths and births within York Meeting has been undertaken and a comparison made with two York parishes. The second will consider whether birth and marriage patterns in York Meeting were a factor in the demographic growth; these are then compared with the two parishes to show the different rates between the three populations. If demographic growth is not the answer to York Meeting's rising membership, a third factor has to be considered: the internal structure of the Meeting. Therefore, an analysis of disownments, admissions and removals in and out of the Meeting has been undertaken, and these results have been compared with BMM.

As table 9 shows, death and birth rates were of major importance for a small Society. If high mortality and low birth rates affected the Society, then the membership would be reduced.

Table 9   YMM deaths and births

	Deaths	Births	Total gain/ shortfall
1780–1790	63	39	-24
1791–1800	46	19	-27
1801–1810	30	18	-12
1811–1820	22	30	+8
1821–1830	53	27	-26
1831–1840	46	16	-30
1841–1850	35	30	-5
1851–1860	50	30	-20

It is clear that natural increase was not the cause of the rise in membership. Only in the decade 1811–20 were there more births than deaths, while the reverse was the case in all other periods. The most surprising and, for the Quaker community, the most alarming feature is the failure of the number of births to rise along with the rise in membership. To explain this, mortality rates for York Meeting have been compared with the two York parishes. These mortality rates have been divided into two sections: infant and child mortality has been worked out both as a percentage of live births and as a percentage of all deaths; adult mortality rates have been calculated separately.

Mortality rates in the adult population indicate that the Quakers were losing proportionately more of their young people than either of the two parishes. Once they had reached the age of twenty-five, however, they were increasingly likely to survive into old age. Over the whole period, York's Quakers had a long life-span, the majority living into their seventies, and there is a noticeable improvement in the numbers reaching their sixties and seventies throughout the whole period. It is probably safe to conclude that they had a longer life expectancy than the population of either of the two parishes.

This longevity amongst the Quakers was probably due to their predominantly middle-class lifestyle. It is unlikely that they enjoyed better sanitary conditions or health care than those in the two parishes (which may account for their high infant mortality), but it is likely that they had a healthier diet and better housing and, for some, an easier lifestyle – all factors which may have contributed to overall improved health. Even so, of those who had a long life, there were some, such as Valentine Johnson, a glover, who were amongst the less well-off members of the Meeting. Quakers themselves claimed that their sober lifestyle led to longevity. Although this might have been a contributory factor, it is unrealistic to imagine that it could be of major significance. Despite this scepticism, as Eversley has argued in his study of the southern rural Quakers (designated SRUR), it does appear that once York's Quakers had survived infancy and childhood, the majority could look forward to a long life and expect to live into a 'ripe old age'.[10]

Table 10   YMM adult mortality rates

	16–25 yrs %	26–40 yrs %	41–55 yrs %	56–75 yrs %	75+ yrs %
1776–1800	16.7	10.6	18.2	37.9	16.6
1801–1839	16.7	12.7	7.8	37.3	25.5
1840–1852	8.2	24.3	10.8	43.2	13.5
1853–1860	0.0	14.7	8.8	50.0	26.5

Table 11   St Mary's, Castlegate, adult mortality rates

	16–25 yrs %	26–40 yrs %	41–55 yrs %	56–75 yrs %	75+ yrs %
1780–1800	9.5	16.9	23.2	33.8	16.6
1801–1820	5.8	24.2	23.4	30.7	15.9
1821–1840	9.7	21.7	20.5	30.6	17.5
1841–1849	8.8	26.4	15.5	33.8	15.5

Table 12   St Michael le Belfrey adult mortality rates

	16–25 yrs %	26–40 yrs %	41–55 yrs %	56–75 yrs %	75+ yrs %
1780–1800	11.4	13.0	20.3	36.5	18.8
1801–1820	9.1	21.8	15.7	36.2	17.2
1821–1840	15.5	16.7	18.9	31.5	17.4
1841–1854	10.3	15.4	19.9	35.2	19.2

(Cholera epidemic 1832)

Although Quakers in York were more likely to live into old age than others in the two parishes, they were equally as likely to die in childhood. To establish a pattern of infant and child mortality, an analysis of infant and child deaths as a percentage of live births was carried out.

Table 13   YMM infant and child mortality rates as a percentage of live births

	0–12 m %	1–4 yrs %	5–9 yrs %	10–14 yrs %
1776–1800	35.5	11.1	11.1	5.5
1801–1860	17.2	10.9	4.6	4.0

These child mortality rates have been compared with those produced by Eversley in his work on the Irish Quakers.[11]

Table 14   SRUR Quakers infant and child mortality rates as a percentage of live births

	0–12 m %	1–4 yrs %	5–9 yrs %	10–14 yrs %
1750–1799	34.3	15.6	6.3	4.0
1800–1850	17.6	9.9	7.0	2.6

The figures for YMM show a remarkable similarity to Eversley's findings and, despite the much smaller sample from only one Meeting, they coincide sufficiently well with Eversley's conclusions to suggest that the sample size has not distorted them.

Eversley suggests that Quaker infant mortality was lower than the general population, but a study of the baptismal records for St Mary's, Castlegate, and St Michael le Belfrey shows that in these parishes the percentage of deaths amongst infants under one-year old between 1780 and 1800 was smaller than in the York Quaker population. In the next age group, Quaker children have a higher survival rate than St Mary's but lower than St Michael's. The toll of Quaker children over five was twice as bad as in either parish and they only fared slightly better in the later period, the two parishes still having a better rate. In the period from 1801 to 1860, although York Quaker infants appear to have a better survival rate than those of St Mary's, they were still worse than

St Michael's and the older Quaker children were still showing a lower rate of survival than those in the parishes.[12] Because the burial registers of YMM do not give any reasons for death, it is difficult to suggest what the causes might have been.

Table 15   St Mary's, Castlegate, infant and child mortality rates as a percentage of live births

	0–12 m %	1–4 yrs %	5–9 yrs %	10–14 yrs %
1780–1800	31.5	15.4	3.9	3.9
1801–1860	30.0	9.8	3.3	1.5

Table 16   St Michael le Belfrey infant and child mortality rates as a percentage of live births

	0–12 m %	1–4 yrs %	5–9 yrs %	10–14 yrs %
1780–1800	18.6	10.3	3.7	2.1
1801–1860	11.8	7.2	1.6	1.3

(St Michael le Belfrey baptismal records have to be treated with caution. Some children, born outside the parish, were christened in the Church because it was fashionable at the time.)

This analysis of infant and child deaths shows that the total mortality rate of children within most age ranges in York Monthly Meeting was significantly different from those in the two parishes. Quaker infants and children were much more likely to die than those living in St Michael's, although, surprisingly, after 1800 their infants did not fare better than those living in St Mary's. In the later period, although Quaker babies had a better chance of survival into the next age group, this simply meant that more of them had survived to then die between the ages of five and fourteen. The reason for this unusual distribution between infant and child deaths is unknown. There could be some aspect of Quaker childcare that helped infants to survive their first year, but no change in practice is recorded to explain the improvement in the second period. Another possible explanation for the low figure for infant deaths in the decades between 1801 and 1837, compared with St Mary's, is the lack of deaths from cholera and smallpox. This could be attributed to the fact that few Quakers lived in the squalid areas such as the Water Lanes and Friargate, off Castlegate (St Mary's parish). Again, the lack of evidence of a cause of death does not allow confirmation of this theory.[13] Moreover, infant and child mortality rates as a percentage of all deaths in YMM averaged about 50%. This is very similar to the figure for St Michael le Belfrey, but St Mary's, Castlegate, as might be expected, had a higher figure of 60%. The lower death rate in YMM and St Michael le Belfrey parish reflects the middle-class lifestyle of the two populations.

Birth and marriage rates

There are known discrepancies present in parochial baptismal records. Omissions can include inaccurate or unrecorded baptisms, unbaptized and illegitimate births and Nonconformists. Record-keeping by Quaker Meetings was extremely efficient and, as Eversley observed: '... Quaker material is more accurate over a longer period of time than all but the best of Anglican registers ...'.[14] It is unlikely that there is significant under-recording in either marriage, birth or death records. However, if there are deficiencies, as is likely, in the recording of baptisms in the records of St Mary's, Castlegate, and St Michael le Belfrey, this means that the birth rate for York Meeting is even lower in comparison with them than is shown in the table. Alan Armstrong has suggested that, in the 1840s and '50s, York did have a lower birth rate than the general population.[15] Figures from Eversley's work on Worcestershire parishes appear to confirm Alan Armstrong's findings.[16] If the birth rate of York Meeting is then compared with the rate for the population of England and Wales, it was significantly lower in all four periods.

Table 17   Birth rates: YMM (as % of membership*) and St Mary's, Castlegate (as % of population)

	1780–1800	1801–1820	1821–1840	1841–1860
YMM	22.6	23.5	13.7	14.2*
St Mary's	—	29.2	29.9	25.6
St Michael's	—	50.1	35.5	35.9**
York	—	—	26.3	31.5
Worcester	35.4	32.6	32.0	31.5

* The figures may be distorted by the larger membership figures for the years 1820–60 and the failure of the number of births to rise.

** Figures for St Michael's are badly distorted by the number of fashionable baptisms taking place at the church. A declining population in 1851, combined with a declining popularity, meant that baptisms had fallen from an average of 69 in 1821–30 to an average of 40 in 1851–60.

Table 18   Birth rate: England and Wales (as % of population)

1799–1803	1809–1813	1819–1823	1841–1851
34.2	33.8	33.4	32.7

Although there is some distortion in the birth-rate figures for York Meeting, the number of births failed to rise at a rate corresponding to the membership. Even allowing for error, the rate is lower in the first two periods – and dramatically lower in the last two – when compared with that of the populations of St Mary's parish, York, Worcester or England and Wales. In no period did it begin to match the other figures. When combined with a high infant mortality rate, a low birth rate had a drastic effect on the growth of the Meeting and was responsible for the overall lack of natural increase in most years. In all probability, this reflects the fertility problems encountered by the late marriage pattern amongst York Quakers. And if this pattern were repeated in other Meetings, it would be an additional reason for the slow growth of the membership of the Society as a whole.[17]

The women of York Monthly Meeting repeatedly practised a pattern of late marriage (see Chapter 4, p. 56). Of the eighteen marriages that took place in the Tuke family between 1765 and 1853, seven of the women were over thirty and four were over twenty-five. The younger a woman was at marriage, the greater the number of years in which she could be expected to produce children and therefore, theoretically, the greater the number of children she could be expected to bear. Davidoff and Hall have shown that middle-class women married significantly later than their lower-class sisters. In their sample, they found that the average marrying age was 26.5 years for women and 29 years for men,[18] both somewhat higher than that of the general population. In Eversley's sample for the SRUR Quakers, both men and women were marrying remarkably late by comparison with either the Davidoff and Hall sample or the general population. This late marrying age reduced the number of years in which the women were fertile; when this age is compared with that of women in St Mary's parish, it is clear that Quaker women were in effect reducing their fertility rate by 4.2 child-bearing years between 1776 and 1820 and by 4.6 years in the later period. Theoretically, this could mean a reduction of up to two children per female. Even by comparison with the slightly more middle-class women in St Michael le Belfrey parish, York's Quaker women were still significantly reducing their potential fertility rate.[19] Although they appear to fit in with Eversley's figures for the SRUR Quakers in the first period, by the later period they were beginning to marry at an earlier age.

Table 19   Average marrying age of men and women: YMM and SRUR Quakers

York Quakers	1776–1820	1821–1860
Women	29.3	27.4
Men	32.6	31.3
SRUR Quakers	1750–1799	1800–1849
Women	28.8	30.2
Men	31.6	32.4

Table 20   Average marrying age: St Mary's, St Michael's, York and national averages

St Mary's	1800–1830	1831–1860
Women	25.1	22.8
Men	27.6	25.0
St Michael's		
Women	21.5	26.4
Men	27.0	29.3
National average	1800–1849	
Women	23.4	
Men	25.4	
York	1838–1865	
Women	25.8	
Men	28.7	

The marriage rate is quite a significant factor affecting fertility: fewer marriages mean fewer children. John S. Rowntree produced figures for Quaker marriages which can be compared with those calculated by Eversley for the population of Worcestershire.[20]

Table 21   Marriage rates: national Quaker rates compared with Worcester parishes (per 1,000 population)

	Quaker	Worcester
1800	4.82	7.89
1810	4.40	7.98
1820	4.78	6.32
1830	4.93	6.67
1840	4.09	

These rates, when compared with those in York Meeting, suggest that the marriage rate in the latter, although higher at times than the national Quaker average, was generally lower than the rate found in the Eversley survey in Worcestershire.

Table 22   Marriage rates: YMM (as % of membership)

1800	6.6
1810	8.3
1820	5.6
1830	3.8
1840	3.1
1850	9.7
1860	3.7

All these factors, combined with the increasingly middle-class nature of York Quakers, ensured the creation of marriage patterns within the Meeting which reduced the potential fertility rates of these couples.[21] And this, added to high infant mortality rates, is of further importance when considering the insignificant level of natural growth in the Meeting.

These demographic analyses demonstrate that it was not natural growth which was responsible for the increases in membership in York Meeting. In fact, it was significantly worse than those of the population of York and very similar to the patterns identified by Eversley in his survey of SRUR Quakers. There must therefore have been a further factor responsible for the expansion and, since it was not demographic, it had to be an internal factor. To identify this, an analysis of the internal structure of the Meeting was carried out.

Disownments and removals

The decline in membership between 1791 and 1800 (table 8) is more than accounted for by a net natural loss of twenty-seven members (table 9), but the gains in other periods are at variance with the shortfall in births over deaths. Other factors must have contributed to the growth of the Meeting. One of these could be the rate of disownment of existing members compared with the rate of admission of newly converted Quakers. Table 23 makes this comparison of disownments and resignations with new admissions.

Table 23   YMM: admissions and disownments

	Admissions	Disownments/ resignations	Gain/shortfall
1780–1790	8	14	-6
1791–1800	10	18	-8
1801–1810	12	10	+2
1811–1820	11	12	-1
1821–1830	7	14	-7
1831–1840	16	11	+5
1841–1850	15	14	+1
1851–1860	19	19	0

We can see from this that the net excess of disownments in the first period of decline, 1790–1800, may have helped to cause that drop, but that the relative level of disownments and admissions does not, on its own, explain the growth of the Meeting.

It would therefore appear that a net surplus of removals into York Meeting, from existing members of the Society of Friends, was the main reason why membership figures rose in all but the two decennial periods (Appendix IX). Reliable statistics for removals in and out for the period to 1800 are unavailable and a gap exists in the Certificates of Removals in the years 1829–41 and 1853–80. However, the Monthly Meeting minutes provide an overall total of removals in and out in the years 1831–40, 1853 and 1860. These figures confirm the hypothesis that it was the high number of existing members entering the Meeting that was the most significant factor in determining changes in the level of membership.

Table 24 shows that, in almost all periods, there was an overall gain in the number of existing members moving into the vicinity of York Meeting.

Table 24   YMM: removals in/out of existing members

	Removals out	Removals in	Gain/shortfall
1800–1825	219	310	+91
1826–1830	67	88	+21
1831–1840	173	187	+14
1841–1853	239	234	-5
1854–1860	142	169	+27

Table 25   YMM: totals of tables 8, 9, 23 and 24

	Change	Deaths/ births	Disownments/ admissions		Existing members in/out
1780–1790	+5	-24	-6		unreliable
1791–1800	-22	-27	-8		unreliable
1801–1810	+17	-12	+2	1800–25	+91
1811–1820	+30	+8	-1		
1821–1830	+2	-26	-7	1826–30	+21
1831–1840	+53	-30	+5	1831–40	+14
1841–1850	0	-5	+1	1841–53	+5
1851–1860	+24	-20	0	1854–60	+27

These statistics suggest why York Meeting was able to maintain and increase its membership in all but two decades of the eighty years under consideration. This was achieved not through natural increase, but by the admission of a relatively large number of newly converted members (sufficient, or almost sufficient, to cancel out a relatively low disownment rate) which combined with the ability of the Meeting and the city to attract existing members from other Meetings.

This theory can now be tested further by reference to membership figures for other meetings. Bristol Monthly Meeting has been chosen because, whilst it was consistently larger than York, it had some similarities. It was an urban Meeting over which a known influential family appeared to have exerted influence. Most importantly, with the exception of membership details, all the records for the Meeting for the period being studied were complete and readily available for study.[22]

Comparison with Bristol Monthly Meeting shows that, unlike York, it suffered a decline in membership from 1790 to 1820, when the overall loss was seventy-nine members. It began to recover during the period 1820–40, when membership reached the figure of 589, but the average figures conceal a steady decline which began in 1833, when membership was 636; this fell to 510 by 1846 and to 380 by 1863, a loss of 256 members in thirty years. At the same time as Bristol numbers were dropping steadily, York was showing a increase in membership.

Bristol Meeting was only one of many within the Society to record a decline in numbers. Marsden Monthly Meeting, within Lancashire Quarterly Meeting, recorded a membership of 345 in 1831, but by 1850 it had fallen to 252.[24] The Society as a whole found that by 1800 it had only 19,800 members; 16,277 by 1840; and 15,345 by 1847.[25]

Table 26   BMM membership statistics

	Membership	Change
1790–1800	555	
1801–1810	496	−59
1811–1820	476	−20
1821–1830	586	+110
1831–1840	589	+3
1841–1850	533	−56
1851–1863	380	−153

(Membership lists for BMM are haphazard: 1790–1800 had to be extracted from an unreliable membership list; 1800–20 are only available for five of the twenty years; and for 1830–46, sufficient information exists only for membership numbers to be averaged[23])

Admissions and disownments as factors in membership growth and decline

The rate at which individual Meetings disowned members was of vital importance to the growth or decline of the Meeting. In most cases, for every member disowned, the Meeting not only lost that individual, but usually also the membership of a husband/wife and any children. Members could be disowned for a whole range of misdemeanours, of which, as John S. Rowntree showed, marriage outside the Society was to prove to be the most damaging.[26] These so-called crimes included business failure, immorality, persistent non-attendance at Meetings for worship, joining another chapel/church, excessive drinking, stealing and dishonesty, joining the Army or Navy, taking oaths and being baptized. Members could also resign – a route often advised by the Meeting for recalcitrant members. Over the period 1780–1820, YMM disowned 41.9% of its membership, and over the next forty years 28.6%. BMM disowned 35.2% in the first forty years and 41.7% in the later period. The percentage differences were not great in the first period but, by the second, York had reduced its disownment rate by 13.3%, whilst Bristol had increased its rate. Bristol, in fact, disowned 406 members over the eighty-year period and the Meeting admitted only 148. The damage that disownment could do to a Meeting is well illustrated. York Meeting provides a strong contrast to this, for whilst it disowned 112 members over the whole period from 1780, it admitted 98, in effect almost cancelling the shortfall caused by the numbers disowned.

Table 27   YMM: disownments (excluding marriage out)

	1780–1800	1801–1820	1821–1840	1841–1860
Business failure	6	3	5	3
Immorality	5	3	0	0
Drink	2	1	1	1
Miscellaneous	1	4	5	1
Resignations	0	1	5	13
Resignations as % of membership	0	0.7	2.7	5.9
Disownment as % of members	11.6	5.4	6.0	2.3

Table 28   BMM: disownments (excluding marriage out)

	1780–1800	1801–1820	1821–1840	1841–1860
Business failure	7	4	9	3
Immorality	5	3	8	2
Drink	3	0	2	0
Miscellaneous	18	38	27	11
Resignations	5	11	38	55
Resignations as % of members	0.9	2.2	6.4	10.7
Disownment as % of members	7.6	11.3	15.0	13.2

The lower rate of disownment in YMM suggests either that the regulations were being relaxed or that misdemeanours were fewer. Whilst the latter might be true, it is impossible to prove the point; but there was a leniency within the Meeting which led to the adoption of a flexible attitude to those suspected of committing so-called crimes.[27] There are several cases where it was only after many weeks – even months – of investigation that disownment or even suspension was carried out. It is probable that the attitude of the Meeting was influenced by the social and economic standing of the individual member. When William Richardson, a tanner and an elder, was disowned in 1831, it took many months to investigate his affairs and several leading members of the Meeting, including Thomas Backhouse, tried to prevent it happening.[28] Undoubtedly, the attitude of the person concerned often influenced the investigating committee. John Linney, a printer, was declared bankrupt in 1848, but because he refused to co-operate with the investigators and would not show them his books, they quickly reached the decision to disown him. And even as the Meeting was beginning to allow civil marriages, they disowned the eccentric John Johnson in 1858 for such a marriage, because he refused to co-operate with the investigating committee.[29]

If these figures are compared with those for Bristol Meeting over the same period, except for the last decades of the eighteenth century, Bristol consistently disowned a higher (and, indeed, until 1840 an increasing) proportion of members than York did. It would be speculative to suggest that the cause was a difference in attitude, but the misdemeanours for which Bristol members were disowned were significantly different from those recorded in York. During the whole period there were no disownments in York Meeting for joining the Army or Navy, despite the fact that York was a garrison town; nor for taking an oath or being baptized, although Joseph King was baptized in St Mary's, Castlegate, in 1788.[30] All these misdemeanours appear on Bristol's list and, despite the long-established availability of affirmation under the 1722 Affirmation Act, the last disownment for oath-taking was as late as 1840. It is possible that the size of Bristol Meeting and, consequently, its more diffuse membership, combined with the attendant opportunities in a port for poorer members to be lured into prostitution or the Navy, could have contributed to the Meeting's inability to maintain discipline.[31] Because of the lack of cases in Bristol where members were forgiven and subsequently reinstated into membership, it has to be concluded that in many cases disownment was used as an example as well as a punishment.

Disownment and marriage out

As John Rowntree demonstrated, the greatest number of disownments throughout the Monthly Meetings was for marriages contrary to the Society's rules. His figures also indicated that there were wide variations in the percentage rate of disownments for marrying out between individual Meetings within the Society as a whole. The figures for Yorkshire Quarterly Meeting for the period studied by Rowntree illustrate this well.[32]

Table 29   Yorkshire Quarterly Meeting: marriages, 1837–1854

Monthly	Av. no. members	No. married to rule	As % of members	No. married against rule	Disowmnents for marriage out as % of members
York	302	28	9.3	11	3.6
Balby	299	31	10.4	20	6.6
Pontefract	430	52	12.1	32	7.4
Brighouse	819	53	6.5	61	7.4
Knaresborough	119	5	4.2	8	6.7
Settle	68	5	7.4	4	5.8
Pickering	155	10	6.5	16	9.0
Hull	154	9	5.8	5	3.2
TOTAL	2, 346	193	8.2	157	6.7

There are noticeable discrepancies between Meetings. Brighouse and Pontefract were both largely urban areas and returned disownment figures which were twice as high as York or Hull, whereas Settle and Balby, which were rural Meetings and therefore perhaps inclined to stricter control, returned lower figures. There is not sufficient consistency within these figures to construct a pattern of disownment which would allow a comparison between rural and urban Meetings, but it could be suggested that the former, because of their size and greater social cohesion, were able to uphold stricter discipline. But, to counter this theory, the urban Meetings of Hull and York show a lower rate of disownment for marriage out than all the other Meetings. Had there been many like Knaresborough, where more members were marrying out than in, the effect on the Society as a whole would have been catastrophic.

A detailed breakdown of disownments for marriage outside the Society for the York and Bristol Meetings over the whole period show the devastating effect that this regulation was having on individual Meetings (see table 30).

In both Meetings, women were more likely to marry out than men, an action which led to automatic disownment. However, table 30 suggests that, at least up until 1840, York was not suffering such great losses as Bristol. The position after 1840 is complicated by the ambiguities in Bristol's record-keeping. There is, nevertheless, some evidence to suggest that York was pursuing a more lenient attitude in these years and keeping disownments to a minimum. When civil marriage became available in 1852, York members marrying in a Registrar's Office were generally

Table 30   YMM and BMM: members disowned for marrying out

| | YMM | | As % of | BMM | | As % of |
	Male	Female	members	Male	Female	members
1780–1800	5	13	14.8	25	20	8.1
1800–1820	2	8	4.9	24	24	9.7
1820–1840	4	5	4.9	23	28	8.6
1840–1860	7	8	6.8	12	1	2.5*

* The low number of female resignations in these years suggests that some women may have been persuaded to resign before marrying out; consequently, this figure is misleading.

not disowned;[33] but this was not the case in Bristol. The attitude of York Meeting to civil ceremonies was summarized in a letter from John Rowntree to his fiancée relating the case of Ann Brown, whose wedding had been conducted in a Registry Office. He wrote that he had told Friends that: ' ... it seemed to me injurious to the individual, harmful to the Society and unauthorised by Scripture' to disown a member for what was, in effect, a moral act. He added, that whilst he had been supported by '... John Ford, my brother, my father and Thomas Coning', he had had to defend himself against an 'onslaught by John Kitching'. Although his ideas with regard to the future discontinuation of this practice had already begun to be formulated and, within York Meeting, he had a good many supporters, he was aware that whilst '... a good deal had been gained', it would take time to have an effect, because, as he wrote, '... this iniquitous practice cannot be overthrown at once – it will probably be a long struggle'.[34]

Removals in and out as factors in membership growth and decline

Appendix IX shows the movement of people into and out of York Meeting already in membership with the Society. Every member who moved in or out of any Monthly Meeting had to have a Certificate of Removal. This were typical of the rigid control exerted over the moral and social welfare of members by the Society and by individual Meetings. Besides introducing a Friend to a new Meeting, the certificate also formed a recommendation as to that person's conduct and his/her clearness from engagements of marriage; it also warned the new Meeting if the member needed any special supervision. When Samuel Smith came to York from Hull Meeting in 1801, his certificate cautioned that he had a record of frequent absence from Meeting; Elizabeth

Ventress, a servant, moved to Pickering Meeting in 1804, which was warned that she '... needs watchfulness against unprofitable company and conversation'; Mary Coning, a servant, was considered to 'dress too un-Quakerly'.[35] By counting these certificates, it has been possible to construct a profile of movements into and out of the Meeting (Appendix IX).[36]

There were several unique factors within York Meeting which appealed to members from other Meetings. The Retreat, opened in 1796, attracted not only patients but also staff, and provided employment for servants, nurses, doctors and general assistants.[37] Trinity Lane School was opened in 1785 and, although it was mainly staffed by existing members of York Meeting, extra servants were employed by Esther Tuke to help with its management. When the Quakers established a girls' school for poor non-Quaker children in the city in 1812, they employed Hannah Wilkinson as the schoolmistress as well as several assistants. With the re-establishment of a Quaker girls' boarding school in York, the Mount School provided employment for at least fifteen female servants and assistants between 1832 and 1860. Bootham School, established in 1823, was also a continual source of employment for a succession of Quaker male teaching assistants and several headmasters. And it may be that many Quaker servants and shop assistants found employment within non-Quaker households as the general population of York expanded.[38]

A study of Quaker wills has shown that members of York Meeting enjoyed increased prosperity during this period.[39] The evidence from this study, combined with a socio-economic analysis of the Meeting, demonstrates that York Meeting had developed a growing middle class by the 1820s. Increasing prosperity resulted in employment for larger numbers of servants and apprentices. Appendix IX indicates that, as members' businesses developed, the employment of apprentices and shop assistants rose pro rata. Joseph Rowntree employed fifty-one shop assistants and apprentices between 1842 and 1859, and John and James Baker employed twelve between 1842 and 1848.[40] Prosperity also led to a rise in the number of house servants employed (see table 5, above). The largest number of people moving in and out of the Meeting were servants or apprentices. Families and individuals account for only a small percentage of these total 'removals in' and 'removals out'.

While the various activities of York Meeting were attracting existing members, newly converted Friends were also being drawn in. These factors, when combined with an ability to uphold the existing membership, helped the overall expansion of numbers. At the same time, resignations from the Meeting were very low by comparison with Bristol Meeting and it was not until the end of the period that they could be considered a significant depleting factor in York Meeting.

Compared with other Meetings, most of which, such as Bristol, were in decline in the crucial forty years to 1860, York was far more successful in keeping its members.

The period of decline suffered by York Meeting in the decades before the turn of the nineteenth century corresponds to the years before the various schools and the Retreat began to offer employment and before growing prosperity increased employment opportunities for servants and apprentices amongst the general population of the Meeting. This period of restricted growth also coincided with a period of doctrinal change; a time before the full effects of the Enlightenment and Evangelicalism had begun to be felt and when remnants of the suffocating effects of Quietism were dying away but had not entirely disappeared.

The period of stagnation between 1840 and 1850 corresponds with the general economic depression of the 1840s. This decline is reflected in the numbers of servants and apprentices entering the Meeting (see Appendix IX). However, although this slowing-down might have been responsible for alerting John S. Rowntree to the decline, the annual figures for numbers leaving and entering the Meeting confirm that it was only at the end of the 1840s, in 1848 and 1850–1, that there were more people leaving the Meeting than entering it. After 1852 it continued to expand, attracting new entrants as well as converting more people than at any other time.

Conclusion

From these analyses, it can be seen that the increase in membership experienced by York Meeting in the period between 1780 and 1860 was not as a result of a high birth rate or a low infant and child mortality rate. Rather, it was caused by the ability of the Meeting to retain its existing membership, attract a large number of new recruits through convincement, and to operate a lenient and benign system of disownment against recalcitrant members. This sympathetic treatment allowed the Meeting to readmit many of those whom it had previously disowned and to hold on to existing members. However, more important than any of these factors was the increased demand for labour, particularly for servants, shop assistants and apprentices, brought about by the establishment of the Retreat and the Quaker Schools; the business acumen of members led to an expansion in business activity and a subsequent rise in income which, consequently, increased prosperity in the home.

These factors support the arguments made in earlier chapters, that there was a powerful internal dynamic within York Meeting which created strong male and female leadership, manifesting itself particularly in a powerful women's ministry. An atmosphere of understanding and cohesion, which allowed members to be innovative and experimental, resulted in the development of a Meeting of ideas, which gave rise to a variety of major projects. And it was these major projects which attracted Friends from other parts of the country into York. At the same time, Quakerism in the city was able to project a high-profile image as an attractive and exciting Meeting, encouraging many non-members to become regular attenders. This, in turn, because of its open-door policy, led to a substantial number of converts, which was responsible for the expansion and development of York Meeting.

Conclusion

The publication of John Stephenson Rowntree's seminal essay in 1859 suggested that York Meeting experienced an atypical growth in its membership in the period 1780–1860.[1] However, whilst his explanation for the decline of the Society of Friends as a whole told some of the story, it did not go far enough and was unable to explain why the trend in York Meeting was so different from most of the others. Analysis of York Meeting's statistics has shown that its growth had nothing to do with internal factors and that, in fact, it suffered worse demographic development than the rest of the city of York;[2] the expansion of the Meeting was entirely due to its own internal dynamics and philosophy. In comparison with Bristol, it appears that York Meeting created an atmosphere of harmony, leniency and tolerance, which ensured that it retained the members it already had, disowning only a comparatively small percentage. At the same time, York was creating a sufficiently vibrant and exciting form of Meeting and ministry to attract a high number of new converts to Quakerism, many more than in Bristol.[3]

Surmounting these internal factors was a government of the Meeting which allowed its members to be experimental and to express and put into action new ideas of humanitarianism and social concern. The results of these endeavours were a range of new opportunities for employment which drew existing Quakers to York. Many jobs were created by the growing wealth and business success of members, but most of all they derived from the establishment of, in the first instance, the Retreat, Trinity Lane School and, in 1829, Bootham Boys' School and, in 1831, the Mount Girls' School.[4]

The transformation of York Meeting began in the last decades of the eighteenth century with the arrival of Esther Tuke in 1765. Her appearance on the scene was highly significant in terms of the future progress of York Quakerism, ushering in a new era of experimental humanitarian reforms and vital changes in internal doctrine and education. Although she was not radical, her views and perceptions, combined with the dynamism of her husband William, helped to form the intellectual basis of the revitalization and rejuvenation of York Meeting.

The socialization and education that they gave to their children and to her stepchildren created men and women who went into the world to preach the distinctive Quaker doctrine which had been engendered within York Meeting. This encouragement of new ministry was reflected in the rise in the number of ministers, especially female, between 1780 and 1820, their revived participation in the Quarterly Meeting for Ministers and Elders, and in the number of journeys that they undertook. The introduction of new doctrine and the expansion of ideas were also manifested in the three major schemes of Ackworth School, Trinity Lane School and the Retreat.[5]

These endeavours not only signalled to the rest of the Society of Friends that York Meeting was making a conscious effort to help revive the flagging ministry and verve of the Society, but also effectively announced to the world at large that Friends had a significant role to play within the spheres of humanitarianism and education.

At the forefront of this rebirth was a conscious elevation of the role of women. The fact that the first school that the Meeting established was for the education of middle-class girls, in order to equip them for a life which, Esther Tuke clearly recognized, would in all likelihood include the ministry, shows how conscious she and other women of the Meeting were that it was a female élite who would be responsible for infusing Meetings with new vitality, enthusiasm and growth. This emphasis on the importance of women as leaders reinforced the existing essential role that they played within the structure of the Society as a whole, and helped to ensure that the rise of a middle-class culture did not erode that role within the organization of the Meeting, but rather enhanced their range of activities by allowing them an entrée into the world of philanthropy and education.[6]

The influence of Evangelicalism and its integration into the doctrine of York Meeting was a vital, dynamic factor in its development and expansion. Not only was it a new and vibrant form of doctrine which drew Quakers closer to other Christians, but it also gave members the intellectual impetus to develop their own humanitarian interests and externalize their concerns, thus increasing the range and opportunities for co-operation with other religious denominations within York's society. Without men such as Henry Tuke and Lindley Murray and women like Esther Tuke, York Meeting would not have been led into a new era of expansion and doctrinal integration. It was they who opened up opportunities for the next generation of Quaker Evangelicals, in particular J. J. Gurney, by allowing Friends to achieve creedal harmony with other Christians without the loss of doctrinal individuality or credibility.

Doctrinal change on its own would not have been sufficient to account for the increasing integration of York's Quakers into the social and political life of the city. Essential to this was economic growth and rising social status. Comparison with Bristol Meeting has shown that, whilst it maintained a high predominance of class III members throughout the period under consideration, York Meeting enjoyed an almost continuous rise in the number of class I and II members which, in the period from 1820–60, ensured that it became dominated by these groups.[7] At the same time that York's Quakers were undergoing socio-economic growth, the city itself was experiencing a similar change – by comparison with Norwich in 1851, York had 6.4% more households with servants. The high rate of domestic labour in York reflected the wealth and extent of the servant-employing middle class.[8] Although it was not subject to the great population growth of the West Yorkshire towns of Leeds, Bradford and Halifax – unlike Norwich, which declined because it failed to attract new industry – York's populace increased steadily, largely due to the influx of Irish labourers attracted by the growth of opportunities for work on the surrounding farms and, from the 1850s, on the railways and in the railway workshops.[9] Undoubtedly, the rise in York's population, accompanied by the continuing railway boom in the 1840s and 1850s, helped to prevent the city from suffering serious economic decline during the depression of the 1840s. The expansion was particularly beneficial to the class of traders with most Quakers and this was reflected in the lack of a serious decline in the number of servants and apprentices that Quakers were taking on in those years.[10]

The existence of comparatively large classes I and II in York – analysis of figures for 1851 shows that 22.05% of the population were in classes I and II and 51.26% in class III – was also a contributory factor in Quaker integration.[11] As Quakers became increasingly middle-class, opportunities for integration and social interaction were created by the presence of a large bourgeois élite within the city with similar interests and concerns. It was they who created such charitable and social organizations as the Philanthropic Society and attracted such prestigious groups as the British Association for the Advancement of Science to York in 1844.[12]

Many of the opportunities for integration also coincided with the rise of Evangelicalism and its use as a form of social control by the ruling élite and the middle classes during the years of the French Revolution and the wars with France. Fears of civil unrest and a breakdown in the social and moral order had produced a number of both national and local reforming and humanitarian societies in York. Participation in the regulation of their parishes as constables and vestry officials led Quakers to support such associations as the Society for the Prevention of Profaneness and Vice, the Vagrancy Office, the York Penitentiary and the various temperance movements.

Throughout the seventeenth and eighteenth centuries, Friends had worked not only within their parishes, but also in the corporation.

The removal of the legal disabilities against Dissenters in the 1820s and '30s enabled them to further their political ambitions. Reforms in local government, together with its increased democratization, allowed Quakers to play an ever more active role in parish and corporate government, while their fight to redraft the 1825 Police Bill drew them into the radical wing of local politics. Their success as Improvement Commissioners, despite the conflicts and turmoil of the first years of their existence, ensured that Quakers were ready to serve as councillors when local government reorganization took place in 1835. Although, after the passing of the Municipal Corporations Act, York city politics settled down to a period of autocratic rule by George Hudson, for Quaker councillors it was both a period of consolidation and political education as well as a period of varied fortunes and conflicts. Throughout the early 1840s they were able to consolidate relations with their political allies, either in coalition against George Hudson or, occasionally, in co-operation with his administration, in order to secure their own as well as the city's future. By 1846, George Hudson's fortunes were on the wane and Liberal Quakers such as Joseph Rowntree had forged useful alliances with the leaders of the Liberal group, George Leeman and Joseph Meek, who were to become key players in York politics in the period up to 1860.[13]

Levels of Quaker integration were directly linked to the homogeneous nature of York society. Christians of all persuasions worked and acted together, particularly in times of crisis, when their middle-class livelihoods and lifestyles were threatened, and in the pursuit of their joint interests; distinctions between denominations were blurred by a range of common self-interests. The weakness of religious polarity ensured that, in York, men were Christians first and Quakers, Methodists or Anglicans second.

The dramatic changes that York Meeting had undergone by the mid-nineteenth century meant that it no longer displayed many of the classic features of a sect as described by Bryan Wilson and Michael Mullett.[14] The move away from sectarianism had been slow but persistent. The most obvious changes were the increased levels of integration with the wider community, which were accompanied by considerable internal changes in doctrine and regulation. By 1860, York Quakerism had abandoned many of its sectarian features: regulations on dress were being relaxed; novels and music were entering Quaker households; and paintings became listed chattels in their wills. At the same time, the Society generally was relaxing its rules in response to demands from a membership no longer willing to tolerate petty restrictions, inhibiting to individual members and harmful and restrictive to the development of the Society as a whole. Disownment for marriage outside the Society was abandoned in 1860 and compilation of the Great Book of Sufferings ceased in 1855. As Elizabeth Isichei noted: '… the sect was rapidly coming to accept the consumption patterns of other middle-class families … and resolved the difficulty by liberalising the conventions which had bound them'.[15] All these changes combined to ensure that, by 1860, Quakerism in York had become but one denomination amongst many.

York Meeting expanded and thrived because it allowed new philosophies and doctrines to enter its consciousness and because its Friends, both men and women, were able to articulate these changes without fear of sanction. The Meeting would have been of no consequence if its members had lacked the vision to see the necessity for change and the wisdom to use the rising doctrine of Evangelicalism for the benefit and use of Quakerism. York Quakers developed and promoted new ideas which accepted that the Society could no longer retain its peculiarities and isolation and survive. It was this message of rebirth that the Meeting was able to develop for its own benefit in the first instance, and for the Society's as a whole in the second. Combined with the growing wealth and rising social status of York's Quakers, this ensured that they became respected and integrated members of York's middle-class élite.

Appendix I

Name (Age at first appearance)	Number of attendances (M: Minister E: Elder)	
1780–1796		
Sarah Priestman	39	M
Ellen Abraham	29	M
Hannah Murray	28	E
Hannah Thurnam	25	
Mary Awmack	23	
Esther Tuke	23	M
Ann Armitage	19	
Rachel Priestman	18	
Sarah Tuke	17	M
Ann Awmack	15	M
Elizabeth Tuke	15	M
Rebecca Doeg	14	
Ann Priestman	14	
Ann Tuke (age 16)	11	M
Mary Hoyle	9	
Hannah Sharp	9	
Mary Maria Tuke	6	
Martha Fletcher	5	
Elizabeth Mason	5	
Sarah Priestman	5	
Jane Taylor	5	
Sarah Awmack	3	
Mabel Tuke (age 19)	3	E
Rebecca Awmack	2	
Elizabeth Lambert	2	
Martha White	2	
Mary Armitage	1	
Sarah Armitage	1	

Naomi Baiston	1	
Elizabeth Coldbeck	1	
Ann Fothergill	1	
Deborah Stansfield	1	

1796–1818

Mary Awmack	20	
Ann Priestman	20	M
Esther Doeg	16	
Catherine Jepson	16	
Martha Fletcher	15	
Esther Tuke	14	M
Martha White	13	
Deborah Sanderson	12	
Martha Richardson	10	
Priscilla Tuke	10	
Mary Camm	9	
Hannah Hall	9	
Sarah Tuke	9	
Mary Flower	8	
Mary Hoyle	8	
Elizabeth Mason	8	
Ann Alexander	7	M
Mary Mildred	7	
Hannah Murray	7	E
Isabel Richardson	7	M
Margaret Wilson	7	
Dorothy Bleckley	6	
Rebecca Fothergill (age 18)	6	
Maria Tuke, jun. (age 18)	6	
Sarah Armitage	5	
Sarah Busby	5	
Rachel Fowler	5	
Sarah King	5	
Katherine Morgan	5	
Sarah Thurnam	5	
Mary Armitage	4	
Elizabeth Mason	4	
Hannah Ponsonby	4	
Katherine Allen	3	
Hannah Galillee	3	
Rebecca Hedley	3	

Elizabeth Lister	3	
Rebecca Webster	3	
Hannah Wilson	3	
Sarah Awmack	2	
Sarah Bevans	2	
Rachel Foster	2	
Elizabeth Fothergill (age 15)	2	
Ann Mason	2	
Deborah Mason	2	
Mary Mason	2	
Ann Rimington	2	
Sarah Sanderson	2	
Ann Woolley	2	
Hannah Woodville	2	
Mary Backhouse	1	E
Hezia Bleckley	1	
Mary Doeg	1	
Mary Doubevand	1	
Mary Fletcher	1	
Alice Horner	1	
Mary Hubert	1	
Ann Knight	1	
Mary Knowles	1	
Catherine Mason	1	
Hannah Richardson	1	
Mary Richardson	1	
Sarah Salthouse	1	
Eliza Sims	1	
Ann Storey	1	
Elizabeth Thurnam	1	
Hannah Thurnam	1	
Mabel Tuke	1	E
Rebecca Tuke	1	

1818–1840

Sarah King	30	
Martha Richardson	24	
Ann Priestman	22	
Hannah Waller	21	
Mary Allis	17	E
Deborah Sanderson	16	
Hannah Wilson	16	

Elizabeth Fothergill	14	
Hannah Scarr	14	
Sarah Allis	13	
Sarah Baker	13	M
Martha Fletcher	13	
Elizabeth Backhouse	10	E
Elizabeth Mason (age 24)	10	
Alice Horner	10	
Barbara Waller	10	
Mary Knowles	9	
Elizabeth Rowntree	9	
Jemima Spence	9	
Sarah Rowntree	8	M
Rebecca Hedley	7	
Mary Hollingsworth	7	
Mary Lay	7	
Hannah Richardson	7	
Maria Tuke	7	E
Helen Burtt	6	
Jane Simpson	6	
Dorothy Bleckley	5	
Elizabeth Kitching	5	
Catherine Mason	5	
Hannah Ponsonby	5	
Katherine Stringer	5	
Sarah Thurnam	5	
Esther Tuke	5	
Charlotte Widdas	5	
Margaret Wilson	5	
Ann Alexander	4	M
Hannah Hall	4	
Hannah Ponsonby	4	
Ann Richardson	4	
Priscilla Tuke	4	
Deborah Backhouse	3	M
Mary Hoyle	3	
Katherine Jepson	3	
Hannah Mennel	3	
Katherine Morgan	3	
Jane Ventress	3	
Mary Backhouse, jun.	2	
Sarah Tuke (age 12)	2	
Anna Allis	1	
Rachel Awmack	1	

Esther Baker	1	
Mary Ann Baker	1	
Margaret Bennington	1	
Ann Briggs	1	
Caroline Crosfield	1	
Hannah Dickenson	1	
Ann Fletcher	1	
Priscilla Fletcher	1	
Rebecca Fothergill	1	
Rachel Hall	1	
Mary Hallersley	1	
Rebecca Johnson	1	
Jane Jowett	1	
Ann Knight	1	
Elizabeth Lister	1	
Mary Mason	1	
Isabella Oddie	1	
Hannah Prier	1	M
Elizabeth Ransome	1	
Ann Scott	1	
Sarah Maria Stackhouse	1	
Rachel Strickney	1	
Guilielma Tuke (age 21)	1	
Rebecca Tuke	1	
Elizabeth Webster	1	
Mary Wheatley	1	
Jean Wilson	1	
Celia Wilcoxs	1	M
Mary Williams	1	
Hannah Woodville	1	

1841–1860

Elizabeth Backhouse (age 18)	15	E
Jemima Spence	14	
Mary Baker	12	
Sarah Rowntree	12	M
Hannah Scarr	12	E
Abigail Taylor	12	
Maria Whitten	12	
Mary Priscilla Fletcher	11	
Hannah King	11	
Bridget Thompson	11	

Sarah King	10	
Jane Robinson	10	
Mary Backhouse	9	E
Mary Hollingsworth	9	
Elizabeth Baker	8	
Rachel Ford	8	E
Caroline Hipsley	8	
Mary Hustler	8	
Elizabeth Priestman	8	E
Martha Richardson	8	
Sarah Richardson	8	
Ann Tuke	8	
Ann Briggs	7	
Helen Burtt	6	
Rachel Mason	6	
Rachel Rowntree	6	
Margaret Spence	6	
Sarah Allis	5	
Sarah Baker	5	M
Jane Johnson	5	
Elizabeth Kitching	5	
Elizabeth Pumphrey	5	
Katherine Stringer	5	
Priscilla Tuke, jun. (age 24)	5	
Maria Tuke	5	E
Charlotte Widdas	5	
Mary Allis	4	
Eleanor Baker	4	
Elizabeth Mason	4	
Deborah Ransome	4	
Elizabeth Ransome	4	
Lydia Richardson	4	
Rebecca Shepherd	4	
Rachel Tregellis	4	
Anna Baker	3	
Esther Baker	3	
Fanny Baker	3	
Elizabeth Brady	3	
Dorothy Brown	3	
Rachel Burgess	3	
Maria Candler	3	
Susanna Fisher	3	
Eliza Stringer	3	
Jane Thornton	3	

Elizabeth J. Tuke	3	
Esther Tuke	3	
Mercy Ward	3	
Mary Anna Williams (age 22)	3	
Grace Wilson	3	
Mary Bellis	2	
Sarah Backhouse (age 20)	2	M
Hannah Benson	2	
Sarah Benson	2	
Hannah Brady	2	
Mary Brady	2	
Mary Casson	2	
Sarah Jane Casson	2	
Martha Fletcher	2	
Mary Flintoff	2	
Elizabeth Fothergill	2	
Jane Hodgson	2	
Maria Jackson	2	
Jane Jowett	2	
Eliza Naylor	2	
Maria Richardson (née Heath)	2	M
Hannah Robinson	2	
Rachel Spence	2	
Jane Ventress	2	
Mary Ann Waller	2	
Mary Alexander	1	M
Abigail Backhouse	1	
Henrietta Baker	1	
Mary Ann Bissell	1	
Fanny Burtt	1	
Martha Cash	1	
Mary Clemesha	1	
Rebecca Constable	1	
Martha Day	1	
Elizabeth Evens	1	
Rachel Ford	1	E
Rachel Goundrey	1	
Lucy Hallam	1	
Mary Hunter	1	
Deborah Hutchinson	1	
Elizabeth Hutchinson	1	
Lydia Hutchinson	1	
Mary Hutchinson	1	
Maria Jackson	1	

Fanny Jacob   1
Judith Ann Linney   1
Sarah Long   1
Hariette Merryweather   1
Sarah Mason   1

1841–1860

Elizabeth Moore   1
Mary Ann Morley   1
Hannah Ponsonby   1
Jane Procter   1
Lucy Reckitt   1
Mary Rhodes   1
Caroline Richardson   1
Elizabeth Rowntree   1
Maria Priscilla Shepherd   1
Rachel Special   1
Hannah Stephenson   1
Elizabeth Stringer   1
Emma Tuke   1
Barbara Waller   1
Sarah Waterfall   1
Mary Wheatley   1
Emma Woodward   1

Appendix II

Male and female ministers appointed within YMM

Female	Date of appointment	Male
Sarah Priestman	1778	
Esther Tuke	1771	
Ann Awmack	1779	
Sarah Tuke	1781	Henry Tuke
Ellen Abraham	1786	
Elizabeth Tuke	1787	Lindley Murray
Ann Tuke	1788	
Mary Tate	1790	
	1796	Benjamin North
	1816	William Bleckly
Isabel Richardson	1818	
Sarah Baker	1820	
Deborah Backhouse	1822	
	1824	James Backhouse
	1825	Samuel Tuke
Hannah Prier	1827	
	1828	John Sanderson
Mary Alexander	1829*	
	1831	Caleb William
	1832	William Baker
Sarah Backhouse	1833	
Elizabeth Janson	1834	
Mary Hustler	1843	
	1846	John Candler
Esther Smith	1847	
Hannah Pierson	1849	
Sarah Rowntree	1855	
Celia Wilcoxs	?*	
Maria Richardson	1858	

* These women were already ministers when they came into York Meeting; the date referred to is that of their Certificate of Removal.

Appendix III

Table 1   Value of Quaker estates, 1780-1860

Name	Occupation	Value of will	Death date
Nathaniel Bell	Bookseller	£100	1778
Isaac Richardson	Tanner	£5,000	1791
John Fothergill	Horn-maker	£2,000 + freehold estate	1807
Thomas Priestman	Tanner	£10,000	1812
Thomas Fox	Whitesmith	£200	1813
Isaac Galilee	Tanner	£600 + tan yard & pits	1814
Henry Tuke I	Tea-dealer	£7,500	1814
Joseph Awmack	Grocer	£1,500	1816
Hannah Galilee		£600	1817
(died intestate, wife of Isaac)			
Parker Busby	Glover	£1,800	1818
Sarah Busby		£1,800	1818
(widow of Parker)			
William Tuke	Tea-dealer	£2,000	1822
John Mason	Tea-dealer	£4,000	1823
Lindley Murray	Gentleman	£14,000	1826
(estate in UK)			
Anne Backhouse		£600	1829
(sister of James & Thomas)			
Rachel Fowler		£400+	1829
(widow of Thomas Fowler, physician)			
Hannah Murray		£4,000	1834
(estate in UK)			
Henry Mason	Druggist	£1,500	
(died intestate)			
Benjamin Horner	Dentist	£35,000	1836
Mary Backhouse*		Railway shares	1838
(mother of Thomas & James)			
Joseph King	Grocer	£4,000	1839

/Cont.

147

Table 1   *Cont.*

Name	Occupation	Value of will	Death date
William Alexander	Bookseller	£3,000	1841
John Tuke	Land-surveyor	£100	1843
Thomas Backhouse	Nurseryman	£60,000	1845
Robert Waller	Gentleman	£25,000	1846
Robert Jackson	Butcher	£600	1848
David Priestman	Gentleman/tanner	£12,000	1851
Christopher Scarr	Merchant	£9,000	1854
Mary Alexander	Schoolteacher	£300	1854
Henry Tuke II	Gentleman	£600	1855
John Bleckley (late grocer & tea-dealer)	Gentleman	£600	1857

Table 2   Wills by valuation shown as a %

Under £500	17.9
£500+	21.4
£1,000+	32.1
£5,000+	10.7
£10,000+	17.9

Base: 28 wills (no value was put on Mary Backhouse's estate, so it was not counted).

Appendix IV

Table 1 YMM average age at marriage of Quaker men and women

	Women	Men		SRUR Women	SRUR Men[1]
1776–1820	29.3	32.6	1750–1799	28.8	31.6
1821–1860	27.4	31.2	1800–1849	30.2	32.4

Table 2 Age at marriage: St Mary's, Castlegate, and St Michael le Belfrey, compared with Armstrong and national averages

	1800–1830		1831–1860	
	Men	Women	Men	Women
St Mary's, Castlegate	27.6	25.1	25.0	22.8
St Michael le Belfrey	27.0	21.5	29.3	26.4
Armstrong[2] (York, 1838–65)	28.7	25.8		
National average (1800–49)	25.4	23.4		

Table 3 Widows and widowers marrying, % of total marriages, 1776–1860

	Widows	Widowers
YMM	2.4	7.3
St Mary's, Castlegate	10.8	21.6
St Michael le Belfrey	3.8	6.8

Table 4   YMM: socio-economic comparison of bride and
              bridegroom at the time of marriage, 1838–1860*

Bride same class as bridegroom	69.0%
Bride lower class than bridegroom	24.1%
Bride higher class than bridegroom	6.9%

* Only for these dates is there reliable information about the occupation of
the bride's father and the bridegroom.

Table 5   Age differences between husband and wife: YMM
              compared with Davidoff and Hall (as %)

Age	YMM	Davidoff and Hall
Wife more than 5 yrs older than husband	8.3	2.0
Wife up to 5 yrs older than husband	13.9	9.0
Same age	11.2	36.0
Husband up to 5 yrs older than wife	38.8	29.0
Husband 5–10 yrs older than wife	22.3	16.0
Husband more than 10 yrs older than wife	5.5	8.0

Apppendix V

Table 1a   YMM: interval between marriage and first birth, as % of all births, 1780–1860

	< 1 yr	< 2 yrs	< 3 yrs	> 3 yrs
	42.3	23.0	26.9	7.7

Table 1b   Interval between marriage and first birth, as average of months

No. of cases	No. of months
1	6.0*
11	10.4
6	16.0
7	28.0
2	44.0

* This was George and Mary Knowles' first child.

Table 2   YMM: average family size

	1st marriage	2nd marriage	SRUR Quakers[3]
1770–1820	3.7	4.6	4.3
1821–1860	3.7	3.5	3.7

Appendix VI

Social and philanthropic organizations in which York Quakers participated, 1740–1860

York County Hospital
York Anti-Slavery Society
York Dispensary
The Retreat (Q)
York Auxiliary Bible Society
York Religious Tract Society
York Association for the Prosecution of Felons & Cheats
York Society for the Prevention & Discouragement of Vice &
  Profaneness
York Benevolent Society
York Charitable Society
Campsall Female Friendly Society
Abbé Carrons Institutions
Society to Assist the Labouring and Poor Classes of York
The Mission to the Indians
The Mission to Africa & The East
Dr Choke's Society for Promoting Schools in Africa
Society for Promoting Permanent & Universal Peace
London Hibernian Society
Society for Promoting the Education of Native Females in India
York Lunatic Asylum
York Board of Guardians
York Vagrant Office
York Soup Kitchen
Yorkshire Philosophical Society
British Association for the Advancement of Science
York Penitentiary Society
The Society for the Prevention of Youthful Depravity
York & District Band of Hope Union
York Temperance Association
Female Temperance Association

The York Society for the Encouragement of Faithful Female Servants
York Mechanics Institute
York Mechanics Friendly Society
York Meeting Sewing Circle for the supply of garments to the poor of
 York (to some extent this was a social gathering for Quaker
 women, specifically designed to allow them more opportunities
 for socializing as well as being a charitable society)

Schools

The Blue Coat School   York Friends Girls' Sabbath
         School (Q)
The Grey Coat School   York Friends Boys' Sabbath
         School (Q)
York Ragged School   The British Girls' School (Q)
Yorkshire School for the Blind

Appendix VII

Table 1a Men attending YMM, 1780–1793

Name	Attendances	Occupation	Comment
Thomas Priestman	34	Tanner	Elder
Robert Pickering	33	Tanner	
James Hessay	30	Gentleman	
John Armitage	29	Cordwainer	Elder
John Fothergill	29	Comb-maker, partner Forbes & Fothergill	
Thomas Doeg	26	Schoolmaster	
Joseph Awmack	19	Grocer/wine merchant	
Thomas Fox	18	Whitesmith	
Nathaniel Bell, jun.	17	Bookseller	
John Thurnam	17	Husbandman	
William Thurnam	17	Yeoman	Elder
Henry Tuke*	16	Tea-dealer	Minister
John Tuke	16	Land-agent	
William Hoyle	15	Husbandman	
William Tuke*	15	Merchant	Elder
William Tuke, jun.	13	Farmer	
John Mason	12	Tea-dealer	
John Sharp	12	Husbandman	
William Baiston	10	Plain-maker	1782[c]
Lindley Murray	9	Grammarian	Minister
John Martin	7	Coal-dealer	
William Awmack	6	Breeches-maker	
William Morley*	6	Linen-draper	
Daniel Peacock	3	Linen-draper	1787[xy]
Timothy White	3	Gentleman	
Daniel Awmack	2	Grocer	
John Moon	2	?	
Joseph Priestman	2	?	

Stephen Procter	2	Carpenter	
William White*	2	Doctor	
John Awmack	1	Husbandman	
John Fothergill, jun.	1	Comb-maker	
George Peacock	1	Dyer	Elder
John Webster	1	Farmer	

TOTAL: 34

x disowned	c convinced member	
y insolvent	* high level of 'public' involvement	

Table 1b Men attending YMM, 1794–1815

Name	Attendances	Occupation	Comment
George Jepson	50	Doctor at Retreat	
Joseph Awmack	48	Grocer/wine merchant	
John Armitage	47	Cordwainer	
David Priestman	40	Tanner	Elder
Thomas Doeg	37	Schoolmaster	
William Hoyle	37	Husbandman	
Thomas Priestman	36	Tanner	
David Doeg	29	Looking-glass maker	
John Martin	29	Gentleman	
Samuel Richardson	27	Tanner	
John Sanderson	27	Woollen-draper	Minister
Robert Pickering	24	Tanner	
Timothy White	24	Gentleman	
John Tuke	21	Land-agent	
William Richardson	20	Tanner	1831^{xy}
John Sharp	20	Husbandman	1810^{xy}
William Tuke	19	Merchant	Elder
Francis Flower	18	Farmer	
Henry Tuke	17	Tea-dealer	Minister
William Alexander*	16	Bookseller/printer	Elder
John Fothergill	14	Combmaker	
Lindley Murray	13	Grammarian	Minister
Stephen Priestman	12	Woollen-draper	

/Cont.

Table 1b   *Cont.*

Name	Attendances	Occupation	Comment
William Bleckley	11	Linen-draper	Minister
Thomas Fox	11	Whitesmith	
Herbert Camm	10	?	
Samuel Tuke*	10	Tea-dealer	Minister
Gervas Elam	7	Farmer	
John Mason	7	Linen-dealer	
William Tuke, jun.	7	Farmer	
Benjamin North	6	?	Minister
Joseph King	4	Grocer	
William Thurnam	3	Yeoman	
James Hessay	2	Gentleman	
John Robinson	2	Cordwainer	
Christopher Scarr	2	Grocer	
Thomas Ventress	2	Gardener	
John Webster	2	Farmer	
Nathaniel Bell	1	Bookseller	
John Bleckley	1	Tea-dealer	
Caleb Fletcher	1	Grocer	Elder
Joseph Hardy	1	Coachman	
Hartas Headley	1	Farmer	
George Knowles	1	Woollen-draper	1813[xz]
John Mason	1	Tea-dealer	
William Simpson	1	Bookseller	
Thomas Sturdy	1	?	

TOTAL: 47

[x] disowned	[z] immorality	
[y] insolvency	* high level of public involvement	

Table 1c   Men attending YMM, 1816–1829

Name	Attendances	Occupation	Comment
David Priestman	33	Tanner	Elder
Joseph King	27	Grocer	
John Sanderson	27	Woollen-draper	Minister
William Richardson	24	Tanner	1831[xy]; 1840[a]

Caleb Fletcher	20	Grocer	
Samuel Tuke*	20	Tea-dealer	Minister
George Jepson	14	Doctor at Retreat	
Thomas Backhouse*	13	Nurseryman	
George Baker	13	Farmer	Elder
John Tuke	13	Land-agent	
William Bleckley	11	Linen-draper	
John Bleckley	10	Tea-dealer (?)	
Joseph Rowntree*	10	Grocer	
William Alexander*	9	Bookseller/printer	Elder
Thomas Allis	9	Superintendent at Retreat	
James Backhouse	9	Nurseryman	Minister
Caleb Williams*	8	Doctor	
Hartas Headley	5	Farmer	
Robert Waller	5	Tea-dealer	
John Clemesha*	4	Hatter	
John Scarr	4	Grocer	
William Simpson	4	Schoolmaster	
William Thurnam	4	Yeoman	
Leonard Johnson	3	Shopkeeper	
Samuel Lay	3	?	
Henry Ransome*	3	Linen-draper	
William Webster	3	Farmer	
William H. Alexander	2	Bookseller	
David Doeg	2	Looking-glass maker	1817[xy]; 1818[a]
Thomas Mason	2	Tea-dealer	
Joseph Awmack	1	Grocer/wine merchant	1820[r]
Francis Carbutt	1	Woollen-draper	
John B. Giles	1	?	
Robert Jackson*	1	Butcher	1829[c]
Robert Leef	1	?	
Thomas Mennell	1	Gentleman	
Stephen Robson	1	Servant	
Joseph Spence*	1	Druggist, partner York Glass Works	
Daniel Tuke	1	Tea-dealer	
William Tuke	1	Merchant	

TOTAL: 40

[x] disowned	[c] convinced member	
[y] insolvency	[r] resigned membership	
[a] reinstated a member	* high level of public involvement	

Table 1d   Men attending YMM, 1830–1836

Name	Attendances	Occupation	Comment
Thomas Allis*	19	Superintendent at Retreat	
David Priestman	18	Tanner	Elder
Thomas Backhouse*	14	Nurseryman	
George Baker	12	Farmer	
John Tuke	11	Land-agent	
Caleb Fletcher	10	Grocer	
Joseph Rowntree*	9	Grocer	
Robert Waller*	9	Tea-dealer	
John Walker	7	?	
Joseph King	6	Grocer	
John Ford	5	Headmaster, Bootham School	
Robert Jackson*	5	Butcher	
Caleb Williams*	5	Doctor	Minister
Samuel Lay	4	?	
Henry Ransome*	4	Linen-dealer	
Stephen Robson	4	Linen-dealer	
William H. Alexander	3	Bookseller	
John Bleckley	3	Tea-dealer	
Thomas R. Hills		?	
Joseph Spence*	3	Druggist	
John Wheatley	3	Farmer	
William Richardson	2	Tanner[xy]	
Holman Sheppard	2	Gentleman	
John Thompson	2	Porter-dealer	
Thomas Bennington	1	?	
John Clemesha*	1	Hatter	
Joseph Flintoff	1	Stonemason	
Leonard Johnson	1	?	1831[x]
Thomas Mason*	1	Tea-dealer	
Henry Richardson	1	Agricultural merchant	
John Sanderson	1	Woollen-draper	Minister
John Scarr	1	Grocer	

[x]   disowned
[y]   insolvent
*   high level of public involvement

William Simpson	1	?	
Samuel Tuke*	1	Tea-dealer	Minister
George Webster	1	Farmer	
William Webster	1	Farmer	
William Wheatley	1	Yeoman	
William Williamson	1	Rope-maker	

TOTAL: 37

Table 1e   Men attending YMM, 1837–1844

Name	Attendances	Occupation	Comment
Thomas Allis*	12	Superintendent at Retreat	
John Ford	12	Headmaster, Bootham School	
David Priestman	11	Tanner	
Joseph Spence*	11	Partner, York Glass Works	
Robert Waller	11	Tea-dealer	
Caleb Fletcher, jun.	9	Thread-maker	
Thomas Backhouse*	8	Nurseryman	
Holman Sheppard	8	Gentleman	
Robert Taylor	8	Butcher (?)	
George Baker	7	Farmer	
Caleb Fletcher, sen.	7	Grocer	
Henry Tuke, jun.	7	Tea-dealer	
Thomas Hills	5	?	
James H. King	5	Grocer	
John Walker	5	?	
James Backhouse*	4	Nurseryman	Minister
John Bleckley	4	Tea-dealer	
Joseph King	4	Grocer	
Joseph Rowntree*	4	Grocer	
John Candler	3	?	
Robert Jackson*	3	Butcher	
John Lewis Linney	3	Printer[xy]	
John Wheatley	3	Farmer	

/Cont.

Table 1e   *Cont.*

Name	Attendances	Occupation	Comment
James Baker	2	Farmer	
William Briggs*	2	Grocer	
Thomas Hattersley	2	Grocer	
Henry Ransome*	2	Linen-draper	
Edwin S. Rickman	2	Teacher	
Samuel Tuke*	2	Tea-dealer	Minister
William Alexander*	1	Bookseller	Elder
John Casson	1	Gentleman	
J. R. Hills	1	?	
William Hipsley	1	Gentleman	
William Sewel	1	Teacher	
Thomas Smith	1	?	
Silvanus Thompson	1	Teacher, Bootham School	
James H. Tuke	1	Tea-dealer	
John Tuke	1	Land-surveyor	

TOTAL: 38

ˣ disowned
ʸ insolvent
* high level of public involvement

Table 1f   Men attending YMM, 1845–1852

Name	Attendances	Occupation	Comment
Caleb Fletcher, jun.	18	Grocer	Elder
Joseph Spence*	16	Partner	
Silvanus Thompson	16	Teacher, Bootham School	
John Ford	12	Headmaster, Bootham School	
Thomas Allis*	9	Superintendent at Retreat	
James Backhouse, jun.	9	Nurseryman	
James H. King	9	Grocer	
Robert Taylor	8	Butcher (?)	
William Briggs*	7	Grocer	

Henry Richardson	6	Owner, Richardson Agricultural Merchants	
Christopher Robinson	6	Tallow-chandler/ soap-boiler	
George Baker, jun.	5	Farmer	
James Baker	5	Farmer	
John Johnson	5	Cabinet-maker [xm]	
Joseph Rowntree*	5	Grocer	Elder
James H. Tuke	5	Artist	
James Mason	4	Tea-dealer	
John Briggs	3	Grocer	
John Candler	3	?	
John L. Linney	3	Printer	1850[x]
David Priestman	3	Tanner	
William Pumphrey	3	Teacher/photographer	
Henry Ransome*	3	Linen-draper	
Henry Tuke, jun.	3	Tea-dealer	
Cornelius Widdas	3	Gentleman	
Thomas R. Hills	2	?	
Charles Jackson	2	Butcher	
John Kitching	2	Doctor at Retreat	
Holman Sheppard	2	Gentleman	
John Thurnam	2	Superintendent at Retreat	
William Wood	2	?	
John Bleckley	1	Tea-dealer	
John Casson	1	Gentleman/farmer	
John Clemesha*	1	Hatter	
Jeffrey Cranswick	1	?	
Henry Hipsley	1	Gentleman/tea-dealer	
Robert Jackson*	1	Butcher	
Joseph Theobald	1	?	
Daniel H. Tuke	1	Doctor	
William M. Tuke	1	Tea-dealer	
Joseph Ventress	1	?	
John Walker	1	?	
Caleb Williams, jun.	1	Doctor	

TOTAL: 43

[x] disowned
[m] marriage out
* high level of public involvement

Table 2a   Voting behaviour of members of YMM, 1774 York election

Candidates: Lord John Cavendish (C) Whig
                Charles Turner (T) Whig
                M. B. Hawke (H) Tory

Quaker	Occupation	Voted for
Daniel Awmack	Whitesmith	C & T
Nathaniel Bell, sen.	Bookseller	C & T
Nathaniel Bell, jun.	Linen-draper	C & T
William Morley	Linen-draper	C & T
Daniel Peacock	Linen-draper	C & T
George Peacock	Tallow-handler	C & T
Robert Pickering	Tanner	C & T
Richard Pickering	Tanner	C & T
Robert Pickering, jun.	Tanner	C & T
John Thurnam	Gentleman	C & T
William Tuke	Tea-dealer	C & T
William White	Doctor	C & T

Table 2b   Voting behaviour of members of YMM, 1807 Yorkshire election

Candidates: William Wilberforce (W)
                Charles W. Wentworth Fitzwilliam, Viscount Milton (M)
                Henry Lascelles (L)

Quaker	Freehold at	Voted for
John Armitage	Fulford	W
Nathaniel Bell	Cottingham	W & M
Isaac Galilee	Whitby	W & L
Daniel Knowles	Ribston	W & L
George Knowles	Ribston	W & L
William Tuke	Fulford	W & L

Wilberforce = 6
Milton = 1
Lascelles = 4

Table 2c   Voting behaviour of members of YMM, 1807 York election

Candidates: William Mordunt Milner (M) Whig
              Mark Masterman Sykes (S) Tory
              Lawrence Dundas (D) Whig

Quaker	Occupation	Voted for
John Armitage	Linen-draper	M & S
Nathaniel Bell, jun.	Linen-draper	M & D
Francis Carbutt	Merchant	M & D
David Doeg	Looking-glass maker	M & D
Thomas Doeg	Schoolmaster	M & D
John Fothergill	Comb-maker	M & D
Thomas Fox	Whitesmith	S
John Mason	Linen-draper	M & D
Daniel Peacock	Linen-draper	M & S
Robert Pickering	Tanner	S
John Tuke	Land-agent	M & S

Whig = 6
Tory = 2
Split = 3

Table 2d   Voting behaviour of members of YMM, 1818 York election

Candidates: Lawrence Dundas (D) Whig
              Mark Masterman Sykes (S) Tory
              William B. Cooke (C) Whig

Quaker	Occupation	Voted for
William Alexander	Bookseller	D & S
John Armitage	Linen-draper	D & S
James Backhouse	Seedsman	D & S
John Bleckley	Grocer	S
Francis Carbutt	Merchant	D
Caleb Fletcher	Grocer	D & S
John Fothergill	Comb-maker	D & C
Hartas Headley	Farmer	D & C
Joseph King	Grocer	D & S
George Knowles	Woollen-draper	S
John Mason, sen.	Tea-dealer	D & S
John Mason, jun.	Tea-dealer	D & S

/Cont.

Table 2d *Cont.*

Quaker	Occupation	Voted for
Thomas Mason	Tea-dealer	D & S
Daniel Peacock	Linen-draper	D & C
George Peacock	Raff-merchant	D & C
John Sanderson	Yeoman	D & C
Joseph Thurnam	Bricklayer	S
William Thurnam	Tanner	S
John Tuke	Land-agent	S
William Tuke	Tea-dealer	S

Whig = 6   Tory = 6   Split = 8

Table 2e   Voting behaviour of members of YMM, 1820 York election

Candidates: Lawrence Dundas (D) Whig
                Lord Howden (H) Whig
                Marmaduke Wyvill (W) Tory (son of Christopher Wyvill)

Quaker	Occupation	Voted for
William Alexander	Bookseller	D & H
John Armitage	Linen-draper	H
Joseph Awmack	Grocer	D & W
John Bleckley	Grocer	H
Francis Carbutt	Merchant	D & W
Caleb Fletcher	Grocer	D & H
Frederick Flower	Farmer	D & W
Hartas Headley	Farmer	D & W
Joseph King	Tea-dealer	D & W
George Knowles	Woollen-draper	H
John Mason, sen.	Tea-dealer	H
John Mason, jun.	Tea-dealer	H
Thomas Mason	Tea-dealer	H
Daniel Peacock	Linen-draper	D & W
George Peacock	Raff-merchant	D & W
John Sanderson	Woollen-draper	D & W
William Thurnam	Tanner	H
Daniel Tuke	Tea-dealer	H
John Tuke	Land-agent	H
William Tuke, jun.	Farmer	D & W
William Williamson	Rope-maker	D & W

Whig = 11   Split = 10

Table 2f   Voting behaviour of members of YMM, 1830 York election

Candidates: Samuel A. Bayntun (B) Tory
               Thomas Dundas (D) Whig
               Edward R. Petrie (P) Whig

Quaker	Occupation	Voted for
Joseph Awmack	Grocer	D & P
George Baker	Farmer	D & P
John Bleckley	Grocer	B
Francis Carbutt	Merchant	D & P
James Cloak	Straw-hat maker	D & P
William Dagnall	Comb-maker	D & P
Caleb Fletcher	Grocer	B & D
Robert Jackson	Butcher	B
Joseph King	Tea-dealer	B & D
George Knowles	Woollen-dealer	B
Thomas Mason	Tea-dealer	D & P
Henry Ransome	Linen-dealer	D & P
William Richardson	Tanner	D
Samuel Richardson	Tanner	D & P
Joseph Rowntree	Grocer	D
John Sanderson	Woollen-draper	D & P
Joseph Spence	Druggist	D & P
Daniel Tuke	Tea-dealer	B
John Tuke	Land-agent	B
William Tuke	Farmer	D & P
William Williamson	Rope-maker	D & P

Whig = 14
Tory = 5
Split = 2

Table 2g   Voting behaviour of members of YMM, 1832 York election

Candidates: Samuel Bayntun (B) Tory
              Edward R. Petrie (P) Whig
              J H. Lowther (L) Tory
              Hon. J. C. Dundas (D) Whig

Quaker	Occupation	Voted for
William Alexander	Bookseller	P & D
Joseph Awmack	Grocer	P & D
John Bleckley	Grocer	B
John Clemesha	Shoe-maker	B & D
James Cloak	Straw-hat maker	P & B
William Dagnall	Comb-maker	D
John Ford	Schoolmaster	P & D
Benjamin Horner	Dentist	P & D
Robert Jackson	Butcher	B & L
George Knowles	Woollen-draper	B & L
George Knowles	Woollen-draper	L & D
William Knowles	Woollen-draper	L
Thomas Mason	Tea-dealer	L
William Moon	?	P & L
David Priestman	Tanner	B
Henry Ransome	Linen-draper	L & D
Joseph Rowntree	Grocer	D
John Sanderson, jun.	Woollen-draper	P & D
Christopher Scarr	Grocer	B & D
Joseph Spence	Druggist	D
William Thurnam	Tanner	P & B
John Tuke	Land-agent	L
William Tuke	Farmer	P & D
Robert Waller	Tea-dealer	D
Caleb Williams	Doctor	D

Whig = 11
Tory = 7
Split = 7

Recorded as not voting: Samuel Tuke
                           James F. Copsie
                           John H Kitching

Table 2h   Voting behaviour of members of YMM, 1835 York election

Candidates: J. H. Lowther (L) Tory
Hon. J. C. Dundas (D) Whig
Charles F. Barkley (B) Whig

Quaker	Occupation	Voted for
William Alexander	Bookseller	D & B
Joseph Awmack	Grocer	D & B
John Clemesha	Shoe-maker	D & B
James Cloak	Straw-hat maker	D & B
William Dagnall	Comb-maker	D & B
Caleb Fletcher	Grocer	D
John Ford	Schoolmaster	D & B
Robert Jackson	Butcher	D & B
George Knowles	Woollen-draper	L
William Knowles	Woollen-draper	L
Thomas Mason	Tea-dealer	L
Joseph Rowntree	Grocer	D
Holman Shepherd	Gentleman	D & B
Joseph Spence	Druggist	D & B
Robert Waller	Tea-dealer	D & B
Caleb Williams	Doctor	D
William Williamson	Rope-maker	L

Whig = 13
Tory = 4

Table 2i   Voting behaviour of members of YMM, 1841 York election

Candidates: J. A. Lowther (L) Tory
H. R. Yorke (Y) Whig
David F. Atcherley (A) Whig

Quaker	Occupation	Voted for
George Baker	Farmer	L
William Briggs	Grocer	Y
Caleb Fletcher	Grocer	Y
Caleb Fletcher, jun.	Thread-maker	Y
Robert Jackson	Butcher	Y
John H. Kitching	Doctor	L & A
George Knowles	Woollen-draper	L & A

/Cont.

Table 2i   *Cont.*

Quaker	Occupation	Voted for
William Knowles	Woollen-draper	L & A
Thomas Mason	Tea-dealer	L & A
David Priestman	Tanner	Y
William Richardson	Tanner	Y
Joseph Rowntree	Grocer	Y
Christopher Scarr	Grocer/brewer	L & A
Joseph Spence	Druggist	Y
William Tuke	Farmer	L & A
William Williamson	Rope-maker	L & A

Whig = 8   Tory = 1   Split = 7

Table 3   Signatories to the petition to the House of Commons from York citizens in 1835, promoted by members of the Society of Friends

Samuel Tuke	Quaker	Tea-dealer
Oswald Allen	Dissenter	Chemist
William Hotham	Dissenter	Lawyer
John Ford	Quaker	HM, Bootham School
Thomas Backhouse	Quaker	Nurseryman
Robert Davis		Town clerk
Benjamin Horner	Quaker	Dentist
Thomas Smith	Alderman	
Revd Charles Wellbeloved	Unitarian minister	
Caleb Fletcher	Quaker	Grocer
David Priestman	Quaker	Tanner
Revd Frederick Calder	Wesleyan minister	
Favill J. Copsie	Quaker	Grocer
Robert Waller	Quaker	Gentleman
Joseph Rowntree	Quaker	Grocer
Varley Beilby		
William Alexander	Quaker	Printer/bookseller
Holman Shepherd	Quaker	Teacher, Bootham School
George Peacock	Alderman	Printer
William Cooper	Alderman	
William Hearon	Alderman	Tea-dealer
Robert Swann	Banker	
Isaac Spencer	Alderman	

Table 4   Quakers serving as chamberlains for York Corporation

Name	Occupation	Date of freedom	Date of service as chamberlain
Isaac Richardson	Tanner	1781	1784
Thomas Priestman	Tanner	1762	1785
William Tuke, jun.	Farmer	1782	1785
Henry Tuke	Tea-dealer	1782	1787
Robert Pickering	Tanner	1784	1795
Joseph Awmack	Grocer	1776	1798
George Peacock	Dyer	1768	1800
Stephen Priestman	Woollen-draper	1794	1804
John Armitage	Cord-wainer	1775	1805
William Bleckley	Linen-draper	1800	1805
John Tuke	Land-agent	1782	1805
John Mason, jun.	Tea-dealer	1811	1812
Daniel Knowles	Glass/china merchant	1811	1813
John Bleckley	Tea-dealer	?	1816
William Alexander	Bookseller	1813	1818
Caleb Fletcher	Grocer	1813	1818
James Backhouse	Nurseryman	1816	1818
John Mason, sen.	Linen-draper/tea-dealer	1786	1818
Daniel Tuke	Tea-dealer	?	1821*
William Thurnam	Tanner	1815	1822
Joseph Rowntree	Grocer	1823	1823
William Richardson	Tanner	1805	1824
Samuel Tuke	Tea-dealer	1822	1828
Christopher Scarr	Grocer	?	1829
William Peacock	Watchmaker	1789	1830

* Daniel Tuke was fined for not paying his exoneration money, but did agree to serve.

Table 5   Early parochial appointments held by York Quakers

Name	Date	Parish
Constables		
Samuel Tuke (I)	1754	Christ Church
John Oddy	1754; 1763	St Peter the Little
William Morley	1755	St Peter the Little
William Tuke	1756	St Mary's, Castlegate
Daniel Awmack	1764; 1765	St John Delpike
Land tax surveyors		
Batty Storr	1765	St Peter's, Liberty
Jonathan Storr	1768–1800	St Peter's, Liberty
Assessors & collectors of the window tax		
Batty Storr	1740–2; 1749–50	St Peter's, Liberty
Nathaniel Bell	1745	All Saints
Robert Pickering	1745; 1754; 1775	St Margaret's
Thos. Hammond	1751	St Michael le Belfrey
William Tuke	1756–7	St Mary's, Castlegate
Thos. Priestman	1766–7	St Margaret's
Joseph Awmack	1767–8; 1774–5	St Margaret's
Jonathan Storr	1772–3; 1774–5	St Peter's, Liberty

Table 6   Parochial appointments held by York Quakers

Date	Name	Post
St Lawrence		
1797	Isaac Galilee	Overseer of the poor
1817	William Peacock	Overseer of the poor
1820	William Thurnam	Overseer of the poor
1826	Samuel Tuke	Overseer of the poor
1847	Cornelius Widdas	Overseer of the poor
St John, Micklegate		
1824–6	Caleb Fletcher	Overseer of the poor

St Mary's, Castlegate

1776	William Tuke	Auditor of Poor Rate A/Cs
1777	William Tuke	Overseer of the poor
1782	Henry Tuke	Overseer of the poor
1782	William Tuke	Auditor of Poor Rate A/Cs
1793–5	Henry Tuke	Auditor of Poor Rate A/Cs
1799	William Tuke	Auditor of Surveyors A/Cs, appointed under 1763 Cleansing Act
1820–1	John Mason	Overseer of the poor
1821–2	John Mason	Auditor of Poor Rate A/Cs
1823–6	Wm. Alexander & John Mason	Auditors of Poor Rate A/Cs
1827–8	Henry Ransome	Auditor of Poor Rate A/Cs
1829	Wm. Alexander & Henry Ransome	Auditors of Poor Rate A/Cs
1830–43	Thomas Mason	Chairman, select vestry; overseer of the poor; guardian to the workhouse

St Martin cum Gregory

| 1828 | John Sanderson | Auditor of Churchwarden's A/Cs |

All Saints, Pavement

| 1824 | Samuel Steers | Overseer of the poor |

Holy Trinity, Micklegate

| 1821 | Thomas Backhouse | Auditor of Poor Rate A/Cs |

St Mary's Bishophill, Senior

| 1783 | Isaac Richardson | Overseer of the poor |

St Michael le Belfrey

1770	Jonathan Storr	Auditor of Churchwarden's A/Cs
1776–9	Jonathan Storr	Churchwarden
1789–90	Jonathan Storr	Auditor of Churchwarden's A/Cs
1792–9	Jonathan Storr	Auditor of Poor Rate A/Cs
1797	Jonathan Storr	Auditor of Lamp A/Cs
1800–3	Jonathan Storr	Churchwarden

Table 7   Sufferings recorded for York Quakers, 1780–1855

KEY:

U = Urban Quaker   TR = Tithe Rent
R = Rural Quaker   M = Militia duty
CR = Church Rates   N = Navy

Name	Suffering	Value
1780–1790		
Grace Hammond (U/CR)	Pewter/silver	£2. 18s.
William Tuke (U/CR)	Cash	£3. 8s. 0¼d.
William White (U/CR)	Silver	£2. 8s. 6d.
William Thurnam (U/CR) (By warrant)	—	£1. 2s.
Thomas Doeg (U/CR) (By warrant)	Goods	15s.
Emanuel Elam (R/TR)	Corn	£3. 17s.
Robert, John & Simeon Webster (R/TR)		£23. 5s.

(The Websters were ejected from their property in 1777 for non-payment after a land enclosure award. Robert Webster also lost his land to the Enclosure Commissioners. They took possession of the estate)

Name	Suffering	Value
John Webster (R/TR)	Cow	£5. 13s. 4d.
John Armitage, jun. (U/M)	Leather	12s.
George Peacock (U/CR)	Hay	£2. 5s.
John & Joseph Armitage (R/TR)	Hay	17s.
Samuel Armitage (R/TR)	Hay	10s.
Thomas Stears (R/TR)	Hay/corn	£3
1791 – 1800		
Lindley Murray (U/CR)	Table/bacon	£5. 3s. 7¼d.
William Tuke (U/CR)	Pewter/silver	£12. 5s. 2¼d.
William & Henry Tuke (U/CR/N)	Cash/pig	£4. 19s. 7½d.
William White (U/CR)	Silver	16s. 6d.
Timothy White (U/CR)	Silver spoons	£2. 1s. 9d.
Thomas Priestman (U/CR)	Leather	£8. 1s. 1d.
John Tuke (U/CR)	4 sheep	£6. 5s.
Thomas Stears (R/TR)	Corn	£9. 2s.
Elizabeth Thurnam (R/TR)	Oats/corn/hay	£21. 9s.

Stephen Priestman (U/CR)	Cloth/cash	£2. 17s. 4¾d.
William Tuke, jun. (R/CR/N)	Wheat/flour	£2. 11s.
Benjamin North (U/CR)	Pewter/ household goods	£3. 3s.
John Mason (U/CR)	Cash/linen cloth	£3. 3s.
John Sharp (R/TR)	Corn/hay	£4. 15s. 6d.
David Priestman (U/M)	Leather	£11. 0s.
John Fothergill (U/M)	Beans	£1. 4s. 10d.
Robert Pickering (U/N)	A hide	£1. 13s.
Joseph Awmack (U/N)	Silver/copper coins	£2. 4s. 3½d.

1801–1810

Herbert Cammal (R/CR)	1 sheep/ wheat/beans	£3. 4s. 6d.

(Cammal's executors had to pay £1. 5s. 6d. in unpaid church rates)

John Sharp (R/CR)	9 bu. barley	£2. 16s. 3d.
John Sanderson (U/CR)	Cash	£2. 3s. 9½d.
Thomas Doeg (U/CR)	Cash/silver/ furniture	£3. 18s.

(Bankers note found by constable after a house search: 3 warrants)

Lindley Murray (U/CR)	Manure	£2. 17s.
Thomas Priestman (U/CR)	Leather	£2. 3s. 9½d.
William Tuke (U/CR)	Cash	£3. 2s. 6d.
William Tuke & Co. (U/CR)	Cash	£3. 4s.
John Mason (U/CR)	Linen cloth	£3. 1s. 11d.
William Alexander (U/CR)	Bacon	£2. 8s. 6d.
David Doeg (U/CR)	Goods/furniture	£6. 7s. 2d.
Thomas & William Procter (R/TR)	Cheeses	£5. 7s. 10d.
Rachel Fowler (U/CR)	Silverplate	£2. 12s. 6d.
Thomas Dearman (U/CR)	Silverplate	£1. 3s.

1811–1820

William Thurnam (U/CR)	3 qrs. oats/a pig	£8. 10s. 6d.
William & Henry Tuke (R/CR) (for land at Naburn)	Gates/cash	£4. 9s.
William Tuke (as treasurer of Retreat) (U/CR)	Hams	£2. 10s. 6d.
William & Henry Tuke (R/TR) (land at Fulford)	Hams	£1. 0s. 6d.
John Sanderson (U/CR)	Cash	£3. 7s.
William Tuke (U/CR) (2 warrants)	Cash	£6. 9s. 5d.
William, Henry & Samuel Tuke (U/CR)	Cash	£4. 4s.

/Cont.

Table 7   *Cont.*

Name	Suffering	Value
John Mason (U/CR)	Linen cloth/ silk goods	£11. 2s. 4d.
William Alexander (U/CR)	Silver spoons/cash	£3. 0s. 7½d.
Henry Tuke (U/CR)	Household goods	£7. 9s.
David Doeg (U/CR)	Household goods/ looking-glass	£9. 1s.
Rachel Fowler (U/CR)	Silverplate	£4. 8s.
David Priestman(U/CR)	Leather	£6. 12s.
Sarah Bevans & Ann Woolley (U/CR)	Brass pans	£2. 2s.
Francis Flower (R/TR)	Bank notes	£7

(The constable & warden, on searching the drawer in the house, found notes.
2 warrants were granted and the officers '… made exorbitant claims for their
trouble')

Thomas & JamesBackhouse (U/CR)	104 st. hay	£2. 12s.

(The constable was a neighbour, so did not charge for collecting the church rate)

William Bleckley (U/CR)	Cash	£2. 1s. 6d.
Lindley Murrary (U/CR)	1 chaldron coal	16s. 6d.

1821–1830

Name	Suffering	Value
William Procter (R/TR)	Hay/wheat beans/cash	£29. 16s.
Ann Webster (R/TR)	Maslen/wheat	£7. 11s.
John & Simeon Webster (R/TR)	Barley	£8. 16s.
Procter Massey & Co. (U/CR)	Barley/linen	£4. 7s. 6d.
William Procter (U/CR)	Cash	£1. 18s.
Thomas Procter (U/CR)	Cash	£2. 12s. 6d.
William Massey (U/CR)	Cash	£2. 12s.
John Bleckley (U/CR)	Cash	£3. 19s. 9d.
John Sanderson (U/CR)	A lamp	£1. 9s.
William Richardson (U/CR)	Leather	£1. 1s. 6d.
William Tuke (U/CR)	Cash	£1. 18s. 3d.
William Alexander (U/CR)	Cash	£1. 1s. 3d.
John Mason (U/CR)	Silk hankies	£2. 8s. 6d.
Hannah Wilson (U/CR)	Bacon/cheese	£2. 3s.
Hartas Headley (U/CR)	Yarn	£1. 10s.
Thomas & James Backhouse (U/CR)	Cash	£1. 18s.
Lindley Murray (U/CR)	Manure	14s. 7d.
David Priestman (U/CR)	Maslen/oats	£3. 17s. 6d.
Thomas Camm (R/M)	A desk	£4. 10s.
Robert Waller (U/CR)	Cash	13s.

Leonard Johnson (U/CR)	Cash	£1
Joseph Rowntree (U/CR)	Cash	£1. 7s.
Henry Ransome (U/CR)	Linen	£1. 7s.
John Scarr (U/CR)	Shoe thread	18s. 5d.
Caleb Williams (U/CR)	Silver spoons	£2
John Parkinson (R/TR)	Wheat	£3. 12s.
Mary Coates (R/TR)	Hams	£1. 8s. 6d.
John Johnson (R/TR)	Wheat	£1. 13s. 2d.
Thomas Wheatley (R/TR)	Wheat	13s.
Elizabeth Dunning (R/TR)	2 heifers/cattle	£31. 11s.
George Johnson (R/TR)	2 heifers/ oats/wheat	£20
Mary Brown (R/TR)	Furniture	19s. 6d.
Sarah Allis (U/CR)	Silver spoons	12s. 6d.
Elizabeth Mason (U/CR)	3 hams	£2. 5s.
Jane & Barbara Procter (U/CR)	Flour	15s.

1831–1840

Sarah Evans (U/CR)	Hams	£1. 6s.
John Hutchinson (U/CR)	Cash	16s.
Thomas R. Hills (U/CR)	Cash	18s.
William Simpson (U/CR) (10s. returned to him)	Silver spoons	£1. 16s.
Fletcher & Scarr (U/CR)	Cash	£1. 17s. 6d.
John Walker (U/CR)	Tea urn/ looking-glass	£4. 15s.
Hannah Murray (U/CR)	Coals	17s.
James Backhouse (U/M)	A clock	£6. 7s. 6d.
William Webster (R/TR)	Wheat/beans	£7. 16s. 9d.
Simeon Webster (R/TR)	Oats	£4. 4s. 6d.
Johnathan Hutchinson (R/TR)	Wheat	£110
(2 years' tithe – distrained under Commutation Act)		
Mary Coates (R/CR)	Wheat	15s. 9d.
Samuel Procter (U/CR)	Ham/candlesticks/ a fender	14s. 8½d.
Robert Jackson (U/CR)	Bacon	£1. 14s. 7½d.
William Alexander (U/CR)	Silver spoons	£2. 11s. 3d.
Hannah Brady (U/CR)	4 spoons /brass pan/clock	£4
Samuel Tuke/James Copsie (U/CR)	Cash	£2. 13s. 6d.
David Priestman (U/CR)	Leather	£3. 3s. 7d.
John Bleckley (U/CR)	Cash	£1. 3s.
William Briggs (U/CR)	Cash	£1. 4s. 6d.

/Cont.

Table 7   *Cont.*

Name	Suffering	Value
1841–1850		
William Briggs (U/CR)	Cash	£1. 2s.
Quaker Girls' School (U/CR)	Silver spoons	£3
Henry Ransome (U/CR)	Linen	£1. 14s. 8d.
Samuel Tuke (U/CR)	Cash	£2. 13s. 6d.
William Fletcher (U/CR)	Cash	11s. 11d.
Thomas Marshall (U/CR)	2 armchairs	14s.
Procter & Co. (U/CR)	Cash	£1. 4s. 2d.
Maria Tuke (U/CR)	12 tumbler glasses	£16s.
Quaker School, Castlegate (U/CR)	2 tablespoons	£2. 15s.
Thomas & James		
Backhouse (U/CR)	Cash	£1. 8s.
Robert Waller (U/CR)	Silver spoons	17s. 2d.
John Wake (R/TR)	Wheat	£4. 2s. 6d.
John Hutchinson (U/CR)	Oats	£3. 14s. 2d.
Mary Hunter/Mercy Ward (U/CR)	Cash	£1. 0s. 1½d.
Quaker Boys' School (U/CR)	Silver spoons	£2. 2s.
Joseph Rowntree (U/CR)	Cash	£1. 1s. 9d.
James H. King (U/CR)	Cash	£2. 2s. 4d.
William Richardson (U/CR)	Cash	£2. 1s.
William Williamson (U/CR)	Cash	19s. 7½d.
Fletcher & Scarr (U/CR)	Cash	£1. 12s. ½d.
George Baker, jun. (R/CR)	Wheat	£8. 11s. 8d.
George Baker, sen. (R/CR)	Wheat	£3. 17s. 6d.
David Priestman (U/CR)	Silver spoons	£1. 5s. 6d.
William Webster (R/TR)	Wheat	£7. 1s.
1851–1855*		
James H. King (U/CR)	Cash	£1. 1s. 2d.
Elizabeth Priestman (U/CR)	Silver soup-ladle	£1. 9s. 10d.
Joseph Rowntree (U/CR)	Cash	£3. 2s. 5d.
William Williamson (U/CR)	Cash	19s. 6d.
John Hutchinson (R/CR/TR)	Wheat/brass kettle/ chairs/2 pans/ candlesticks/13 cheeses/ 177 bu. wheat	£108. 4s. 2d.
Friends Boys' School (U/CR)	Cash	£1. 5s.
William Briggs (U/CR)	Cash	£1. 1s. 1d.
James Baker (U/CR)	Cash	£1
William Webster (R/TR)	Beans	£7. 4s.

* Great Book of Suffering ceases in 1855

Appendix VIII

Map 1   York and Thirsk Monthly Meetings in 1773

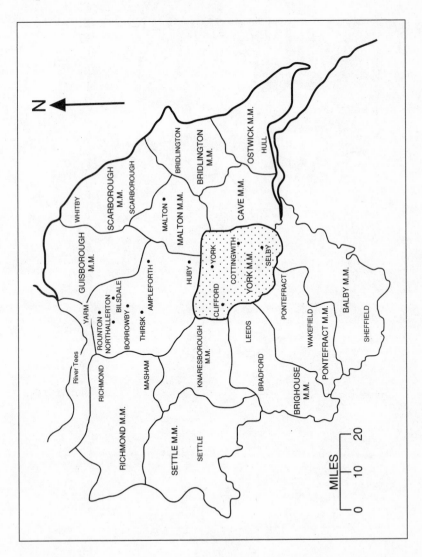

Map 2   York and Thirsk Monthly Meetings in 1827

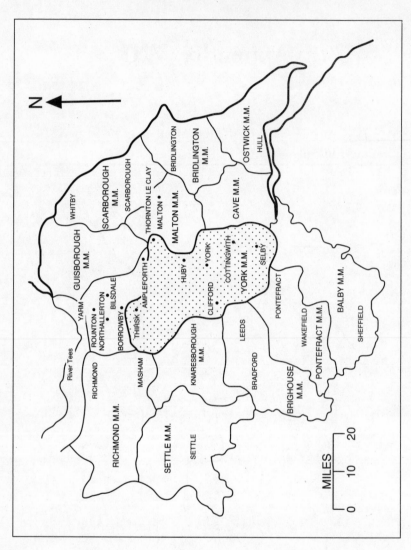

Appendix IX

Removals in and out of YMM

	1780–99[y]	1800–25	1826–30	1831–40	1841–53	1854–60[x]
Removed out						
M	1	67	24	—	111	—
F	6	90	29	—	100	—
Total	7	157	53	173	211	142
Removed in						
M	50	90	38	—	99	—
F	85	137	35	—	122	—
Total	135	227	73	187	221	169
Families						
In	0	23(83)	4(15)	—	7(22)	—
Out	10(34)	15(62)	3(9)	—	9(28)	—
Servants						
In	10	112	36	—	106	—
Out	6	71	9	—	112	—
Apprentices						
In	11	28	8	—	30	—
Out	8	17	9	—	33	—
No. of others of known occupation						
In	10	21	7	—	14	—
Out	6	9	0	—	4	—

[y] Certificates of Removal are almost non-existent for this period.

[x] There is a gap in the Certificates of Removal for the years 1830–41 and 1853–74.

Figures in brackets indicate the number of individual family members.

Appendix X

Frequency of occupations in YMM

Social Class	Occupation	1780–1820	1821–1860
I	Dentist	1	—
	Doctor	2	4
	Gentleman	4	5
	Manager	1	2
	Farm-manager	—	1
	Surveyor	—	1
	Surgeon	—	1
II	Bookseller	2	1
	Schoolmistress	1	3
	Schoolmaster	1	6
	Grocer	6	10
	Wine merchant	1	1
	Nurseryman	2	2
	Draper (employer)	7	4
	Tea-dealer	4	6
	Looking-glass manuf.	1	—
	Comb-manufacturer	1	—
	Farmer (land-owning)	3	3
	Tanner	5	3
	Matron (Retreat)	1	—
	Corn & ham factor	1	—
	Druggist	1	1
	Coal-dealer	1	—
	Agricultural merchant	—	1
	Printer (employer)	—	1
	Glass manufacturer	—	1
	Flannel manufacturer	—	1
	Artist	—	1

III	Shoe-maker	1	—
	Husbandman	5	—
	Breeches-maker	1	—
	Plane-maker	1	1
	Draper (not employer)	2	2
	Mantua-maker	2	—
	Glover	2	—
	Nitrol-manufacturer	1	—
	Horn-maker	1	—
	Whitesmith	1	—
	Carpenter	2	—
	Poster-maker	1	—
	Cabinet-maker	—	1
	Confectioner	—	2
	Butcher	2	3
	Glass & china dealer	1	—
	Woollen-draper	1	2
	Stay-manufacturer	—	1
	Dyer	1	—
	Watchmaker	2	—
	Tailor	—	1
	Raff-merchant	—	1
	Stone-mason	—	1
	Rope-maker	—	1
	Tallow-chandler/soap-boiler	1	1
IV	Hatter	1	—
	Carpenter	1	—
	Bricklayer	—	1
	Flax-dresser	1	—
	Servants	numerous	
	Apprentices	ditto*	
V	Labourer	1	1
	Hawker	1	1

* In terms of classification, to put apprentices in this category could be misleading, since many were the sons of wealthy, middle-class Quakers, but since the social origins of many are unknown, they have been categorized thus.

SOURCE: A. Armstrong, in E. A. Wrigley, ed., *Nineteenth Century Society: Essays in the use of Quantitative Methods for the study of Social Data* (Cambridge, 1972).

Appendix XI

Principal Members of YMM, 1780–1860

KEY:

M = Minister
E = Elder
f = gained freedom
ch = appointed chamberlain
sh = Sheriff
ald = Alderman
m = married to
d = death date
b = birth date
s = son
da = daughter
w = widow

sis = sister
app = apprentice/apprenticed to
dis = disowned
r = resigned
rein. = reinstated a member
C = 'convinced' a Quaker
> = came to York Meeting
< = left York Meeting
MM = Monthly Meeting
LMM = Leeds Monthly Meeting
YMM = York Monthly Meeting

William ABBOTT	Schoolmaster
Ellen ABRAHAM	M; single
James ADCOCK	?
Ann (Tuke) ALEXANDER	M; m. William Alexander 1796; d.1849
Mary ALEXANDER	Schoolmistress; sis, William; d.1854
William ALEXANDER	E; bookseller/printer/schoolmaster; f.1813; ch.1818; d.1841; m. Ann Tuke 1796; 2s. William Henry, Joseph, d.1810
Ann ALLEN	Confectioner; >York 1848
Thomas ALLIS	Superintendent at Retreat; m. Sarah; 2s. Thomas Henry, Charles b.1820

182

	d.1824; 4 da. Mary, Sarah b.1818 d.1824, Elizabeth, Anna
Thomas Henry ALLIS	App.Tuke & Co. 1838
John ARMITAGE	E; cordwainer; >1790; f.1775; ch.1805; dis; w. Ann d.1790; da. Sarah
Sarah ARMITAGE	d.1804
Francis ARNITT	Schoolmaster; d.1832; w. Mary; 3s. William, John, Thomas; 2 da. Francis, Hannah
John H. ASHFORD	App. Joseph Rowntree; >1850; <1855
Ann AWMACK	M; d.1787
Daniel AWMACK	Whitesmith; d.1784; m. Sarah
Edwin AWMACK	App.Thomas Smith; >1851; <1857
John AWMACK	Husbandman; w. Mary
Joseph AWMACK	Grocer/British wine merchant m. Mary Collier (LMM); f.1766; ch.1798; d.1816; 3s. Joseph b.1780, John b.1783, Josiah b.1790 d.1790; 2 da. Sarah b.1785, Ann b.1787
Joseph AWMACK	Looking-glass maker; f.1802; r.1820
Sarah AWMACK	m. Daniel; d.1787
William AWMACK	Breeches-maker
Deborah BACKHOUSE	M; m. James Backhouse
James BACKHOUSE	M; nurseryman; >1816; d.1869; f.1816; ch.1818; m. Deborah; 1s. James b.1825; 2 da. Elizabeth b.1823 m. Joseph Crosfield 1847, Sarah
James BACKHOUSE, jun.	Nurseryman/schoolmaster; f.1857; m. Mary 1855; Mary Louisa b.1857
Joseph BACKHOUSE	>1825; w. Mary Ann; da. Jane Eliza b.1827
Sarah BACKHOUSE	M
Thomas BACKHOUSE	Nurseryman; >1816; d.1845; m.(i) Hannah; m.(ii) Abigail d.1841; 3s. James, Joseph, Thomas b.1840; 4 da.

Mary b.1827, m. W. J. Ecroyd 1851,
Elizabeth, Sarah Jane b.1838, Ann

William BAISTON

Plane-maker; dis; d.1804; m. Naomi
Wilkinson 1782 d.1786; 3s. James,
William b.1783, Daniel 1785 d.1785;
1 da. Sarah b.1785 d.1785

George BAKER

E; farmer; >1820; d.1850; m. Sarah
Hedley 1803; 18 children

James BAKER

Draper; >1838; m.(i) Fanny Burtt
1847 d.1853; 3s. David, Thomas,
George; m.(ii) Elizabeth Morris 1858;
s. James (surgeon); da. Sarah Ann

Sarah BAKER

M; m.(i) George Baker; m.(ii) George
Benson 1856

William BAKER

Farmer; d.1851; m. Sarah; 1s. Joseph;
3 da. Ann, Hannah, Henrietta

Hannah BARRON

?

Ann Mercy BELL, jun.

m. William Richardson 1793

Ann Mercy BELL

M; w. Nathaniel Bell

Nathaniel BELL

E; bookseller; >1739; f.1768;
ch.1757; d.1778; m. Ann Mercy
Ellwood; 1s. Nathaniel m. Judith
Heron d.1815; 3 da. Rachel,
Margaret, Ann Mercy

Nathaniel BELL, jun.

Bookseller/alehouse keeper; dis.
1768; rein. 1778; d.1828

Samuel BELLIS

dis. 1832; 2s. Samuel, Edward;
1 da. Mary

George BENSON

Farmer; m. Sarah Ellis Baker w.
William Baker 1856; 2s. William
b.1857, George b.1857

John BLECKLEY

>1803; ch.1816; d.1851

Joseph BLECKLEY

Servant

William BLECKLEY

M; linen-draper/tea-dealer; >1801;
f.1800; ch.1805; master, Worshipful
Company of Merchant Tailors 1805;
m. Dorothy Clemesha 1800; 1s.

	Henry; 3 da. Sarah and Elizabeth b.1804, Maria b.1806
Samuel BOWLAND	Labourer; d.1796; m. Rebecca d.1796
Elizabeth BRADY	Headmistress, York Girls' School 1842–9; established private girls' school in Edgbaston, Birmingham 1849; > 1842; < 1849; sis. William; 2 da. Elizabeth, Anna
Hannah BRADY	w; schoolmistress; 1 da. Henrietta m. Abraham Sewell of Malton 1842
William BRADY	Draper; >1853; d.1857; m. Mary Benson; 1s. William d.1859; 1 da. Emily d.1857
John BRIGGS	Grocer; > 1835; m. Caroline Jackson 1840; 12 children, 7s., 5 da.
Ralph BRIGGS	> 1850; d.1851; m. Elizabeth
William BRIGGS	m. Ann 1838
Dorothy BROWN	Mantua-maker
Mary BROWN	Mantua-maker
Fletcher BURTT	>1844
Helen BURTT	> 1845; sis. Fletcher
Jonathan BURTT	>1832; m. Elizabeth 1853; Lucy b.1833
Parker BUSBY	Glover; d.1818; m. Sarah d.1818
Herbert CAMM	Yeoman; d.1810
Joseph CAMM	1s. Thomas; 3 da. Sarah, Ann, Mary
John CANDLER	M.
Francis CARBUTT	Woollen-draper; app. to John Bagley; f.1782; < LMM 1813; >1823
John CASSON	> 1833; < 1850
Thomas CHIVERS	Farmer; d.1825; m. Sarah d.1821
John CLEMESHA	Hatter/shoe-maker; f.1823; C. 1823; m. Mary; 5s. Frederick d.1830, Edward, John d.1830, William, Charles d.1836; 1 da. Elizabeth

Thomas CONING — Grocer; f.1852; app. James H. King 1832; m. Mary Clark 1856; 4s. Joseph f.1882, Thomas f.1890, George f.1891, William f.1901

James Favell COPSIE — Grocer; partner with Samuel Tuke, Tuke, Favell, Copsie, 1820

Jeffrey CRANSWICK — C. 1832; d.1859

Elizabeth DEARMAN — Servant

Thomas DEARMAN — Nitrol-manufacturer; m. Phobe; 1s. Thomas; 4 da. Ann b.1807, Deborah Maria b.1811, Jane, Elizabeth

David DOEG — Looking-glass maker; f.1798; dis. 1817; rein.1818; m. Elizabeth 1800; 4s. William, Henry, David, Robert; 4 da. Rebecca, Elizabeth b.1810, Priscilla b.1812, Jane b.1814

Mary DOEG — m. John Pierson 1805

Thomas DOEG — Schoolmaster; f.1776; d.1814; m. Rebecca Torr d.1796; 1s. David, 1 da. Mary

Gervais ELAM — Farmer

Caleb FLETCHER — E; wholesale grocer; partner, Fletcher & Scarr; f.1813; ch.1818; d.1864; m. Mary d.1849; 1s. Caleb b.1815; 1 da. Mary b.1813

Caleb FLETCHER, jun. — Thread-maker/merchant; f.1838; d.1852

Martha FLETCHER — Teacher, Trinity Lane School; d.1854

Francis FLOWER — Farmer; m. Mary; 1s. George; 1 da. Ann

John FORD — Headmaster, Bootham School; m. Rachel

Rachel FORD — E; w. John Ford

John FOTHERGILL — Horn-maker; partner, Forbes & Fothergill comb-makers; f.1789; d.1807; m. Mary Ann; 4s. Charles,

	John, Samuel b.1778, Alexander; 3 da. Elizabeth, Margaret, Mary Ann
John FOTHERGILL, jun.	Comb-maker; f.1799; m. Rebecca; 2s. John Alexander b.1804, George William b.1813; 6 da. Rebecca b.1802, Mary Ann b.1807, Elizabeth b.1808, Anna b.1810, Margaret b.1812, Charlotte b.1817
Rachel FOWLER	w. Thomas Fowler, surgeon; d.1829
Thomas FOX	Whitesmith; f.1789; m. Mary; 2s. George b.1785 d.1786, George b.1787; 1 da. Mary b.1783 d.1784
Isaac GALILEE	Tanner; f.1807; m. Hannah d.1817
Charles GALLEWAY	Draper; >1859; app. James Baker 1846–52
Robert GRUBB	E; m. Sarah Tuke 1782
Sarah (Tuke) GRUBB	M; m. Robert Grubb of Clonmel MM 1782; d 1790
David HALL	Carpenter/joiner; f.1785; app. Stephen Procter, carpenter; d.1833; m. Hannah d.1835
Elizabeth HALL	Servant at the Retreat
Rachel HALL	Assistant at the Retreat; m. James Mason 1842
Joseph HARDY	Coachman to Lindley Murray
Isaac HARTAS	m. Mary Massey 1848
Hartas HEADLEY	Flax-dresser/farmer; m. Rebecca; 3s. James, William, Isaac
Joseph HEIGHINGTON	Porter and wine merchant; <LMM 1813; d.1835
James HESSAY	Gentleman
Thomas HILLS	>1830; <1845;. m. Sarah Maria; 1s. Edward
Henry HIPSLEY	Gentleman; m. Caroline; 2s. Richard, John

Benjamin HORNER

Dentist; f.1822; sh.1830; ald.1835; d.1836; m. Alice; 3s. William b.1806, Charles b.1817, Edward; 1 da. Sarah Jane b.1806 d.1828

William HOYLE

Husbandman; m. Mary; 1 da. Mary m. Samuel Lay 1823

Mary HUSTLER

M.

Jonathan HUTCHINSON

E.

Charles JACKSON

Butcher; f.1837; >1839; m. Hannah d.1854; 8 da.

Robert JACKSON

Butcher; C; f.1825; d.1825; m. Ann; 1s. William b.1831; 3 da. Ann b.1825, Elizabeth and Catherine b.1829

Robert JACKSON, jun.

Butcher; m. 1842 Maria; d.1848; 1s. William; 1 da. Sarah

Elizabeth JANSON

M; >1828; d.1839; 1s. William; 1 da. Elizabeth

George JEPSON

Manager, the Retreat; m. Katherine Allen 1806

John JOHNSON

E; cabinet-maker; >1842; d.1881; m.(i) Jane Ventress 1845 d.1855; m.(ii) Elizabeth (separated)

Leonard JOHNSON

Shopkeeper; dis.1831

Valentine JOHNSON

Corn and ham factor; m. Ann Tessyman 1788; in Retreat from 1822; d.1828

Henry KING

Grocer; m. 1825 Esther Richardson Sewell; 1s. William; 2 da. Mary Jane, Henrietta

James Harison KING

Grocer; f.1841; d.1845; m. Hannah m. William Brady 1846

Joseph KING

Grocer; f.1811; m. Sarah Awmack 1810; 5s. Joseph b.1813, James Harrison b.1817, William b.1819, Henry b.1821, Edward b.1822; 2 da. Mary b.1818, Sarah Ann b.1829

John KITCHING	Superintendent at Retreat; >1850; m. Elizabeth; 3s., 5 da.
Daniel KNOWLES	Glass/china-dealer; f.1811; ch.1813; d.1817
George KNOWLES	Woollen-draper; f.1807; ch.1810; master, Worshipful Company of Master Tailors 1811; m. Mary Nicholson 1807; dis.1808; rein.1819; 2s. Thomas, William b.1809; 1 da. Mary b.1813
William KNOWLES	Woollen-draper; f.1830; dis.1848; d.1879
John LEE	Haberdasher; d.1828
Mary LEE	w. John Lee; r.1845; <1855; 1 da. Priscilla r.1854
George LINNEY	Tailor/teacher of PE at the Mount School from 1852; C. 1829; m. Elizabeth Howden; 2 da. Sarah, Ann
John Lewis LINNEY	Printer; >1837; C.1840; dis.1850; m. Mary; 2s. James, John; 6 da. Judith, Elizabeth, Jane, Ann, Mary, Lucy
Elizabeth LISTER	Mantua-maker
Jean MACDERMID	Confectioner; >1859
John MARTIN	Flax-dresser/gentleman
Ann MASON	m. Benjamin, Trusted Tanner of Wellington, Somerset 1816
Deborah MASON	m. Henry Ransome, linen-draper
Henry MASON	Druggist; f.1821; d.1829
James MASON	Manager of the farm at the Retreat; d.1876; m. Rachel Hall 1842
John MASON	Linen-draper; f.1789; ch.1818; m. Elizabeth d.1844; 3s. John b.1789, Thomas b.1793, Henry b.1799; 5 da. Deborah b.1788, Ann b.1791, Mary b.1792, Margaret b.1796, Elizabeth b.1794

John MASON	Tea-dealer; f.1811; ch.1812; d.1827; m. Catherine Smart of Warwick MM
Margaret MASON	m. William Smee
Mary MASON	m. Jonathan Shackleton of LMM 1830
Thomas MASON	Tea-dealer; 3s. Thomas b.1818, John, William; 1 da. Elizabeth
James MASTERMAN	Butcher; d.1807
Charles MENELL	Clerk; f.1859
Thomas MENELL	Woollen-draper; >1822; m. Emma; 2s. Thomas, Charles.
William MORLEY	Linen-draper; d.1784; m. Sarah d.1787
Hannah MURRAY	E; d.1834; m. Lindley Murray
Lindley MURRAY	M; gentleman; grammarian; >1785 from New York; d.1826; m. Hannah
John NEILD	Shoe-maker; d.1807; m. Naomi d.1818
Ann NORTH	E; m. Benjamin North
Benjamin NORTH	M; m. Ann
Mary ODDY	w; caretaker at Meeting House; d.1793; 1 da. Ann
Daniel PEACOCK	Linen-draper; f.1811; m. Mary; 5s. Thomas b.1771, George b.1774, George II b.1778, Daniel b.1779, Jonathan b.1782; 1 da. Mary b.1781
George PEACOCK	E; tallow-chandler; f.1768; d.1781 m. Mary; 2s. George, William b.1775; 1 da. Elizabeth
John PEACOCK	Dyer; f.1779; m. Rebecca Carbutt 1779; 1s. William b.1782; 2 da. Elizabeth b.1780, Sarah b.1784
Jonathan PEACOCK	Glover; f.1812
William PEACOCK	Watchmaker; f.1789; ch.1830
Robert PICKERING	Tanner; f.1784; ch.1795; app. to Timothy Hudson 1772–3; m. Mary;

	2s. Richard b.1774, John b.1777; 2 da. Mary b.1779, Elizabeth b.1784
Hannah PIERSON	M; m. Thomas Pierson
Thomas PIERSON	Draper; 1 da. Esther 1842
Hannah PRIER	M.
David PRIESTMAN	E; tanner
Sarah PRIESTMAN	M; m. William Richardson of Durham MM 1804
Stephen PRIESTMAN	Woollen-draper; f.1794; ch.1804; dis.; m. Mary Tatham from LMM 1796
Thomas PRIESTMAN	E; tanner; f.1762; ch.1785; d.1812; m. Sarah; 3s. David, Daniel, Joseph b.1771; 4 da. Ann, Rachel b.1765, Sarah, Hannah b.1774
Elizabeth PROCTER	?
Isaac PROCTER	Carpenter; f.1791; <London
Peter PROCTER	Husbandman
Stephen PROCTER	Carpenter; f.1758; app. George Pierson; d.1805; m. Rebecca; 2s. William, Isaac; 1 da. Sarah
William PUMPHREY	Photographer/teacher; m. Elizabeth Allis 1851; 2 da.
Henry RANSOME	Linen-draper; f.1828; >Yarmouth MM 1823; m. Deborah Mason; 1s. John d.1823; 2 da. Margaret, Elizabeth
Sarah RICCALTON	r.1839
Henry RICHARDSON	Agriculturalist; d.1893; m. Maria Heath
Isaac RICHARDSON	Tanner; f.1781; ch.1784; m. Sarah Mayleigh Oliver d.1828; 3s.William b.1781, Samuel, Henry b.1790
Maria RICHARDSON	M; d.1911; friend of Josephine Butler and campaigner for repeal of Contagious Diseases Act

Samuel RICHARDSON   Tanner; f.1810

William RICHARDSON   Tanner, f.1810; ch.1824; dis.1831;
                       rein.1838; m. Martha Mildred 1811;
                       2s. William b.1817, Henry b.1813;
                       2 da. Lydia b.1812, Sarah

Edwin S. RICKMAN   Teacher, Bootham School

Christopher ROBINSON   Tallow-chandler; >1853 LMM

John Stephenson ROWNTREE   Grocer; f.1840; d.1907; m. Elizabeth
                           Hotham; 9 children

Joseph ROWNTREE   E; grocer; >1822 Scarborough MM;
                       f.1823; d.1859; m. Sarah Stephenson
                       1832; 3s. John S. b.1834, Joseph
                       b.1836, Henry Isaac b.1838;
                       2 da. Hannah b.1840, Sarah b.1834

Joseph ROWNTREE, jun. Grocer; b.1836; d.1925; m.(i) Julia
                       Seebohm 1858 d.1863; m.(ii) Emma
                       Antoinette Seebohm 1867; 5s., 1 da.

Sarah ROWNTREE   M; m. Joseph Rowntree

Morgan RYAN   Lace-weaver; m. Ann; 2s. Jeremiah
                       b.1780, George b.1781

John SANDERSON   M; woollen-draper; f.1806; ch.1812;
                       m. Deborah Gates 1808; 2s. Thomas
                       b.1812, John b.1815; 3 da. Mary Ann
                       b.1814, Margaret b.1815, Sarah
                       b.1818

Mary Ann SANDERSON   m. Henry Hipsley

Sarah SANDERSON   m. John Allis Bristol MM 1812

Christopher SCARR   Grocer; partner, Fletcher & Scarr;
                       ch.1829; d.1853; m. Elizabeth

Hannah SCARR   E; w. John Scarr; >1821

John SHARP   Husbandman; m. Hannah;
                       1 da. Elizabeth

Mark SHEPHERD   > 1831; m. Rebecca

Holman SHEPPARD   Gentleman
William SIMPSON   Schoolmaster; >1823; m. Jane; <
                       1833 Brighouse MM; >1855; <1859

Joseph SPENCE	E; druggist/partner, York Glass Works; >1828; f.1828; d.1872; m. Jemima Mariott 1834; 2 da. Charlotte b.1847, Margaret
Samuel STEARS	Linen-draper; f.1779; dis.; d.1796; m. Mary; 2 da. Sarah b.1773, Mary
Batty STORR	Watchmaker; d.1793; 1s. Jonathan
Jonathan STORR	Watchmaker
John TATE	Coal-dealer; m. Mary
Mary TATE	M; w. John Tate
Abigail TAYLOR	>1821
Sylvanus THOMPSON	Schoolmaster, Bootham School; m. 1848 Bridget; 4s; 2 da.
Sylvanus Philips THOMPSON	Scientist
William THURNAM	Tanner; f.1815; ch.1822
John THURNAM	Husbandman; ch.1771; m. Elizabeth 2s. William, John; 2 da. Elizabeth, Hannah
John THURNAM	Doctor at the Retreat
Elizabeth TUKE	M; d.1826; m. Joshua Wheeler 1795
Esther TUKE	M; m. William Tuke d.1794
Henry TUKE	M; tea-dealer; f.1782; ch.1787; d.1814; m. Mary Maria Scott 1781; 3s. Samuel b.1784, William b.1786 d.1799, Henry b.1787 d.1788, Henry b.1789 d.1799; 2 da. Esther b.1782, Maria b.1790
John TUKE	Land-agent; f.1782; ch 1805; m. Sarah Mildred 1783; 2s. Daniel, Robert b.1789; 5 da. Lydia b.1785, Rebecca b.1786, Elizabeth b.1793, Ann b.1795, Esther b.1798
Mabel TUKE	E; d.1864; m. John Hipsley 1804
Maria TUKE	E; d.1848
Mary Maria TUKE	m. Henry Tuke 1781 b.1748 d.1815

Robert TUKE   Farmer; f.1820; >1826; < 1835
Pontefract MM.; m. Mable;
4s. Daniel, Henry, Robert, Edward
b.1826; 3 da. Sarah, Lydia, Elizabeth

Samuel TUKE   M; f.1822; ch.1828; d.1857;
m. Priscilla Hack of Chichester MM
1810; d.1828; 13 children

William TUKE   E; grocer; f.1753; d.1822 m.(i)
Elizabeth Hoyland 1754; m.(ii)
Esther Maud of Bradford MM 1765;
4s. Henry b.1755, William b.1758,
John b.1759 d.1736, Samuel b.1766
d.1767; 4 da. Sarah b.1756, Elizabeth
b.1760, Ann b.1767, Mabel b.1770

William TUKE, jun.   Mealman/farmer; m. Rachel
Priestman 1789; 1s. Thomas b.1791;
2 da. Sarah b.1790, Esther b.1793

Benjamin TRUSTED   Flannel-manufacturer; m. Ann Mason

Thomas VENTRESS   Gardener/shopkeeper; m. Jane;
1 da. Mary b.1803

John WALKER   >1830; <1845; m. Hannah; 2s.
Charles, Frederick; 1 da. Arabella

Robert WALLER   Tea-dealer; >1818; d.1846; m.
Hannah

James WALTON   Warehouseman; 1 da. Ann 1803;
d.1802

Juliana WALTON   w; 2s. John app. to Henry Tuke,
George; 1 da. Ann

John WEBSTER   Farmer; m. Mary; 4s. Isaac, Simeon,
John, George; 2 da. Mabel, Mary

George WELLS   Plane-maker; C.1859; f.1837; app.
William Dibb; m. Sarah

William WEST   Labourer; m. Eleanor; 1 da. b.1803

John WHEATLEY   Farmer; >1831; d.1854; m. Mary
1834; 1s. John; 2 da. Jane, Mary

Thomas WHEATLEY   Mason; >1827; m. Mary; >1847;
1s. William; 2 da. Mary, Rachel

Ann WHITE   C. 1801

Martha WHITE   sis. William White d.1820

Timothy WHITE   Gentleman

William WHITE   Doctor; f.1771; b.1743; d.1790;
                            1s. Timothy

Charlotte WIDDAS   Stay-maker; d.1874

Cornelius WIDDAS   Gentleman; d.1876; m. Charlotte;
                            2s. George b.1842, Daniel b.1845

Caleb WILLIAMS   M; doctor; f.1824; >1824; m. Mary
                            Mennell; 2s. Isaac, Caleb; 3 da.
                            Emma, Mary Anna, Frances Maria

Caleb WILLIAMS, jun.   Doctor

Emma WILLIAMS   m. William Murray Tuke 1848;
                            1 da. Mary Maria b.1847

Mary WILLIAMSON   Attendant at the Retreat/matron,
                            Croyden School

William WILLIAMSON   Joiner/sail-maker; f.1811; app. to
                            William Wilkinson; m. Sarah;
                            4 da. Mary, Rachel, Sarah, Amelia

James WILSON   Book-keeper; f.1857

Bibliography

MANUSCRIPT SOURCES

Manuscripts held at the Borthwick Institute of Historical Research, York (BI)

York Monthly Meeting (on microfilm)

Monthly Meeting Minute Book, Vol.5 (1755–77); Vol.6, (1777–93); Vol.7 (1793–1815)
Preparative Meeting Minute Book, Vol.5 (1787–1842)
Preparative Meeting: Legacy Fund Account Book, Vol.1 (1707–1849)
Meeting of Ministers and Elders Minute Book, Vol.1 (1709–75); Vol.2 (1776–1856)
Certificates of Friends travelling in the Ministry (1697–1861)
Accounts of the Sufferings of Friends (1793–1865)
Women's Monthly Meeting Minute Book, Vol.2 (1767–96); Vol.3 (1796–1818)
Women's Preparative Meeting Minute Book, Vol.1 (1707–75); Vol.2 (1775–1841)
List of Members, Vol.1 (1790–1841)
Declarations of intentions and consents to marriage, Vol.1. (1681–1846)
Applications for membership; disownments; documents of discipline etc., Vol.1 (1672–1797)
Catalogue of books, register of loans (1710–1840)
Ann Mercy Bell: Journal and correspondence (1745–86)

Yorkshire Quarterly Meeting (on microfilm)

Meeting of Ministers and Elders Minutes Book, Vol.1 (1689–1798); Vol.2 (1798–1867)
Record of Ministers and Elders (1785–1876)
Record of the Sufferings of Friends, Vol.5 (1749–80); Vol.6 (1781–92); Vol.7 (1793–1821); Vol.8 (1822–7)

Gifts and legacies for charitable purposes left to Monthly and Preparative Meetings in Yorkshire (1765–82)
Letters and papers relating to the Lothersdale prisoners (1794–8)
Ecclesiastical prosecutions (1741–74)
Petitions to the judges etc. and various papers relating to Sufferings (1682–1810)

Parish Records

St Mary's, Castlegate
    Baptismal, Burial and Marriage Registers (1780–1860)
    Churchwardens A/Cs (1750–1877)
    Overseers (1741–1856)
    Surveyors (1760–1822)
    Vestry Minutes (1762–1800; 1831–56)
    Land Tax (1749–1805) (1810–24)
St Michael le Belfrey
    Baptismal, Burial and Marriage Registers (1780–1860)
    Vestry Minutes (1751–85; 1786–1817)
    Overseers (1794–1805)
    Poor Rate Assessment (1792–9)
All Saints, Pavement
    Churchwardens A/Cs (1790–3)
    Overseers of the Poor (1823–6)
Holy Trinity, Goodramgate
    Constables A/Cs (1636–1770)
    Overseers A/Cs (1777–1867)
    Surveyors (1770–1824)
Holy Trinity, Micklegate
    Churchwardens A/Cs (1780–1850)
    Overseers (1810–37)
    Vestry Minutes (1788–1850)
St Lawrence
    Churchwardens A/Cs (1750–1850)
    Overseers of the Poor (1784–1837)
    Vestry Minutes (1821–1852)
St Martin cum Gregory
    Churchwardens A/Cs (1750–1850)
    Constables (1796)
    Overseers (1834–8)
    Vestry Minutes (1823–1954)
St Olaf's
    Church A/Cs (1818–79)

St Helen's, Stonegate
    Assessors for the Lighting of Lamps and the Land Tax (1810–15)
St Mary's, Bishophill Senior
    Overseers (1761–89)
The Methodist Records for York Circuit
The Tuke family papers
The Blue Coat Boys' School
    Committee Meeting Minutes (1780–5)
    List of Subscribers (1828–49)
The Grey Coat Girls' School
    Minutes of the Ladies' Committee (1790–1814)

Manuscripts held at the Brotherton Library, Leeds University (BL)

York Monthly Meeting

Monthly Meeting Minute Book, Vol.8 (1815–29); Vol.9 (1829–36); Vol.10 (1844–52); Vol.11 (1853–60)
Preparative Meeting Minute Book, Vol.5 (1842–60)
Preparative Meeting: Legacy Fund Account Book, Vol.2 (1849–1948)
Preparative Meeting: Sewing Meeting (Friendly Society for Benevolent Objects) Minutes and Proceedings (1834–48); Vol.2 (1848–80)
Meeting of Ministers and Elders Minute Book, Vol.3 (1857–76)
Reports and papers received (from ministers) (1837–53)
Women's Monthly Meeting Minute Book, Vol.4 (1818–40); Vol.5 (1841–60)
Women's Preparative Meeting Minute Book, Vol.3 (1841–70)
List of Members, Vol.2 (1842–59)
Declarations of intentions and consents to marriage, Vol.2 (1846–8)
Applications for membership; disownments; documents of discipline etc., Vol.2 (1800–48)
Birth notes (1825–9; 1832–7)
Removals, births, marriages and burials, etc., Vol.3 (1823–58); Vol.4 (1858–83)
Burial notes (1837–61)
Rawdon School: General Meeting of Women Friends: Minute Book (1840–65)
Rawdon School: Women's Committee Minute Book (1840–65)

Manuscripts held at Bristol City Archives (BA)

Bristol Monthly Meetings

Monthly Meeting Minute Books, 8 Vols (1786–1864)

Women's Monthly Meeting Minute Books, 8 Vols (1786–1864)
Minutes of the Meeting of Ministers and Elders (1780–1805; 1813–25)
Women's Preparative Meeting Minute Books (1780–99)
Women's Meeting Account Book (1792–1825)
Members Lists (incomplete) (1790–1863)

Manuscripts held at the British Library (BML)

Diaries of Quaker Women: MFR/2791/1–5

Manuscripts held at Friends' House Library, Euston Road (FHL)

John Stephenson Rowntree manuscripts
The Great Book of Sufferings, Vols.27–44 (1780–1856)
York Tract Association Committee Minutes (1843–86)
Diary of Henry Wormwald, Lothersdale prisoner

Manuscripts held at Sheffield City Library

Wentworth Woodhouse manuscripts (microfilm)

Manuscripts and records held at York City Archives (YA)

Chamberlains' Account Books
Minute Books of the Commissioners appointed under the 1825 Police
    Act, Vols.1–3
York Dispensary Report (1782; 1802)
York City Council Minute Books, Vols.1–4
York Female Friendly Society: List of General Members (1789); Orders
    and Memoranda (1794–1818)
Foss Navigation Committee: General Minutes (1793–1853)
York Board of Guardians: Minute Books (1835–46)
York Glass Works: Business Records
City of York House Books, Vols.44–50
York Mechanics Institute: Book of the Report and Committee
    Proceedings (1832)
Ouse Navigation Commissioners Minute Books (1772–8; 1833–41)
Registers of Apprentices
York Society for the Prevention and Discouragement of Vice and
    Profaneness: Committee Meeting Reports (1808); Annual Reports
    (1808–39; 1842; 1843); Subscribers' Lists (1801–5; 1830)

York Association for the Prosecution of Felons and Cheats: Minute
    Book (1800–49); Subscribers' List (1800–5)
York Female Penitentiary Society (1822–42)
York Penitentiary Society Minute Books: Men's Committee (1844–57);
    Ladies' Committee (1845–64); Visitors' Books (1846–61)
York Friends Adult School: Register (1856)
York British Girls' School: Minutes of Managers (1812–22), with sub-
    scribers; General Meeting of Subscribers (1812); Quarterly Meeting
    of Female Subscribers (1813); Minutes of Managers (1822–35;
    1836–60)
First Day School, York: Minute Book of Teachers' Meeting (1848–50)
York Friends Boys' Sabbath School: Register (1860–9); Minute Book of
    Teachers' Meeting (1859–64)
York Friends Girls' Sabbath School:Report (1859) in Men's Minute Book
The Society for the Prevention of Youthful Depravity: Minute Book
    (1859–63)

Manuscripts and records held at York Public Library (YPL)

Ninth Report of the Committee of the York Society for the Encour-
    agement of Faithful Female Servants
Requisition for an Anti-Slavery Meeting by the Inhabitants of York and
    Vicinity to the Lord Mayor (March 1824)
British Association for the Advancement of Science Meeting (1844)
York Auxiliary Bible Society: Proceedings and Resolutions of the
    Meeting on the Formation of an Auxiliary Bible Society (1812),
    including addresses by leading participants; lists of subscribers
    (1833; 1834)
York Philosophical Society: Ladies' Subscribers' List (1855)
York Vagrant Office: Half-Yearly Report (1822)
York Temperance Society: 14th Annual Report (1850); 16th Annual
    Report (1852)
York Temperance Band Of Hope: 11th Annual Report (1858); 12th
    Annual Report (1859); 16th Annual Report (1863)
York Penitentiary Society Annual Report (1861), including report of the
    Society for the Prevention of Youthful Depravity and subscribers'
    list
York Ragged Schools: 1st Annual Report (1848)
York Trade Directories (1781; 1784; 1796; 1805; 1809–11; 1816–17;
    1818; 1828–9; 1843; 1849; 1851)
York Poll Books (1774; 1807; 1818; 1820; 1830; 1832; 1835; 1841)
Yorkshire Poll Book (1807)
York Mechanics Institute: Report of Annual Meeting (1836)

Private papers

The Richardson family papers

PRINTED SOURCES

Newspapers and Periodicals

At York Public Library

York Gazette, York (1780–1860)
York Herald, York (1790–1860)
Courant, York (1780–1848), amalgamated with *Herald*
Yorkshireman, York (1834–58), incorporated with *Herald*
Gentleman's Magazine (1800–20)

At the British Library

Eclectic Review (1800–10)
Christian Observer (1800–10)

At John Rylands Library, Manchester

Methodist Magazine (1820–30)
Bible Christian Magazine (1823–24)
Primitive Methodist Magazine (1823)

PRINTED CONTEMPORARY SOURCES

Alexander, W., *Address to the Public on the Present State of the Question relative to Negro Slavery in the British Colonies* (York, 1828)
A Journal of the Life, Labours, Travels and Sufferings in and for the Gospel of that Ancient Servant and Faithful Minister of Jesus Christ, John Banks (London, 1798)
Barclay, R., *An Apology for the True Christian Divinity: Being an Explanation and vindication of the principles and doctrines of the people called Quakers* (London, 1841)
Braithwaite, J. B., *Memoirs of J. J. Gurney: with selections from his Journal and Correspondence*, 2 Vols (Norwich, 1854)

Cappe, C., *Thoughts on the Desirableness and Utility of Ladies Visiting Female Wards of Hospitals and Lunatic Asylums* (York, 1816)

Corder, S., *Life of Elizabeth Fry: Compiled from her Journals as edited by her daughters* (London, 1853)

Epistles from the Yearly Meeting of Friends (London, 1858)

Fox, G., *A Collection of Many Select and Christian Epistles*, Vol.2 (London, 1698)

—— *A Journal or Historical Account of the Life, Travels, Sufferings, Christian Experiences and Labour of love in the work of the Ministry of that ancient, eminent and faithful servant of Jesus Christ, G. Fox*, Vol.2 (London, 1827)

Gillman, F. J., *The Story of the York Adult School Movement from Commencement to the Year 1907* (York, 1907)

Gospel Privileges Exemplified in the Life of Ann Scott, tracts published by the York Friends Tract Association (York, 1857)

James, J. A., 'The Family Monitor', in J. F. James, ed., *The Works of John Angel James* (Birmingham, 1860)

Memoir of the Life of Elizabeth Fry with extracts from her Journal and Letters, edited by her daughters, Vols.1 and 2 (London, 1847)

Memoirs of the Life and Writings of Lindley Murray in a series of letters written by himself (York, 1826)

Murray, L., *Biographical Sketch of Henry Tuke* (York, 1827)

—— 'The Power of Religion on the Mind in Retirement Affliction and the Approach of Death, 1787', in *Testemonies of Experience* (York, 1820)

—— *A Compendium of Religious Faith and Practice* (York, 1815)

—— *The Duty and Benefit of a Daily Perusal of the Holy Scriptures in Families* (York, 1817)

Pickwell, W., *The Temperance Movement in York* (York, 1886)

Richard, H., *Memoirs of Joseph Sturge* (London, 1864)

A Brief Memoir of the late Rev. William Richardson, sub-chanter of York Cathedral etc., 2nd edn (York, 1822)

Rowntree, J. S., *Quakerism Past and Present: Being an inquiry into the causes of its decline in Great Britain and Ireland* (London, 1859)

Rowntree, J. W., *Essays and Addresses*, ed. J. S. Rowntree (1905)

Rowntree, J. W. and Binns, H. B., *A History of the Adult School Movement* (London, 1903)

A Selection from the Letters of the Late Sarah Grubb (London, 1848)

Smith, F., *On the Duty of a Wife* (London, 1810)

Some Account of the Life and Religious Labours of Sarah Grubb (London, 1776)

Some Account of the Life and Religious Experiences of Mary Alexander, Late of Needham Market (York, 1811)

Strangers Guide Through the City of York and its Cathedral, 3rd edn (York, 1829)

The Journal of the Life, Travels and Religious Labours of William Savery (London, 1844)

Tuke, H., *The Principles of Religion as Professed by the Society of Christians, usually called Quakers* (York, 1819)

Tylor, C., ed., *Memoirs of Elizabeth Dudley* (London, 1861)

—— ed., *Samuel Tuke: His Life, Work and Thoughts*

Wakefield, P., *Reflections on the Present Condition of the Female Sex with Suggestions for its Improvement* (London, 1798)

Wilberforce, W., *Practical View of the Prevailing Religious System of Professed Christians in the Higher & Middle Classes of this Country Contrasted with real Christianity* (London, 1797)

Winskill, P. T., *The Temperance Movement and its Workers: A Record of Social, Moral, Religious and Political Progress* (Blackie, 1892)

PRINTED SECONDARY SOURCES

Abbatt, J. D., *A Victorian Quaker Courtship: Lancashire Love Letters of the 1850s* (York, 1988)

Allott, S., *Friends in York: The Quaker Story in the Life of a Meeting* (York, 1978)

Armstrong, A., *Stability and Change in an English Country Town: A Social Study of York, 1801–1851* (Cambridge, 1974)

Banks, J. A., *Prosperity and Parenthood: A Study of Family Planning Among the Victorian Middle-class* (London, 1954)

—— *Victorian Values: Secularisation and the Size of Families* (London, 1981)

Barbour, H., *The Quakers in Puritan England* (New Haven, 1964)

—— 'Quaker Prophetesses and Mothers in Israel', in C. and J. Stoneburner, eds, *The Influence of Quaker Women on American History* (Lewiston, 1986)

Barry, J., 'The Parish in Civic Life: Bristol and its Churches 1640–1750', in S. Wright, ed., *Parish Church and People* (London, 1988)

Basch, F., *Relative Creature: Victorian Women in Society and the Novel* (London, 1974)

Bebbington, D. W., *Evangelicalism in Modern Britain: A History from the 1730s to 1980s* (London, 1989)

Best, G., 'Evangelicalism and The Victorians', in A. Symondson, ed., *The Victorian Crisis of Faith* (London, 1970)

Billington, L. and R., 'A Burning Zeal for Righteousness: Women and the British Anti-Slavery Movement, 1820–1860', in J. Rendall, ed., *Equal or Different: Women's Politics 1800–1914* (Oxford, 1987)

Binfield, C., *So Down to Prayers: Studies in English Non-Conformity 1780-1920* (London, 1977)

Bossy, J., *The English Catholic Community 1570-1850* (London, 1975)

Boulding, E., 'Mapping the Inner Journey of Quaker Women', in C. and J. Stoneburner, eds, *The Influence of Quaker Women on American History* (Lewiston, 1986)

Bradley, I. C., *The Call to Seriousness: The Evangelical Impact on the Victorians* (London, 1976)

Bradley, J. E., *Religion, Revolution and English Radicalism: Nonconformity in Eighteenth Century Politics and Society* (Cambridge, 1990)

Braithwaite, W. C., *The Second Period of Quakerism* (Cambridge, 1981)

Branca, P., *Silent Sisterhood: Middle Class Women in the Victorian Home* (London, 1975)

Brett, P., *The Rise and Fall of the York Whig Club 1818–1830*, Borthwick Paper No.76 (York, 1989)

Brontë, A., *The Tenant of Wildfell Hall* (Penguin, 1979)

Brontë, C., *Jane Eyre* (Penguin, 1966)

Brown, E. K., *Women of Mr. Wesley's Methodism: Studies in Women in Religion* (New York, 1983)

Brown, F. K., *Fathers of the Victorians: The Age of Wilberforce* (Cambridge, 1961)

Burdett, G. B., *The Story of Quakerism in Scotland, 1650–1850* (London, 1952)

Cammage, W., *York Ragged School* (York, 1907)

Christie, I. R., *Wilkes, Wyvill and Reform: The Parliamentary Reform Movement in British Politics 1760–1785* (London, 1962)

Corfield, K., 'Elizabeth Heyrick: Radical Quaker', in G. Malmgreen, ed., *Religion in the Lives of English Women, 1760–1930* (London, 1986)

Corfield, P. J., *The Impact of English Towns* (Oxford, 1982)

Cott, N. F., *The Bonds of Womanhood: 'Woman's Sphere' in New England 1780–1835* (London, 1977)

Cowherd, R. G., *The Politics of English Dissent: The Religious Aspects of Liberal and Humanitarian Reform Movements from 1815 to 1848* (London, 1959)

Davidoff, L. and Hall, C., *Family Fortunes: Men and Women of the English Middle Class 1780–1860* (London, 1987)

Davis, S., *Quakerism in Lincolnshire* (Lincoln, 1989)

Dews. D.C., 'Ann Carr and the Female Revivalists of Leeds', in G. Malmgreen, ed., *Religion in the Lives of English Women, 1760–1930* (London, 1986)

Digby, A., *Madness, Morality and Medicine: A Study of the York Retreat 1796–1914* (Cambridge, 1985)

—— *From York Lunatic Asylum to Bootham Park Hospital*, Borthwick Paper No.69 (York, 1986)

Dinwiddy, J. R., *Christopher Wyvill and Reform 1790–1820*, Borthwick Paper No.39 (York, 1971)

Edkins, C., 'Quest for Community: Spiritual Autobiographies of Eighteenth Century Quaker and Puritan Women in America', in E. Jelenek, ed., *Women's Autobiography: Essays in Criticism* (Bloomington, 1980)

Eliot, G., *Middlemarch* (Penguin, 1965)

Eliot, G., *Adam Bede* (Penguin, 1980)

Eversley, D. E. C., 'A Survey of the Population in an Area of Worcestershire from 1660–1850', in D. V. Glass and D. E. C. Eversley, *Population in History: Essays in Historical Demography* (London, 1965)

—— 'The Demography of the Irish Quakers 1650–1850', in J. M. Goldstrom and L. A. Clarkson, eds, *Irish Population Economy & Society: Essays in Honour of the Late K. H. Connell* (Oxford, 1981)

Feinstein, C. H., 'Population, Occupations and Economic Development 1831–1981', in C. H. Feinstein, ed., *York 1931–1981: 150 Years of Scientific Endeavour and Social Change* (York, 1981)

Finnegan, F., *Poverty & Prostitution: A Study of Victorian Prostitutes in York* (Cambridge, 1979)

Frazer, D., *Urban Politics in Victorian England: The Structure of Politics in Victorian Cities* (Leicester, 1976)

Frost, J. W., *The Quaker Family in Colonial America* (New York, 1973)

Gash, N., *Politics in the Age of Peel* (London, 1953)

Gorham, D., *The Victorian Girl & the Feminine Ideal* (London, 1982)

Hamm, T. D., *The Transformation of American Quakerism: Orthodox Friends, 1800–1907* (Bloomington, 1988)

Harrison, B., *Drink and the Victorians: The Temperance Question in England 1815–1872* (London, 1971)

Heasman, K., *Evangelicals in Action: An Appraisal of their Social Work in the Victorian Era* (London, 1962)

Hylson-Smith, K., *Evangelicals in the Church of England 1734–1984* (London, 1988)

Isichei, E., *Victorian Quakers* (Oxford, 1970)

Jay, E., *The Religion of the Heart: Anglican Evangelicalism and the Nineteenth Century Novel* (Oxford, 1979)

Jones, R. M., *The Later Periods of Quakerism* (London, 1921)

Krause, J. T., 'The Changing Adequacy of English Registers 1650–1837', in D. V. Glass and D. E. C. Eversley, *Population in History: Essays in Historical Demography* (London, 1965)

Lamb, C., *Elia and The Essays of Elia* (Oxford, 1987)

Levy, B., *Quakers and The American Family: British Settlement in The Delaware Valley* (Oxford, 1988)

Mack, P., 'Gender and Spirituality in Early English Quakerism

1650–1665', in E. Potts-Brown and S. M. Stuard, eds, *Witnesses for Change: Quaker Women over Three Centuries* (London, 1989)

Mahood, L., *The Magdalenes: Prostitution in the Nineteenth Century* (London, 1990)

Malmgreen, G., 'Domestic Discords: Women and the Family in East Cheshire Methodism, 1750–1830', in J. Obelkovich, L. Roper and R. Samuel, eds., *Disciplines of Faith: Studies in Religion, Politics and Patriarchy* (London, 1987)

Manning, B., *The Protestant Dissenting Deputies* (Cambridge, 1952)

Mill, J. S., *The Subjection of Women* (London, 1983)

Morrow, T., *Early Methodist Women* (London, 1967)

Muldowney, J. E. and Cade, C. A., *Strange Infatuation: The Curious Tale of Hannah Beedham, forgotten Prophetess of York and Kelfield* (York, 1989)

Nead, L., *Myths of Sexuality: Representations of Women in Victorian Britain* (Oxford, 1988)

Nussbaum, F. A., *The Autobiographical Subject: Gender and Ideology in Eighteenth Century England* (Baltimore, 1989)

Owen, A., *The Darkened Room: Power and Spiritualism in Late Nineteenth Century England* (London, 1989)

Peacock, A. J., 'George Leeman and York Politics, 1833–1880', in C. Feinstein, ed., *York 1831–1981: 150 Years of Scientific Endeavour and Social Change* (York, 1981)

Phillips, N. C., *Yorkshire and English National Politics 1783–84* (Canterbury, NZ, 1961)

Pollock, J., *Wilberforce* (Tring, 1977)

Porter, R., *English Society in the Eighteenth Century* (London, 1982)

Pratt, D.H., *English Quakers and the First Industrial Revolution: A Study of the Quaker Community in four Industrial Counties: Lancashire, Yorkshire, Warwickshire and Gloucestershire, 1750–1830* (New York, 1985)

Prochaska, F. K., *Women and Philanthropy in Nineteenth Century England* (Oxford, 1980)

Reay, B., *The Quakers and the English Revolution* (Oxford, 1969)

Rendall, J., *The Origins of Modern Feminism: Women in Britain, France and the United States, 1780–1860* (London, 1985)

Rosman, D., *Evangelicals and Culture* (London, 1984)

Royle, E., *Nonconformity in Nineteenth Century York*, Borthwick Paper No.68 (York, 1985)

—— *The Victorian Church in York*, Borthwick Paper No.64 (York, 1983)

—— 'Religion in York, 1831–1981', in C. Feinstein, ed., *York 1831–1981: 150 Years of Scientific Endeavour and Social Change* (York, 1981)

Royle, E. and Walvin, J., *English Radicals and Reformers 1760–1848* (Brighton, 1982)

Scott, D. A., *Quakerism in York, 1650–1720*, Borthwick Paper No.80 (York, 1991)

Sessions, W. K. and E. M., *The Tukes of York: Mainly an Account of Three Generations* (York, 1987)

Barbara Smith, ed., *Truth, Liberty and Religion. Essays Celebrating Two Hundred Years of Manchester College* (Oxford, 1986)

Smith, E. A., *Whig Principles and Party Politics: Earl Fitzwilliam and the Whig Party 1784–1833* (Manchester, 1975)

Spacks, P. M., *Imagining Self: Autobiography and the Novel in Eighteenth Century England* (Harvard, 1976)

Stone, L., *Road to Divorce: England 1530–1987* (Oxford, 1990)

Tate, W. E., *The Parish Chest* (Cambridge, 1969)

Taylor, B., 'The Woman Power: Religious heresy and feminism in early English socialism', in S. Lipshitz, ed., *Tearing the Veil: Essays on Femininity* (London, 1978)

Trevett, C., *Women and Quakerism in the Seventeenth Century* (York, 1991)

Tyrell, A., *Joseph Sturge and the Moral Radical Party in Early Victorian Britain* (London, 1987)

Valenze, D. M., *Prophetic Sons and Daughters: Female Preaching and Popular Religion in Industrial England* (Princeton, 1985)

Vann, R. T., *The Social Development of English Quakerism 1655–1755* (Harvard, 1969)

Vernon, A., *A Quaker Businessman: The Life of Joseph Rowntree 1836–1925* (York, 1987)

The Victoria County History of Yorkshire: The City of York (Oxford, 1961)

Wagner, G., *The Chocolate Conscience* (London, 1987)

Walkowitz, J. R., *Prostitution and Victorian Society: Women, Class and the State* (Cambridge, 1980)

Webb, K. A., *One of the Most Useful Charities in the City: York Dispensary, 1788–1988*, Borthwick Paper No.74 (York, 1988)

Weber, M., 'The Protestant Sects and the Spirit of Capitalism', in H.G. Gerth and C. Wright-Mills, eds, *From Max Weber: Essays in Sociology* (London, 1948)

Wells, R.V., 'Quaker Marriage Patterns in a Colonial Perspective', in N. F. Cott and E. H. Pleck, eds, *Work and Feminism in America* (New York, 1980)

ARTICLES

Bacon, M. H., 'Quaker Women in Overseas Ministry', *Quaker History: The Bulletin of the Friends Historical Association*, 77 (1988)

Bradley, J., 'Whigs and Non-conformists: "Slumbering Radicalism" in

English Politics 1739–1789', *Eighteenth Century Studies*, 9 (1975)

Cadbury, H. J., 'John Woolman in England 1772', *Journal of the Friends Historical Society* (a documentary pamphlet, 1971)

Carre, B., 'Early Quaker Women in Lancaster and Lancashire', *Early Lancaster Friends* (Centre for NW Regional Studies), University of Lancaster Occasional Paper No.5 (1975)

Christie, I. R., 'Sir George Saville, Edmund Burke and The Yorkshire Reform Programme, February 1780', *Yorkshire Archaeological Journal*, 40 (1959–60)

—— 'The Yorkshire Association, 1780–4: A Study in Political Organisation', *Historical Journal*, 3 (1960)

Collie, R., 'The Quakers of Tottenham, 1775–1825', *Edmonton Hundred Historical Society Occasional Paper*, New Series, No.37 (1979)

Cott, N. F., 'Passionlessness: An Interpretation of Victorian Sexual Ideology 1790–1850, *Signs*, 4 (1978)

David, T. M., ed., 'Committees for Repeal of the Test and Corporation Acts, Minutes 1786–90 and 1827–8', *London Records Society*, 14 (1978)

Degler, C., 'What Ought to Be and What Was: Women's Sexuality in the Nineteenth Century', *American Historical Review*, 79 (1974)

Edwards, G. W., 'Quakers as Church Wardens', *Journal of the Friends Historical Society*, 52 (1968)

Evans, E. J., 'Our Faithful Testimony: The Society of Friends and Tithe Payments, 1690–1730', *Journal of the Friends Historical Society*, 2 (1969)

Ford, H., 'Friends and Authority: a consideration of attitudes and expedients with particular reference to Derbyshire', *Journal of the Friends Historical Society*, 70 (1988)

Goodyear, I. R., 'Wilson Armistead and the Leeds Antislavery Movement', *Thorseby Society Miscellany*, 16 (1979)

Grubb, M., 'The Beacon Separation', *Journal of the Friends Historical Society*, 55 (1988)

Isichei, E., 'From Sect to Denomination in English Quakerism with Special Reference to the Nineteenth Century', *British Journal of Sociology*, 15 (1964)

Loft, L., 'Quakers, Brissot and Eighteenth Century Abolitionists', *Journal of the Friends Historical Society*, 55 (1989)

Mack, P., 'Women as Prophets during the English Civil War', *Feminist Studies*, 8 (1982)

Malmgreen, G., 'Ann Knight and the Radical Subculture', *Quaker History*, 71 (1982)

Mortimer, R. S., 'Quakers in the Diocese of Salisbury, 1783', *Journal of the Friends Historical Society*, 50 (1962)

Mullett, C., 'The Corporation Act and The Election of English

Protestant Dissenters to Corporation Offices', *Virginia Law Review*, 21 (1935)

Mullett, M., 'From Sect to Denomination? Social Developments in Eighteenth-Century English Quakerism', *Journal of Religious History*, 13 (1984)

Phillips, N. C., 'Country against Court: Christopher Wyvill, a Yorkshire Champion', *Yorkshire Archaeological Journal*, 10 (1962)

Seed, J., 'Gentlemen Dissenters: The Social and Political Meanings of Rational Dissent in the 1770s and 1780s', *Historical Journal*, 28 (1985)

Shorter, E., 'Female Emancipation, Birth Control and Fertility in European History', *American History Review*, 78 (1973)

Sonderland, J. R., 'Women's Authority in Pennsylvania and New Jersey Quaker Meetings, 1680–1760', *William & Mary Quarterly*, 44 (1987)

Swift, D. E., 'Charles Simeon and J. J. Gurney: A Chapter in Anglican–Quaker Relations', *Church History*, 29 (1960)

Swift, W., 'The Women Itinerant Preachers of Early Methodism', *Proceedings of the Wesley Historical Society*, 29 (1953)

Tholfsen, T. R., 'The Origins of the Birmingham Caucus', *Historical Journal*, 2 (1959)

Thomas, K., 'Women and the Civil War Sects', *Past & Present*, 13 (1958)

Tual, J., 'Sexual Equality and Conjugal Harmony: The Way to Celestial Bliss', *Journal of the Friends Historical Society*, 55 (1988)

Tyrell, A., 'Woman's Mission and Pressure Group Politics in Britain (1825–60)', *Bulletin of the John Rylands Library*, 63 (1980–1)

Wells, R. V., 'Family History and Demographic Transition', *Journal of Social History*, 9 (1975)

Wilson, B. R., 'An Analysis of Sect Development', *American Sociological Review*, 24 (1959)

Wright, S., 'Quakerism and its Implications for Quaker Women: The Women Itinerant Ministers of York Meeting, 1780–1840', *Studies in Church History*, 27 (1990)

THESES AND UNPUBLISHED ARTICLES

Bailey, M. H., 'The Contribution of Quakers to some aspects of Local Government in Birmingham, 1828–1902', unpublished MA thesis (University of Birmingham, 1952)

Bradley, I. C., 'The Politics of Godliness: Evangelicals in Parliament 1784–1832', unpublished D.Phil thesis (University of Oxford, 1974)

Bradley, J., 'The Legal Status, Social Structure and Ideology of Nonconformity', unpublished paper (n.d.)

Corfield, P. J., 'The Social and Economic History of Norwich, 1650–1850: A Study in Urban Growth', unpublished Ph.D. thesis (University of London, 1975)

Cumming, S. L., 'Evangelicals in York: The public activities of a group of leading churchmen 1771–1865', unpublished M.Phil. thesis (University of York, 1990)

Morgan, N., 'The Quakers and the Establishment 1600–1730, with specific reference to the North-West of England', unpublished Ph.D. thesis (University of Lancaster, 1985)

Peacock, A. J., 'York in the Age of Reform', unpublished D.Phil. thesis (University of York, 1973)

Price, F. C., 'The Parliamentary Elections in York City, 1754–1790', unpublished MA thesis (University of Manchester, 1958)

Scott, D. A., 'Dissent, Politics and Quakerism in York, 1640–1700', unpublished D.Phil. thesis (University of York, 1990)

Walsh, J. D., 'The Yorkshire Evangelicals in the Eighteenth Century, with especial reference to Methodism', unpublished Ph.D. thesis (University of Cambridge, 1956)

Notes

INTRODUCTION

1   W. C. Braithwaite, *The Second Period of Quakerism* (Cambridge, 1981); H. Barbour, *The Quakers in Puritan England* (New Haven, 1964); R. T. Vann, *The Social Development of English Quakerism 1655–1755* (Cambridge, Mass, 1969); B. Reay, *The Quakers and the English Revolution* (Oxford, 1984).

2   D. A. Scott, 'Dissent, Politics and Quakerism in York 1640–1700', unpublished D.Phil. thesis (University of York, 1990); N. Morgan, 'The Quakers and the Establishment 1600–1730 with specific reference to the North-West of England', unpublished Ph.D. thesis (University of Lancaster, 1985).

3   C. Trevett, *Women and Quakerism in the Seventeenth Century* (York, 1991).

4   E. Isichei, *Victorian Quakers* (Oxford, 1970); R. Jones, *The Later Periods of Quakerism* (London, 1921).

5   S. Allott, *Friends in York: The Quaker Story in the Life of a Meeting* (York, 1978); and T. D. Hamm, *The Transformation of American Quakerism: Orthodox Friends, 1800–1907* (Indiana, 1988).

6   J. W. Frost, *The Quaker Family in Colonial America* (New York, 1973); B. Levy, *Quakers and the American Family: British Settlement in the Delaware Valley* (Oxford, 1988).

7   *The Victoria County History of Yorkshire: The City of York* (Oxford, 1961).

8   A. Armstrong, *Stability and Change in an English Country Town: A social study of York, 1801–1851* (Cambridge, 1974).

9   E. Royle, *Nonconformity in Nineteenth Century York*, Borthwick Paper No.68 (1985); E. Royle, *The Victorian Church in York*, Borthwick Paper No.64 (1983); E. Royle, 'Religion in York 1831–1981', in C. H. Feinstein, ed., *York 1831–1981: 150 Years of Scientific Endeavour and Social Change* (York, 1981); S. L. Cumming, 'Evangelicals in York: The public activities of a group of leading churchmen 1771–1865', unpublished M.Phil. thesis (University of York, 1990).

10 J. S. Rowntree, *Quakerism Past and Present* (London, 1859).

213

CHAPTER 1

1   *The Victoria County History of Yorkshire: The City of York* (Oxford, 1961), pp.207–53.
2   Ibid., p.253.
3   The school still exists within the city.
4   *Victoria County History*, op.cit., pp.251–2.
5   Ibid., p.257.
6   A. Armstrong, *Stability and Change in an English Country Town* (Cambridge, 1974), p.45.
7   *Victoria County History*, op.cit., p.259.
8   *York Courant*, 24 September 1833.
9   E. Royle, *Nonconformity in Nineteenth Century York*, Borthwick Paper No.68 (1985), p.2.
10 Ibid.
11 Richardson became the focus for other Evangelical ministers. His brother James came to York in 1785, first to St Maurice's, then in 1804 to St John's, Micklegate; his nephew, Thomas Richardson, became a curate at St Martin's, Micklegate in 1819.
12 Royle, op.cit., pp.5–10.
13 James Martineau attended the college from 1822–7. See also Barbara Smith, ed., *Truth, Liberty and Religion. Essays Celebrating Two Hundred Years of Manchester College* (Oxford, 1986).
14 The extension was to accommodate the larger Quarterly Meeting which met in York.
15 *Victoria County History*, op.cit., p.269.
16 J. S. Rowntree, *Quakerism Past and Present* (London, 1859), p.34.
17 W. K. and E. M. Sessions, *The Tukes of York* (York, 1987), p.34.
18 *Epistles from Yearly Meeting of Friends 1681–1857* (London, 1858), pp.139; 141.
19 Ibid., p.26. *Epistles* for 1725, 1731, 1737, 1755, 1760, and 1770 were concerned with regulations on conversation and conduct; reminders on plainness of dress were issued in 1718, 1739, 1743, and 1753; that reading should exclude plays and romances in 1720 and 1769; regulations on mourning in 1724, 1745 and 1751.
20 R. Barclay, *An Apology for the True Christian Divinity: Being an explanation and vindication of the principles and doctrines of the people called Quakers* (London, 1841), p.211.
21 In 1797 Henry Tuke of York Meeting and George Millar travelled to Scotland and Northern England in an attempt to revive Meetings.
22 S. Allott, *Friends in York* (York, 1978), pp.1–2.
23 York Friends Meeting House is still in Friargate.
24 K. Thomas, 'Women and the Civil War Sects', *Past & Present*, 13 (1958), pp.44–62.
25 G. Fox, *A Collection of Many Select and Christian Epistles*, Vol.2 (London, 1867), p.33.

26   G. Fox, *A Journal or Historical Account of the Life, Travels, Sufferings, Christian Experiences and Labour of love in the work of the Ministry of that ancient eminent and faithful servant of Jesus Christ, G. Fox*, Vol.2 (London, 1827), pp.324–43.

27   Minutes of the Meeting of Ministers and Elders (1709–1775), York Monthly Meeting, MFR/18.

28   Esther Tuke to Henry Tuke, letter dated 8/7/1785: Tuke family papers, box 4. She commented that 'The concourse was so great and such numbers ... that it was at times a tumult ... what made it still more were the fears ... least the floors should breakdown.'

29   WMMM, Vol.2, 4 January 1781, f.67; and July 1785, f.111.

30   I have developed this theme further in S. Wright, 'Quakerism and its Implications for Quaker Women: The Women Itinerant Ministers of York Meeting, 1780–1840', *Studies in Church History*, 27 (1990), pp.403–14.

31   Allott, op.cit., p.32. Typical of this confusing rhetoric was this report in 1781 by Esther Tuke from the Women's Quarterly Meeting: '... much caution and counsel was opened ... [on the] great revoltings of many amongst us joining themselves in fellowship with the world, its customs and fashions and ... the necessity of laying these things to heart, lest a day of sore judgment [*sic*] should overtake us with others, when those who had partook of the pleasures of a wicked and delusive world will also partake of their sorrow, if they repent not', WMMM, 4 January 1781, f.66.

32   British Library, MFR/2791/1. Diary of Susanna Boone of Birmingham Monthly Meeting, 1773–89. It was not only other Quakers who undermined Quaker confidence. Charles Lamb wrote a thinly veiled attack on Quaker women preachers in 1821, portraying their ministry as 'a trembling female, generally ancient, voice is heard' and with 'a quaking diffidence' – a clear attack on the role that Quaker women were given within the Meeting and a male fear that this was subversive to the role that was increasingly being assigned to women. C. Lamb, 'A Quaker's Meeting', in *Elia and The Essays of Elia* (Oxford, 1987), p.54.

33   Allott, op.cit., p.29.

34   D.A. Scott, 'Dissent Politics and Quakerism in York, 1640–1700', unpublished D.Phil. thesis (University of York, 1990), p.16.

CHAPTER 2

1   For a discussion of the effects of Evangelicalism on American Quakerism, see T. D. Hamm, *The Transformation of American Quakerism: Orthodox Friends, 1800–1907* (Bloomington, 1988).

2   See *Gentleman's Magazine* for March 1803, p.249; July 1806, p.639; and May 1807, p.432. These accusations were based on the fact that

Quakers did not subscribe to the supremacy of the Scriptures. See J. Bossy, *The English Catholic Community 1570–1850* (London, 1975), p.391, for his definition of Protestant.

3   Ibid., p.393. Bossy argues that Quakers and Catholics had geographical links, as well as an '… archaic character more reminiscent of pre- than post-Reformation Christianity'.

4   R. Barclay, *An Apology for the True Christian Divinity: Being an explanation and vindication of the principles and doctrines of the people called Quakers* (London, 1841), p.66.

5   Ibid., p.67.

6   R. M. Jones, *The Later Periods of Quakerism*, Vol.1 (London, 1921), p.276.

7   D. E. Swift, 'Charles Simeon and J. J. Gurney: A Chapter in Anglican–Quaker Relations', *Church History*, 29 (1960), pp.173–4.

8   D. W. Bebbington, *Evangelicalism in Modern Britain: A history from the 1730s to 1980s* (London, 1989), p.5. G. Best, 'Evangelicalism and the Victorians' in A. Symondson, ed., *The Victorian Crisis of Faith* (London, 1970), p.38. Swift, op.cit., p.173.

9   See p.86; see also D. A. Scott, 'Dissent, Politics and Quakerism in York 1640–1700', unpublished D.Phil. thesis (University of York, 1990).

10   A. Digby, *Madness, Morality and Medicine: A study of the York Retreat 1796–1914* (Cambridge, 1985).

11   See pp.100–4.

12   *Gentleman's Magazine*, March 1803, p.249.

13   *Epistles from the Yearly Meeting of Friends*, Vol.2 (London, 1858), p.247.

14   It has been argued that Evangelicalism and the Evangelicals had no significant influence on Quakerism until about 1835. See M. Grubb, 'The Beacon Separation', *Journal of the Friends Historical Society*, 55 (1988), p.191.

15   Ackworth School was initiated by Dr John Fothergill, a London Quaker, at Yearly Meeting in 1777. Plans for its foundation were taken up by William and Esther Tuke and it was they who worked to rally the Meetings of Yorkshire to the cause. After a hesitant start, they succeeded in raising the necessary finance of £7,000 and the school opened in 1779.

16   Esther, Ann, Sarah and Elizabeth Tuke founded the school in Trinity Lane which subsequently became the Mount School. For their interest in the Retreat, see Digby, op.cit., p.15.

17   *Memoirs of the Life & Writings of Lindley Murray in a series of letters written by himself* (York, 1826).

18   L. Murray, *Biographical Sketch of Henry Tuke* (York, 1827).

19   W. K. and E. M. Sessions, *The Tukes of York: Mainly an Account of three Generations* (York, 1987), p.18. See also papers, letters and correspondence of Mary Maria Tuke: Tuke family papers, box 8–12, BI.

20   Sarah Lynes Grubb came from Clonmel Monthly Meeting and must have had many debates with Sarah Tuke Grubb who, throughout her

time at Clonmel, struggled to 'awaken the dead' within her adopted Meeting. She started a Quaker school for Quaker children, run along similar lines to Trinity Lane in York, and advised Scripture education for the children.

21   *A Selection from the Letters of the Late Sarah Grubb* (London, 1848), p.17.

22   Swift, op.cit., p.181.

23   Henry Tuke manuscripts: Tuke family papers, box 71, BI. Zachary Macaulay, a leading member of the Clapham Sect, founded the *Christian Observer* in 1802.

24   *Christian Observer*, Vol.II (1803), p.595.

25   Ibid., p.719; Vol.III (1804), p.71; Vol.IV (1804), p.714.

26   Henry Tuke manuscripts: Tuke family papers, box 71, BI.

27   *Christian Observer*, Vol.V (1805), p.714. Henry Tuke manuscripts, op.cit.

28   H. Tuke, *The Principles of Religion as Professed by the Society of Christians, usually called Quakers* (York, 1819), pp.16–17.

29   Ibid., pp.42–3.

30   Henry Tuke manuscripts, op.cit.

31   Letter from an unknown New York Friend to Henry Tuke, 24 August 1806: Tuke family papers, box 9, BI.

32   *Christian Observer*, Vol.V (1805), p.168. For a similar comment, see also *Gentleman's Magazine*, Vol.75 (April 1805), p.351.

33   *Christian Observer*, Vol.IV (1804), p.604.

34   This culminated in the schism within Lancashire Monthly Meeting in 1835/6 caused by Isaac Crewdson, the author of the controversial *Beacon*, in which he espoused extreme Evangelical views. Yearly Meeting set up an investigating committee carefully chosen to represent all shades of Quakerism. Samuel Tuke and J. J. Gurney represented the Evangelical Quakers and their open-minded assessment helped to avoid a more serious split in English Quakerism. Much of the concern over Crewdson and *The Beacon* reflected English Quaker fears for the development of a 'Hicksite' style schism within English Quakerism. See Grubb, op.cit., pp.193–6, who considers it was the presence of uncommitted Quakers that prevented schism. See also Alan P. F. Sell, *Church Planting. A Study of Westmorland Nonconformity* (Worthing, 1986), pp.102–4, for the situation in Kendal. However, for Samuel Tuke's obvious sympathies with Isaac Crewdson, see Samuel Tuke to Elizabeth Hack, letter dated 8 February 1836: Tuke family papers, box 19. For the development of the relationship between J. J. Gurney and Evangelical Anglicans, see D. Swift, pp.167–86.

35   Jones, op.cit., p 286.

36   L. Murray, 'The Power of Religion on the Mind in Retirement Affliction & the Approach of Death, 1787', in *Testemonies of Experience* (York, 1820). *Gentleman's Magazine* (November 1803), p.1055.

37   L. Murray, *A Compendium of Religious Faith and Practice* (York, 1815).

38   L. Murray, *The Duty and Benefit of a Daily Perusal of the Holy Scriptures in Families* (York, 1817), p.8.

39   Systematic study of the Scriptures was not introduced at Ackworth School until 1816. This was at the instigation of the Management Committee, which included Samuel Tuke and J.J. Gurney. Samuel Tuke had been a member of a conference at the school in 1813 which had tried to introduce religious instruction. He commented at the time that Charles Parker opposed the idea, but that 'He was ... in great measure, alone and the general opinion ... was in favour of some additional means being introduced ... Our women Friends ... were unanimously in favour of improvement.' These included Ann Maud (Bradford), Mary Camm and Martha Fletcher from York. Samuel Tuke to Priscilla Tuke, letter dated 23 April 1813: Tuke family papers, box 21. For J.J. Gurney's involvement, see J. B. Braithwaite, *Memoirs of Joseph John Curney: with selections from his journal and correspondence*, Vol.I (Philadelphia, 1857), pp.176–83.

40   'Proceedings and Resolutions of the Meeting held at the Assembly Rooms in York, the 29th day of January 1812, on the formation of an Auxilliary Bible Society for the City of York and its vicinity', Henry Tuke's address to the meeting, p.25, MS at YPL.

41   Ibid., p.25.

42   Ibid., p.27. Letter from Lindley Murray to the Meeting.

43   Quakers present at the inaugural meeting were: William Tuke, William Thurnam, Samuel Tuke, John Tuke, William and Samuel Richardson, Thomas Priestman, William and Ann Alexander, Joseph Awmack, Martha Fletcher, George Jepson and Joseph King. Also present were Evangelical Anglicans Faith and William Gray, the Revd William Richardson, Dr Withers, Cordelia Withers, Martha Richardson and the Unitarian minister, Charles Wellbeloved. Quakers also supported the York Religious Tract Association and by 1843 22 of them were either committee members or members of the association: *York Gazette*, 10 November 1827. By 1821 there was a Ladies' Bible Association which distributed tracts/Bibles; Priscilla Tuke was one of the workers. Priscilla Tuke to Esther Tuke, letter dated 1821: Tuke family papers, box 25. Members of the York Auxiliary in Aid of the Conversion of the Jews included William Alexander (Quaker) and Anglicans William and Jonathan Gray, the Revd T. Richardson, the Revd J. Graham and the Independent minister, the Revd J. Parsons: *York Gazette*, 21 November 1829.

44   D. Swift, 'Charles Simeon and J.J. Gurney', op.cit., p.182. Swift suggests that because J.J. Gurney's work was admired by many Quakers, his popularity and influence as a minister drew in new members to Norwich Meeting in the mid-1820s which helped its numerical growth.

CHAPTER 3

1   E. Isichei, *Victorian Quakers* (Oxford, 1970), pp.107–10. Since most
    historians of English Quakerism have concentrated on the seven-
    teenth century, including Keith Thomas, Jacques Tual and, especially,
    Phyllis Mack, and only a few on Quaker women, comparative work
    for the eighteenth and nineteenth centuries comes mainly from
    America.

2   A. Tyrrell, *Joseph Sturge and the Moral Radical Party in Early Victorian
    Britain* (London, 1987), p.66.

3   See p.51.

4   B. Carre, 'Early Quaker Women in Lancaster and Lancashire', in
    Early Lancaster Friends (Centre for NW Regional Studies), University
    of Lancaster Occasional Paper No.5 (1975), p.43.

5   Great Book of Sufferings, Vols.22–5, 31, 34, 38 and 44. See also
    Appendix VII, table 7.

6   R. T. Vann, *The Social Development of Englidsh Quakerism 1655–1755*
    (Harvard, 1969), pp.101–21.

7   The average known age at marriage for women who served YWMM
    between 1800 and 1830 was 31.1 yrs.; 1830–60, 28.4 yrs. Several,
    particularly Tuke women, remained unmarried into their mid-thirties.
    Bristol Meeting repeats this pattern and only leading women
    members were involved in the organization of the Women's Meeting.
    See also J. R. Sonderland, 'Women's Authority in Pennsylvania
    and New Jersey Quaker Meetings, 1680–1760', *William & Mary
    Quarterly*, 3rd Series, 44 (1987), pp.728–9, where he found that 80%
    of female leaders were the wives of prominent members of the Men's
    Meeting whom, he suggests, did not become active participants until
    they had married.

8   Esther Tuke, supported by eight English and four American women
    Friends, won the right for English women Friends to have a separate
    Yearly Meeting in 1784. This allowed them to meet separately and
    issue their own Yearly Epistle: W. K. and E. M. Sessions, *The Tukes of
    York* (York, 1987), pp.30–1.

9   *Epistles from the Yearly Meeting Concerning the Regulation of The Society*
    (London, 1792), p.211.

10 YWMM, Vol.3 (1796–1818), MFR/10, BI.

11 Convincement involved attendance at First Day Meeting on a
    continuous basis; being judged by the inspectors truly to espouse the
    beliefs of, and adhere to the rules and regulations of, Quakerism.

12 YWMM, Vol.3, op.cit., and YWMM, Vol.4 (1818–40), BL.

13 See below, Chapter 7, table 23, for admissions into YMM.

14 Many came to work at the Quaker schools and the Retreat. Ann Scott
    came to work for a Quaker household in 1825 and was converted in
    1830: see p.41.

15 YWMM, Vol.3, op.cit..

16   Quakers were anxious that members should not apply to the parish for poor relief and probably served as overseers in vestries partly to ensure they did not.

17   Applications for membership; disownments; documents of discipline, etc., Vol.2 (1800–48), MFR/19. Letter dated 4 May 1826, BL.

18   Bristol Meeting established its own workhouse in 1696, giving the Meeting a further source of help to its poor: BWMM, SF/A2/1B.

19   YWPM, Vol.2 (1775–1841), MFR/22, BI.

20   Ibid.

21   BWPM had large funds. The balance in the account book regularly averaged £50 between 1792 and 1830 and could rise to £100. The money was from bequests: Susanna Rodgers left £20 in 1780; Betty Green £20 in 1794; Rachel Crosby £50 in 1799.

22   Joseph Hardy became Lindley Murray's coachman in 1800.

23   In 1798 the fund paid Sarah Sharp's apothecary bill of £1. 13s. 3d; gave Sarah Peacock clothing worth £3. 8s. 9d.; it paid Caleb Williams' bill (the Quaker doctor) of £3. 14s. for attending Margaret Wilson: YPM, Legacy A/C Book, Vol.1 (1707–1849), MFR/22, BI.

24   Dorothy Brown was in business as a mantua-maker, but her business failed. In 1845 she was employed as a servant with Samuel Tuke: YMM Members List, Vol.2 (1842–59), BL. In Bristol in August 1780 Friends found a new post for Hester Davies because her non-Quaker employer would not let her attend Meeting: BWMM (1764–81), SF/A2/1B.

25   The fees were £10. 14s. 4d. at Ackworth for poor Friends.

26   YMM, Robert Waller's Education Fund Ledger (1845–1934), BL. This fund was for the education of Friends at Rawdon School, Leeds. Quaker women from the Quarterly Meetings of Yorkshire were on the joint committee which ran the school.

27   Applications for membership, disownments, documents of discipline, etc., op.cit. In Bristol, Mary Clapp was on poor relief from 1808 but was disowned for marrying out in 1813, and Hannah Dorrington had received intermittent relief for 20 years when she resigned her membership in 1822: BWMM Account Book, SF/F8/4, BA.

28   Applications for membership, disownments, documents of discipline, etc., op.cit.

29   Ibid. See below, Chapter 7, tables 28 and 30, for disownments in BMM.

30   In York Meeting women were generally more vulnerable to disownment than they were in Bristol. See below, Chapter 7, table 30.

31   There was an increase in the number of resignations in Bristol Meeting. Possibly this was the result of exerting pressure on those inclined to marry out to resign. The original objection to marriage out was that it implied marriage by a priest not, as it became interpreted in the eighteenth century, marriage to a non-Quaker. See M. Mullett, 'From Sect to Denomination? Social Developments in

Eighteenth-Century English Quakerism', *Journal of Religious History*, 13, 2 (1984), p.177.

32 Yearly Meeting, held in May each year, was the social occasion of the year and involved a continuous round of tea and dinner parties. When Joseph Rowntree was a boy, he recalled Quarterly Meeting being a time of frantic entertaining by his parents, with seven or eight people staying in the cramped house in Parliament Street and thirty sitting down to dinner in relays: A. Vernon, *A Quaker Businessman: The Life of Joseph Rowntree 1836–1925* (York, 1987), p.19.

33 Applications for membership, disownments, documents of discipline, etc., Vol.1. The Society established the 'Fund for the Encouragement of Marriage amongst people of low circumstances, members of the Society of Friends, commonly called Quakers' in 1817. The fund aimed to help young men in a position with little opportunity to save enough to marry and it had a scale of grants for those who married within the Society. Those with property to the value of £10 received £10; those with £20 received £6; those with £20–30, £3: Gifts and Legacies, YPM (1765–82), MFR/12, BI.

34 Applications for membership, disownments, documents of discipline, etc., Vol.2 (1800–48), BL.

35 YWMM, Vol.5 (1841–60), F25, BL.

36 Ibid. Three other women were married in a Registrar's Office before the change in the marriage rule in 1860. None of them was disowned. Elizabeth Bellis married in 1854; Priscilla Pilmoor in 1857; and Sarah Wells in 1857. But John Johnson, who married Elizabeth Steel (not a Friend) in a Registrar's Office in 1858, was disowned, probably because he refused to co-operate with the investigating committee.

37 YWPM, Vol.2, BL.

38 Applications for membership, disownments, documents of discipline, etc., Vol.1, BL.

39 L. Davidoff and C. Hall, *Family Fortunes* (London, 1987), p.87.

40 Applications for membership, disownments, documents of discipline, etc., Vol.1. Her letter was written in response to one from the Men's Meeting dealing with her husband Samuel's case. The loss of financial support resulted in her own eventual disownment for debt.

41 Ibid.

42 Martha Richardson to George Richardson, letter dated 6 October 1832: Richardson family papers (in private hands).

43 Bristol Women's Meeting had access to more funds than York. As a result, they had greater autonomy because they did not have to ask the Men's Meeting for any large sums of poor relief.

44 N. F. Cott, *The Bonds of Womanhood: 'Woman's Sphere' in New England, 1780–1835* (London, 1977), pp.126–9.

45 Methodism had many female class leaders. At New Street Chapel, York in 1789, 3 out of 8 class leaders were women. By 1812, the figures

were 6 out of 17, and by 1822, 8 out of 22 were women. Membership had increased from 231 in 1791 to 731 by 1814 and 919 by 1822: Methodist Records, MRC1/1/1–4, BI.

46   G. Fox, *A Collection of Many Select and Christian Epistles*, Vol.2 (London, 1698), p.244.

47   R. Barclay, *An Apology for the True Christian Divinity* (London, 1841), p.310.

48   Ibid., p.311.

49   There are no journals available for male York Friends. Where possible, letters have been used to supplement published journals.

50   Women's journals in particular suffer from editorship, reflecting male notions of what should be rather than what was. George Fox often censored manuscripts and by the eighteenth century a male committee at Yearly Meeting edited all publications of the Society.

51   P. M. Spacks, *Imagining Self: Autobiography and the Novel in Eighteenth Century England* (Harvard, 1976), p.55. See also F. A. Nussbaum, *The Autobiographical Subject: Gender and Ideology in Eighteenth Century England* (London, 1989), p.157.

52   D. Rosman, *Evangelicals and Culture* (London, 1984), pp.13–14.

53   C. Edkins, 'Quest for Community: Spiritual Autobiographies of Eighteenth Century Quaker and Puritan Women in America', in E. Jelenek, ed., *Women's Autobiography: Essays in Criticism* (Blooming-ton, 1980), p.41. For women, journals were a legitimate source of expression through which they could make themselves heard and have the truth about their work known.

54   Ibid., p.45. She incorrectly asserts that women became members of the Society when they first stood up to speak during Meeting. Most women and men were birthright members and standing up in Meeting was initiation into the ministry not into the Society.

55   Lower-class Quakers had fewer opportunities to write, and by the eighteenth and nineteenth centuries very few were ministers.

56   *Some Account of the Life and Religious Labours of Sarah Grubb* (London, 1776), p.4.

57   Ibid., p.6.

58   Ibid., p.9.

59   *Some Account of the Life and Religious Experience of Mary Alexander Late of Needham Market* (York, 1811), p.24.

60   Both J. J. Gurney and Elizabeth Fry record the tests required to give up these un-Quakerly activities.

61   *Gospel Privileges Exemplified in the Life of Ann Scott*, in tracts published by the York Friends Tract Association (York 1857), p.4.

62   Elizabeth Tuke, first wife of William Tuke, had a correct presenti-ment of death whilst expecting her fifth child in six years of marriage in 1760. Eliza Sturge also foretold her own death in childbirth just ten months after her marriage to Joseph in 1834: Tyrell, op.cit., p.62.

63   *A Journal of the Life Labours, Travels and Sufferings in and for the Gospel*

of that Ancient Servant and Faithful Minister of Jesus Christ, John Banks
(London, 1798), p.42.

64   J. B. Braithwaite, *Memoirs of Joseph John Gurney* (Norwich, 1854),
       p.84.

65   *The Journal of the Life, Travels and Religious labours of William Savery*
       (London, 1844), pp.2–3.

66   D. M. Valenze, *Prophetic Sons and Daughters: Female Preaching and
       Popular Religion in Industrial England* (Princeton 1985), p.143.

67   E. K. Brown, *Women of Mr. Wesley's Methodism: Studies in Women in
       Religion*, Vol.2 (New York, 1983), p.203.

68   Ibid., p.206.

69   *Bible Christian Magazine*, Vol.2 (1823–4), p.93.

70   Quoted in B. Taylor, 'The Woman Power', in S. Lipshitz, ed., *Tearing
       The Veil: Essays on femininity* (London 1978), p.120.

71   Minutes of the Meeting of Ministers and Elders (1709–75): YMM,
       MFR/18, BI.

72   Ibid., Vols.1 and 2 (1776–1856), MFR/18, BI. For women travelling in
       the ministry, see M. H. Bacon, 'Quaker Women in Overseas Ministry',
       Quaker History: The Bulletin of the Friends Historical Association, Vol.77,
       2 (1988), pp.93–109; and H. Barbour, 'Quaker Prophetesses and
       Mothers in Israel', in C and J. Stoneburner, eds, *The Influence of Quaker
       Women on American History* (Lewiston, 1987), pp.57–79.

73   D. C. Dews, 'Ann Carr and the Female Revivalists of Leeds', in
       G. Malmgreen, ed., *Religion in the Lives of English Women, 1760–1930*
       (London, 1986), p.71. This had probably been in response to the
       behaviour of women such as Hannah Beedham of York. Ex-
       communicated in 1833 by the Wesleyan Methodists, she prophesied
       that she would die at 9 p.m. on Thursday, 1 August 1833 at Kelfield.
       Thousands followed her and waited nine days for her to die.
       She didn't and, not surprisingly, lost her credibility as a preacher:
       J. E. Muldowney and C. A. Cade, *Strange Infatuation: The Curious Tale
       of Hannah Beedham, forgotten Prophetess of York and Kelfield* (York, 1989).

74   G. Malmgreen, 'Domestic Discords: Women and the Family in East
       Cheshire Methodism, 1750–1830', in J. Obelkevich, L. Roper and
       R. Samuel, eds, *Disciplines of Faith: Studies in Religion, Politics and
       Patriarchy* (London, 1987), pp.55–6; E. Dorothy Graham, 'Chosen by
       God: The female travelling preachers of early Primitive Methodism',
       Proceedings of the Wesley Historical Society, XLIX, 3 (October, 1993),
       pp.77–95.

75   Dews, op.cit., p.73.

76   P. Mack, 'Women as Prophets during the English Civil War', *Feminist
       Studies*, 8 (1982), pp.19–47. She suggests that women were particularly
       receptive to God's word because of their natures. This observation is
       valid for late eighteenth-century Quaker women, but the expression
       of their receptivity was quite different, being more calmly and quietly
       expressed and with the greater discipline required by a Society no

longer welcoming prophetic preaching or ecstatic behaviour and the bad publicity which might result from this behaviour. See also A. Owen, *The Darkened Room: Power and Spiritualism in Late Nineteenth Century England* (London, 1989); P. Mack, 'Gender and Spirituality in Early English Quakerism 1650–1665', in E. Potts-Brown and S. M. Stuard, eds, *Witnesses for Change: Quaker Women over Three Centuries* (London, 1989), p.34.

77 Ann Mercy Bell's style of preaching was to hold impromptu Meetings on street corners, often up to six or more times a day. Her style when preaching in Leadenhall Market was described thus: 'Entering in at the lower end of the poulterers market, she went thro' calling for repentance as she passed, with uncommon force and solemnity; and coming to a convenient place in the Leather Market, after the people, who poured in at every avenue, were gathered round her, she had a large and favourable opportunity with them': Journal and Correspondence of Ann Mercy Bell (1745–86), YMM, MFR/13, BI, p.4.

78 YMMME, Vols.1 and 2, MFR/18, BI.

79 C. Tylor, ed., *Memoirs of Elizabeth Dudley* (London, 1861), p.33. Her mother, Mary Dudley, was a minister in Clonmel Meeting, Southern Ireland, having been convinced into Quakerism in 1773. As a Methodist, she had been a friend of John Wesley. Ann Alexander preached to tin miners at Pyrden, Cornwall in October 1794: Ann Alexander to Henry Tuke, letter dated 22 October 1794: Tuke family papers, box 17, BI.

80 Tylor, op.cit., p.33.

81 Ibid. This report was by a member of the audience, not a Friend.

82 Posters were displayed, such as one announcing: 'A Sermon will be preached by an American Lady Minister, Rebecca Collins of the Friends Society at the Burdett Hall, Burdett Road, Limehouse on Sunday Evening May 12th. Service commencing at 7 o'clock. All are welcome': no date, f.N/135d., FHL.

83 Ann Alexander to Henry Tuke, letter dated 31 September 1797: Tuke family papers, box 17, BI.

84 *Life and Religious Experience of Mary Alexander*, op.cit., p.143.

85 *The Primitive Methodist Magazine*, Vol.4, p.1823.

86 W. Swift, 'The Women Itinerant Preachers of Early Methodism', *Proceedings of the Wesley Historical Society*, 29 (1953), p.80.

87 *Bible Christian Magazine*, Vol.2 (1823–4), p.169.

88 Ibid., p.267.

89 All these denominations used similar language to express their conversions and their beliefs.

90 Sarah Tuke Grubb to Tabbitha Hoyland, letter dated 12 April 1774: Tuke family papers, box 14, BI.

91 Sarah Tuke Grubb to Tabbitha Hoyland, letter dated 1778: Tuke family papers, box 14, BI.

92 *Some Account of Sarah Grubb*, op.cit., p.149.

93 Mary Alexander moved to York in the 1830s to run the Quaker girls' school. She moved to Birmingham in 1848 to open a girls' school and died in 1854.

94 Ann Tuke Alexander to Henry Tuke, various letters: Tuke family papers, box 17, BI.

95 YMM certificates of ministers travelling in the ministry. This is not to suggest that these women left their children lightly. For Quaker women and children, see E. Boulding, 'Mapping the Inner Journey of Quaker Women', in C. and J. Stoneburner, eds, op.cit., pp.115–29.

96 *Some Account of Sarah Grubb*, op.cit., p.42.

97 Swift, op.cit., p.80.

98 *Some Account of Sarah Grubb*, op.cit., p.159.

99 Henry Tuke to William Tuke, letter dated 8 August 1797: Tuke family papers, box 4, BI.

100 *Some Account of Sarah Grubb*, op.cit., p.46. See also G. B. Burdett, *The Story of Quakerism in Scotland, 1650–1850* (London, 1952), who suggests that, by the mid-eighteenth century, Quakerism in Scotland was in decline and had almost died out. Scottish Friends had sent no representative to Yearly Meeting for some years. Efforts to revive the Society in the 1780s, which included this trip by Henry Tuke and George Millar in 1797, failed.

101 Davidoff and Hall, op.cit., p.138.

102 Dews, op.cit., p.68. See also T. M. Morrow, *Early Methodist Women* (London, 1967), p.15.

103 Women preachers of the Bible Christian Connexion only served for short periods: of the 71 women ministers in 1819, 27 served for 3 years or less. Their numbers were to decline from about 1825 to a point where, by 1844, there were only 6 women preachers working on the Bible Christian circuit: Swift, op.cit., p.76. Women preachers of Primitive Methodism also served for very short periods: of the 21 women who are listed as having preached on a regular basis, Elizabeth Bultitude, who was active on the East Anglian circuit for over 30 years, was the only woman who worked for more than 10 years; 5 women served for up to 5 years; 3 for between 5 and 10 years; the majority served for 1 or 2 years. Elizabeth Bultitude carried on preaching until 1862. Primitive Methodist Ministers, list compiled by W. Leary (1970–7) in unpublished MS held at John Rylands Library, Manchester.

104 Because Quaker preachers were middle-class, they could afford the servants necessary to care for children while they were away on ministering journeys.

105 Images of Quaker women have been used to create powerful stereotypes of pure, saintly, plain women, but by constructing Quaker-like attributes, novelists also projected, on a subliminal basis, the other roles of Quaker women – the public and the authoritarian roles. Thus the imagery expresses alternative ideas about women's role within

society, hinting at the possibility of transcending the traditional women's sphere. In Charlotte Brontë's case, they reflect her own frustrations when faced with the lack of choice of occupation as a single woman and her dislike of what John Stuart Mill in 1861 called the 'exaggerated self-abnegation which is the present artificial ideal of feminine character': J. S. Mill, *The Subjection of Women* (London, 1983), p.77. These descriptions of heroines as Quaker-like were used by Charlotte Brontë in a secular context in *Jane Eyre* (London, 1966), pp.130, 287, to describe Jane's dress and general deportment; and by George Eliot in her description of Dorothea Brooke in *Middlemarch* (London, 1965), p.29, and in her description of the minister, Dinah Morris, in *Adam Bede* (London, 1980), pp.67, 77–82.

CHAPTER 4

1   L. Davidoff and C. Hall, *Family Fortunes* (London, 1987).
2   From W. Cowper (1731–1800), 'The Task'.
3   J. A. James, 'The Family Monitor', in T. S. James, ed., *The Works of John Angell James* (Birmingham, 1860), p.56.
4   D. Gorham, *The Victorian Girl & The Feminine Ideal* (London, 1982), p.4.
5   Several other Quaker women also worked in the family business until the 1830s, including Mary Steers, Mary Armitage and Maria Tuke. There were 6 businesses run by Quaker women between 1780 and 1860: 3 confectioners; 2 mantua-makers and a stay-maker, Charlotte Widdas, who supported her husband all his life.
6   D. Gorham, op.cit., pp.8–10; P. Branca, *Silent Sisterhood: Middle Class Women in the Victorian Home* (London, 1975), pp.40–59.
7   Ibid., p.40.
8   Gorham, op.cit., pp.10–11. Acquisition of middle-class status was conferred when a family employed a servant, even if it was only a girl who came in to clean during the day.
9   Samuel Tuke built a second home, a country cottage at Deighton, in 1820.
10   See below, Chapter 7, table 5.
11   Richardson papers, in private hands.
12   The maids earned between £6. 6s. and £8. 8s. in 1800–7 and up to 10 guineas by 1814. Murray paid his coachman £21 in 1800 and this had risen to £26. 5s. by 1809; the gardener earned £14. 14s.
13   Priscilla Tuke to Esther Tuke, no date, 1813: Tuke family papers, box 25.
14   Governesses were employed by Elizabeth Harris, John Kitching, Samuel Tuke, Joseph Rowntree and Robert Saunders.
15   For a discussion on the education of women, see J. Rendall, *The Origins*

of Modern Feminism: Women in Britain, France, and the United States, 1780–1860 (London, 1985), pp.108–25.

16 P. Wakefield, *Reflections on the Present Condition of the Female Sex: with Suggestions for its Improvement* (London, 1798).

17 The curriculum at Trinity Lane was generally wider than that offered by the local dame-schools and included reading, writing, English grammar, geography, history and arithmetic. French was an extra, for which parents paid fifteen shillings per annum.

18 D. Rosman, *Evangelicals and Culture* (London, 1984), pp.97–118.

19 Priscilla Tuke to Samuel Tuke, various letters, 1810: Tuke family papers, box 23.

20 Rendall, op.cit., p.75.

21 Husbands were expected to allow their wives to travel in the ministry and any who complained could expect a rebuke from the Monthly Meeting. See J. W. Frost, *The Quaker Family in Colonial America* (New York, 1973), p.178.

22 B. Levy, *Quakers and the American Family: British Settlement in the Delaware Valley* (Oxford, 1988), p.72.

23 Isabel Richardson of Hull Meeting came to York Meeting aged 17, and went initially to act as unpaid housekeeper to her cousins Samuel and William Richardson, tanners; then to nurse her uncle, Thomas Priestman of Hull. Her only independence came from her work as a minister.

24 YQM Marriage Registers (1720–1860).

25 Parish Registers, St Mary's, Castlegate, PR/Y/MC/141/142/143 (1799–1859).

26 Davidoff and Hall, op.cit., p.222.

27 See pp.119–21.

28 See D. E. C. Eversley, 'The Demography of the Irish Quakers 1650–1850', in J. M. Goldstrom and L. A. Clarkson, eds, *Irish Population, Economy & Society: Essays in Honour of the Late K. H. Connell* (Oxford, 1981), p.65. Comparative work has been done on eighteenth-century American Quakerism which gives an age of first marriage of 22.8 years for a woman and 26.5 years for a man. This would suggest that the colonial experience was significantly different from English Quakerism. See R. V. Wells, 'Quaker Marriage Patterns in a Colonial Perspective', in N. F. Cott and E. H. Pleck, eds, *Work and Feminism in America* (New York, 1980), pp.82–3.

29 See pp.46–7.

30 YQM Marriage Registers.

31 Marriage Registers for St Mary's, Castlegate.

32 Davidoff and Hall, op.cit., p.222.

33 J. A. Banks, *Prosperity & Parenthood: A Study of Family Planning among the Victorian Middle Class* (London, 1954), pp.36–7.

34 Although most would be allowed to attend Meeting and were often readmitted to membership in due time.

35   Marriage Registers, St Mary's, Castlegate.
36   Wells, op.cit., p.85, has shown that the colonial experience was very similar.
37   YQM Marriage Registers.
38   F. Basch, *Relative Creatures: Victorian Women in Society and the Novel* (London, 1974), p.27.
39   Mary Maria Tuke to Henry Tuke, various letters: Tuke family papers, box 10–12. For Quaker courtship, see J. D. Abbatt, *A Victorian Quaker Courtship: Lancashire Love Letters of the 1850s* (York, 1988).
40   K. Thomas, 'Women and the Civil War Sects', *Past & Present*, 13 (1958), p.47.
41   J. Tual, 'Sexual Equality and Conjugal Harmony: The Way to Celestial Bliss. A View of Early Quaker Matrimony', *Journal of Friends Historical Society*, 55 (1988), p.162.
42   F. Smith, *On the Duty of a Wife* (London, 1810), pp.5–8. He was a Quaker.
43   G. Malmgreen, 'Ann Knight and the Radical Subculture', *Quaker History*, 71 (1982), pp.100–13. Ann Knight never married, preferring the 'single blessedness'. She ridiculed the 'difficulties imposed on her friends by their domestic obligations'. Writing in 1840 to Maria West Chapman, whose domestic duties precluded her attending the anti-slavery convention, she commented: 'Ah, that thou hadst not married. That thy "proper sphere" at this juncture should have been nature's recess instead of reason's exercise ...' (p.103).
44   Wakefield, op.cit., p.86.
45   Tuke family papers, box 71. Quaker wills are held at the Borthwick Institute.
46   Letter from Nathaniel Bell to his children, dated August 1774: Journal and correspondence of Ann Mercy Bell, MF/13.
47   Davidoff and Hall, op.cit., pp.219–22. As Lawrence Stone has suggested, middle-class marriage arrangements began to ape the aristocracy as property became increasingly important and as middle-class families became wealthier. L. Stone, *Road to Divorce: England 1530–1987* (Oxford, 1990), p.327.
48   Jacques Tual has argued that seventeenth-century Quaker marriages were based on 'mutual love' and '... relinquished mercenary considerations and developed into a union founded on reciprocal love rather than financial attraction': Tual, op.cit., p.164. But Frost argues that social and financial considerations were very important in seventeenth-century Quaker marriage: Frost, op.cit., pp.156–7.
49   Frost, op.cit., pp.164–5. Esther Maud to William Tuke, 1764: Tuke family papers, box 1, BI.
50   Frost, op.cit., p.157.
51   YQM Marriage Registers, BI.
52   Samuel Tuke asked James Hack's permission in May 1809. On 10 June 1809, his father Henry wrote to James Hack setting out Samuel's

financial situation, telling him that he would have £1,000 upon marriage and an increased share in their business. Henry Tuke to James Hack, letter dated 10 June 1809: Tuke family papers, box 4, BI.

53 Henry Tuke to Samuel Tuke, letter dated 29 May 1809: Tuke family papers, box 8, BI.

54 Samuel Tuke to Priscilla Hack, letter dated 5 June 1810: Tuke family papers, box 21, BI.

55 Samuel Tuke to Priscilla Hack/Priscilla Hack to Samuel Tuke, various letters, 1809: Tuke family papers, box 23, BI.

56 Barbara Scott to Mary Maria Scott, letter dated 1780: Tuke family papers, box 52, BI.

57 Samuel Tuke to Priscilla Tuke, letter dated 3 August 1817: Tuke family papers, box 21, BI. This comment reinforces the idea that for Quaker women, marriage was not the only role they expected in life.

58 For Joseph Rowntree's views on this subject, see below.

59 Sarah Richardson to Robert Coates, letter dated 1 October 1850: Richardson papers, in private hands.

60 E. Shorter, 'Female Emancipation, Birth Control and Fertility in European History', *American History Review*, 78 (1973), p.612. Also Banks, op.cit., pp.139–68. Banks has shown that there was no noticeable decline in family size until post-1861: J. A. Banks, *Victorian Values: Secularisation and the Size of Families* (London, 1981), p.40. For a discussion of Quaker fertility and birth-control, see R. V. Wells, 'Family History and Demographic Transition', *Journal of Social History*, 9 (1975), pp.1–20.

61 Not all Quaker women enjoyed children. Elizabeth Fry wrote that she did not 'experience that joy some women describe when my husband first brought me my little babe': *Memoir of the Life of Elizabeth Fry with extracts from her journal and letters*, Vol.1, edited by her daughters (London 1847), p.106.

62 Priscilla Tuke and her daughters went swimming on holiday at Scarborough; she and Samuel climbed Skiddaw on their honeymoon in the Lake District and ministering women rode hundreds of miles around Britain and Europe on horseback.

63 It is known that Elizabeth Tuke died in childbirth in 1760 and Priscilla Tuke in 1828. Guilielma Tuke to Samuel Tuke, letter dated 27 April 1845, describes the still birth of a son to her sister Hannah: Tuke family papers, box 26, BI.

64 N. F. Cott, 'Passionlessness: An Interpretation of Victorian Sexual Ideology 1790–1850', *Signs*, 4 (1978), pp.219–36. She has used the word 'passionlessness' to argue that, with Evangelicalism, came a view of women as lacking either sexual aggression or sexual appetite, thus creating the ideal of women made for God's, not man's, purposes and therefore the upholders of the morals of society. For a somewhat different view, see C. Degler, 'What Ought to Be and What Was: Women's Sexuality in the 19th C.', *American Historical Review*, 79

(1974), pp.1467–90. He suggests that there was no consensus on the subject of women's sexuality and that there was plenty of literature which suggested that women had strong sexual feelings.

65 Wakefield, op.cit., p.22. She suggested that by using wet-nurses, women were encouraging harm to their own babies by leaving them hungry and badly cared-for.

66 A. Vernon, *A Quaker Business Man: The Kife of Joseph Rowntree* (York, 1987), pp.14, 18–20.

67 It is difficult to suggest that this was general practice, but Jonathan Gray, son of Faith Gray, was born on 3 August 1779 and weaned at six months on 3 February 1780: Diary of Faith Gray, Acc. 5 & 6, YA.

68 Maria Tuke to Henry Tuke, letter dated 3 November 1786: Tuke family papers, box 10, BI.

69 When baby John Linney died at six months in July 1841, his mother was already pregnant and gave birth to a girl in January 1842. This might indicate wet-nursing, but could also suggest the failure of the contraceptive effect of breast-feeding.

70 Maria Tuke to Barbara Scott, letter dated 1787: Tuke family papers, box 10, BI.

71 Vernon, op.cit., p.29. Joseph Rowntree took his son Joseph to Ireland during the famine; this had a permanent effect on Joseph II, creating in him an intense sympathy for the poor throughout the rest of his life.

72 Maria Tuke to Esther Tuke, letter dated 14 June 1802: Tuke family papers, box 8, BI.

73 Elizabeth Tuke died in childbirth in 1760, after five pregnancies in six years.

74 See p.47.

75 Vernon, op.cit., p.21.

76 Ibid., p.24.

77 *Methodist Magazine*, Vol.56 (1833), p.405.

78 Maria Tuke to Barbara Scott, undated letter 1799: Tuke family papers, box 12, BI.

79 Diary of Faith Gray, op.cit.

80 Maria Tuke to Favilla Scott, letter dated 2 February 1799: Tuke family papers, box 12, BI.

81 Ibid., p.65.

CHAPTER 5

1 For the work of the York Penitentiary Society, see F. Finnegan, *Poverty & Prostitution: A study of Victorian Prostitutes in York* (Cambridge, 1979). For prostitute reform, see J. R. Walkowitz, *Prostitution and Victorian Society: Women, Class and the State* (Cambridge, 1980), and L. Mahood, *The Magdalenes: Prostitution in the nineteenth Century* (London, 1988).

For how contemporary perceptions of prostitutes were formed, see L. Nead, *Myths of Sexuality: Representations of Women in Victorian Britain* (Oxford, 1988), pp.91–155. For the Retreat, see A. Digby, *Madness, Morality & Medicine: A Study of the York Retreat 1796–1914* (Cambridge, 1985). For the Ragged School in York, see W. Cammage, *York Ragged School* (York, 1907). For temperance, see W. Pickwell, *The Temperance Movement in York* (York, 1886).

2   D. E. Swift, 'Charles Simeon and J. J. Gurney: A Chapter in Anglican-Quaker Relations', *Church History*, 29 (1960), p.177.

3   E. Isichei, *Victorian Quakers* (Oxford, 1970), p.214.

4   A. Digby, *From York Lunatic Asylum to Bootham Park Hospital*, Borthwick Paper No.69 (York, 1986), p.10.

5   Romans, 2: 23.

6   W. Wilberforce, *Practical View of the Prevailing Religious System of Professed Christians in the Higher & Middle Classes of this Country Contrasted with real Christianity* (London, 1797), p.26.

7   Ephesians, 2: 10.

8   Wilberforce, op.cit., p.148.

9   Quoted in F. K. Prochaska, *Women and Philanthropy in Nineteenth-Century England* (Oxford, 1980), p.9.

10   This emphasis on, and enthusiasm for, conversion, it has been suggested, began to cause embarrassment to moderate Evangelicals: see E. Jay, *The Religion of the Heart: Anglican Evangelicalism and the Nineteenth-Century Novel* (Oxford, 1979), p.60.

11   Hannah More castigated herself for not meditating during a migraine attack: D. Rosman, *Evangelicals and Culture* (London, 1984), p.58.

12   J. B. Braithwaite, *Memoirs of J. J. Gurney*, Vol.I (Norwich, 1854), pp.56–7, 80.

13   Isichei, op.cit., p.214; G. Wagner, *The Chocolate Conscience* (London, 1987).

14   H. Richard, *Memoirs of Joseph Sturge* (London, 1864), p.48.

15   York Meeting provided for their own poor in times of distress and individuals contributed to charities in the city; e.g. William White gave £25 in 1790 to St Mary's, Castlegate, for distribution among the poor.

16   For discussion of the shortcomings of Evangelical attitudes to philanthropy, see K. Hylson-Smith, *Evangelicals in the Church of England 1734–1984* (London, 1988), p.89; I. C. Bradley, 'The Politics of Godliness: Evangelicals in Parliament 1784–1832', D.Phil. thesis (University of Oxford, 1974), p.192; I. C. Bradley, *The Call to Seriousness: The Evangelical Impact on the Victorians* (London, 1976), pp.106–8; F. K. Brown, *Fathers of the Victorians: The Age of Wilberforce* (Cambridge, 1961), p.50, criticizes the Clapham Evangelicals for deliberately constructing their Evangelicalism to appeal to the great, never attacking their debauchery. He ignores Hannah More's tracts which persuaded the rich to change their habits.

17   M. Mullett, 'From Sect to Denomination? Social Developments in Eighteenth-Century English Quakerism', *Journal of Religious History*, 13, 2 (1984), p.174.

18   The York British Girls' School was supported entirely by Quakers; the Female Friendly Society by Evangelical Anglicans.

19   K. A. Webb, *One of the Most Useful Charities in the City: York Dispensary 1788–1988*, Borthwick Paper No.74 (York, 1988).

20   Prochaska, op.cit., p.9.

21   The frequency with which James had to preach on the 'proper' role of women indicates that he was not preaching to the converted but preaching to convert.

22   S. Corder, *Life of Elizabeth Fry*, compiled from her journals as edited by her daughters (London, 1853).

23   C. Cappe, *Thoughts on the Desirableness and Utility of Ladies visiting Female Wards of Hospitals and Lunatic Asylums* (York, 1816).

24   Ninth Annual Report of the Committee for the York Society for the Encouragement of Faithful Female Servants (1829), YPL.

25   Although Catherine Cappe advised against women becoming involved in mixed charitable concerns, she and Faith Gray worked on mixed-sex committees. Lindley Murray contributed 10 guineas p.a. from 1802. See Lindley Murray's Executorship A/Cs: Tuke family papers, box 73, BI. Donors included John Mason, Daniel Peacock and William Tuke.

26   York Dispensary Report (1806–8), Acc.27/60, YA.

27   Lindley Murray supported Clapham Sect organizations, including the missions to the Indians established by Wilberforce; the missions in Africa and the East, which became the Church Missionary Society established by Wilberforce and Venn in 1799. Most of the members of York Meeting contributed to a collection for the mission to the Indians in 1806 which raised £68. 10*s*.: MF/183, BI. Samuel Tuke supported Wilberforce's society to stop the use of boy chimney-sweeps

28   See pp.101–4.

29   By 1809 the society included Faith Gray (Evangelical Anglican), Catherine Cappe (Unitarian), and ten Quakers, including David Doeg, John Mason, William and Samuel Richardson, Thomas Priestman, Lindley Murray. Henry Tuke donated the profits of £21 from his book, *Duties of Religion & Morality*, to the society: Annual Report, York Society for the Prevention and Discouragement of Vice and Profaneness (1809), YA.

30   Ibid. The National Society for Promoting Observance of the Sabbath was established in 1809, and the Lord's Day Observance Society in 1831.

31   Ibid. Report of committee appointed 29 February 1808: Acc.212/204, YA.

32   See pp.87–91 for Quaker participation in parish affairs and the policing of this area. Several members of the parish vestry were also members of the Society.

33 York Vagrant Office, Half-Yearly Report of the Committee of Twenty-four (1822), YPL.

34 Finnegan, op.cit., pp.164–211.

35 The York Society for the Encouragement of Faithful Female Servants (founded 1820) was another attempt by Quakers and Evangelicals to try to stop girls being drawn into prostitution. Many of the cases coming into the penitentiary were female servants, violated by male servants or employers and forced to leave their place of employment.

36 York Female Penitentiary Society, Subscribers' List, Acc.212.40, YA.

37 By 1880 the society had workers touring the streets seeking out girls to bring into the penitentiary.

38 York Female Penitentiary Society, Minutes Book (February 1823), Acc.212.39/i, YA.

39 Ibid. (1822–42), Acc.212.40/ii, YA.

40 Ibid. (1844–57, November 1855), Acc.212/1, YA.

41 Ibid. (September 1854).

42 Ibid.

43 B. Harrison, *Drink and The Victorians: The Temperance Question in England 1815–1872* (London, 1971), p.94. For Evangelicals and temperance, see K. Heasman, *Evangelicals in Action: An Appraisal of their Social Work in the Victorian Era* (London, 1962), pp.126–47.

44 Both locally and nationally, Quakers had banned rum from slave-grown sugar-cane and Joseph Sturge refused to sell malt or supply grain to distilleries: Richard, op.cit., p.53.

45 The York Temperance Society distributed a free journal, *The York Temperance Visitor*, containing articles on the evils associated with drink. By 1855 4,000 people had taken the pledge.

46 Many of the Quakers involved in the temperance movement were dealers in tea, coffee and cocoa, e.g. Joseph Fry, Richard Cadbury and Joseph Rowntree. Rowntree set up carts in York dispensing cheap coffee as an alternative to beer. Temperance was also helped by reductions in tax on tea and coffee.

47 York Temperance Society Report (1850), YPL.

48 Ibid., Subscribers' List.

49 P. T. Winskill, *The Temperance Movement & Its Workers: A Record of Social, Moral, Religious & Political Progress* (Blackie, 1892), p.216. Joseph Spence was a founder of the Friends' Temperance Society, vice-president of the British League, and a subscriber to the United Kingdom Alliance.

50 York Temperance Band of Hope, 16th Annual Report (31 December 1863), Subscribers' List, YPL.

51 Quaker brewers resisted any suggestion that the Society adopt teetotalism.

52 Female novelists often portrayed alcoholism and gambling as the height of male villainy: see A. Brontë, *The Tenant of Wildfell Hall* (London, 1979).

53   A spinning school was established in 1784; a knitting school in 1786.

54   Blue Coat Boys' and Grey Coat Girls' Schools, charity schools, Committee Meeting Minutes (1780–84), BCS 6/9; Benefactors to the two charity schools of York (1785), BCS 1, BI.

55   Lindley Murray Executorship A/Cs: Tuke family papers, box 73, BI.

56   The 1836 report of the Manchester Statistical Society on education in York shows that, before 1820, there were 10 dame-schools, 5 common boys' schools, 2 common girls' schools, 1 private boys' school and 4 private girls' schools. It also showed that in 1836 there were 15 Established Church Sunday schools, 4 Wesleyan, 2 Independent, 2 Methodist and 1 Unitarian – 16 of which had been established before 1820.

57   The Royal Lancasterian Schools Society system was founded in 1810 and one of its founders was William Allen, a leading London Quaker who was also a member of the anti-slavery campaign.

58   British Girls' School, Formation Meeting (21 October 1812), Acc.118/254, YA.

59   Ibid., General Meeting of Subscribers (17 June 1813), Acc.118.

60   British Girls' School Quarterly Meeting of Female Subscribers (17 February 1813), Acc.118.

61   Priscilla Tuke to Samuel Tuke, letters dated 8 July and 10 July 1813: Tuke family papers, box 23, BI.

62   York Meeting provided an advance of two-thirds of the cost of the building (not to exceed £200); the school raised the rest of the finance. Under the 1870 Act, school inspectors condemned the siting of the school as highly undesirable and insanitary.

63   Children paid 1*d*. or 3*d*. for tuition; fees were based on the ability to pay.

64   York Education Statistics, compiled by the Manchester Statistical Society (1836), p.xv.

65   The school taught reading, writing, arithmetic and religious instruction, but the unique feature was the teaching of the use of the electric telegraph. Equipment was loaned to the school by the Electric Telegraph Company and the pupils were then employed by the company as clerks.

66   York Education Statistics, op.cit., pp.ii, iv, vi.

67   Ibid., p.vii.

68   York Ragged School, First Annual Report (22 February 1848), YPL.

69   Robert Jackson, Quaker butcher, donated several dinners. Under the 1854 Education Act, it became an industrial school: *The Victoria County History* (Oxford, 1961), p.459.

70   Isichei, op.cit., pp.258–79.

71   York Mechanics Institute, Report of Annual Meeting (1836), YPL.

72   First Day School, Minute Book of Teachers Meeting (1848–50), Acc.118/1, YA.

73   Friends' First Day School Conference (1849), p.15, FHL.

74   Report of the Friends' First Day School Conference (1852), p.35.
      F. J. Gillman, *The Story of York Adult Schools from Commencement to the
      Year 1907* (York, 1907), p.6.
75   No pupils under 8 years of age were admitted.
76   In February 1848 it was decided to register 100 scholars; 80 was the
      optimum number, but they made an allowance for drop-outs.
77   By the 1830s York Religious Tract Society (founded 1799) was
      dominated by Quakers: Samuel Tuke, Thomas Backhouse Joseph
      Rowntree; and Evangelicals: William Gray, James Richardson,
      Jonathan Gray, John Graham. A library was formed, which in
      November 1848 had 110 volumes.
78   Deposits of not less than 1*d*. and not more than 2*s*. were allowed, with
      interest paid at 4% p.a. Sums withdrawn within a year received no
      interest.
79   York Friends Boys' Sabbath School Register (1860–9), Acc.118/3, YA.
80   Ibid.
81   Report of the Friends First Day School Association Conference
      (1859), p.37.
82   Ibid., pp.45–6.
83   Isichei, op.cit., p.275.
84   Ibid., p.260.
85   Some Evangelical Quakers did open Sunday schools in Leeds and
      Manchester. The extreme Evangelicals, the Beaconites, opened a
      large Sunday school in Manchester: ibid., p.260.

CHAPTER 6

1   P. J. Corfield, *The Impact of English Towns* (Oxford 1982), p.2.
2   J. Seed, 'Gentleman Dissenters: The Social and Political Meanings
     of Rational Dissent in the 1770s and 1780s', *The Historical Journal*, 28
     (1985), p.314.
3   D. A. Scott, 'Dissent, Politics and Quakerism in York, 1640–1700',
     unpublished D.Phil. thesis (University of York, 1990), p.101. Also
     D. A. Scott, *Quakerism in York 1650–1720*, Borthwick Paper No.80
     (York, 1991).
4   N. Morgan, 'The Quakers and the Establishment 1600–1730 with
     specific reference to the North-West of England', unpublished Ph.D.
     thesis (University of Lancaster, 1985), p.28.
5   M. Weber, 'The Protestant Sects and the Spirit of Capitalism', in
     H. G. Gerth and C. Wright-Mills, eds, *From Max Weber: Essays in
     Sociology* (London, 1948), p.306.
6   Esther Tuke to Yorkshire Quarterly Meeting: Tuke family papers,
     box 74.
7   R. T. Vann, *The Social Development of English Quakerism 1655–1755*
     (Harvard, 1969), pp.105–21.

8   J. S. Rowntree, *Quakerism Past & Present* (London, 1859), p.58.

9   D. Frazer, *Urban Politics in Victorian England: The Structure of Politics in Victorian Cities* (Leicester, 1976), p.9. The political careers of several York politicians started in the parishes. Seth Agar (Roman Catholic) was surveyor of the land tax from 1822 in St Helen's, Stonegate; Christopher Cattle (Anglican), a surveyor under the 1763 Cleansing Act (1794–99), became a common councilman.

10   Ibid., p.2.

11   W. E. Tate, *The Parish Chest* (Cambridge, 1969), p.18.

12   The visitation of Bishop Shute Barrington in Salisbury in 1783 reveals various attitudes to Quakers in the parishes in the Salisbury diocese. The local parson in Lacock parish described his only Quaker resident as 'a gentleman of considerable landed property in this parish, a quiet man and a good neighbour'. Conversely, another priest wrote that there were '… too many of these [Quakers] and none more obstinate than Mr Sutton's bailiff, a large farmer'. R. S. Mortimer, 'Quakers in the Diocese of Salisbury, 1783', *Journal of the Friends Historical Society*, 50 (1962), pp 153–7.

13   Scott, 'Dissent, Politics and Quakerism', op.cit., p 102.

14   Church Accounts, St Olaf's, PRY/OL/18; Church Accounts, Holy Trinity, Micklegate, PRY/HTG/14 BI.

15   Church Rate Accounts Book, Holy Trinity, Micklegate, PRY/HTM/19 (1830–52), BI.

16   Jonathan Storr paid 1776–1805; William Richardson, 1808–36; James Backhouse, 1819; David Priestman, John Tuke, Isaac Richardson, 1835: PRY/MBps/17, Church Rate A/Cs (1808), PRY/OL/20, BI. There seem to be geographic as well as urban/rural differences in the strength of witness against tithes and in the size of tithe demands. For geographic differences, see E. J. Evans, 'Our Faithful Testimony: The Society of Friends and Tithe payments, 1690–1730', *Journal of Friends Historical Society*, 2 (1969), pp.106–21; H. Ford, 'Friends and Authority: a consideration of attitudes and expedients with particular reference to Derbyshire', *Journal of Friends Historical Society*, 70 (1988), pp.61–75; R. Collie, 'The Quakers of Tottenham 1775–1825', *Edmonton Hundred Historical Society Occasional Paper*, New Series No.37 (1979), p.10. In rural areas around York (see Appendix VII, table 7), tithe demands were higher and more rigorously applied than church-rate demands. Between 1795–8, eight Quakers from Settle Meeting were incarcerated in York gaol for non–payment on the warrant of George Markham, curate of Carlton, near Selby. One of the prisoners subsequently died in prison. For YMM support of the prisoners, see MS diary of Henry Wormall (1795–8), one of the prisoners: box K17, FHL.

17   Church Rate Accounts Book, Holy Trinity, Micklegate, BIHR, PRY/HTM/19. Years unpaid: 1818, 1824, 1829; Great Book of Sufferings, Vol.36. Quakers who joined this campaign were: John Fothergill, Elizabeth Janson, John Walker, Henry, Hannah and Christopher

NOTES TO CHAPTER 6

Scarr, Sarah Allis, Martha Fletcher, Thomas Marshall and Joseph Rowntree.

18   G. W. Edwards, 'Quakers as Church Wardens', *Journal of the Friends Historical Society*, 52 (1968), pp.48–53.

19   Appendix VII, table 5, shows that Jonathan Storr's father had begun the family's involvement in parish service.

20   PRY/MB/36; PRY/MB/37; PRY/MB/95; PRY/MB/75.

21   Minutes of the Vestry Meeting, St Mary's, Castlegate, PRY/MC/111 (3 October 1831).

22   Ibid. (29 May 1834).

23   Ibid. (27 November 1834).

24   Ibid. (21 January 1843).

25   J. E. Bradley, 'The Legal Status, Social Structure and Ideology of Nonconformity', unpublished paper, pp.32–3. Stockport, Cheshire, had a Quaker mayor in 1721: J. E. Bradley, *Religion, Revolution and English Radicalism: Non-conformity in Eighteenth Century Politics and Society* (Cambridge, 1990), p.71. In some towns, e.g. Hull and Norwich, it has been suggested that the corporation ignored or rejected the Test and Corporation Act. See C. Mullett, 'The Corporation Act and the Election of English Protestant Dissenters to Corporation Offices', *Virginia Law Review*, 21 (1935), p.643.

26   The corporation tried and failed on three occasions to elect Dissenters illegally to corporate offices – cases brought against them either failed or were dismissed: Joshua Drake, Mercer (Nonconformist), elected sheriff 1694; Roger Shackleton (Quaker), elected sheriff 1734; Oswald Allen, Methodist, elected sheriff 1821. See C. Mullett, op cit., p.652.

27   Parochial offices such as constable and assessors for the various taxes had also required an oath.

28   *Strangers Guide Through the City of York and Its Cathedral*, 3rd edn (York 1829).

29   Chamberlains' Accounts are extant for 1780–1835: CB, YA.

30   For the seventeenth-century York experience, see Scott, 'Politics, Dissent and Quakerism', op.cit., p.91.

31   York Corporation House Book, Vol.45 (1780–92), ff.94–5, YA.

32   YMMM, MF 183, BI.

33   William Hotham was a JP and in partnership with the Quakers Samuel Tuke and Parker Busby. He was also an executor of several Quaker wills.

34   York Corporation House Book, op.cit., f. 90. John Fothergill was a Quaker but Charles Forbes, his brother-in-law, was an Anglican. Charles Forbes was also a common councilman in 1782–92 and no doubt helpful in furthering their business interests. Their business was one of the largest in the city, taking on 33 apprentices in the years 1789–1808: Register of Apprentices Indentures (1787–1816), MS.D15, YA.

35   York Corporation House Book, op.cit., f.25; York Corporation House Book, Vol.49 (1818–27), f.172.

THE DYNAMICS OF QUAKER REVIVAL 1780–1860

36 Samuel Tuke to Priscilla Tuke, letter dated 27 January 1825: Tuke family papers, box 21, BI.

37 York Corporation House Book, vol.47, op.cit., f.183; York Corporation House Book, Vol.48, (1812–21), f.122.

38 The Lothersdale prisoners were Quakers from Settle Meeting who had been imprisoned in York gaol for non-payment of tithes. York Quakers secured support from many sources, including articles in the *Analytical Review* and *The British Critic*. George Markham, the prosecuting curate, was denounced by both journals and the Justices for making excessive tithe demands.

39 Wentworth Woodhouse Muniments, Sheffield City Libraries, WWM/MF46, f.67/38.

40 Henry Tuke to Lindley Murray, letter dated 26 May 1808: Tuke family papers, box 73.

41 Frazer, op.cit., pp.91–2. He points out that whilst the commissioners were not a truly political body, their existence created a rival to local corporations, causing jealousies and antagonisms. In York, Improvement Commissioners were elected in vestries and ratepayers qualified for election either by being occupants of freehold property or occupants of leasehold property to the value of £20. In the parish of St Mary's, Castlegate, only 10 inhabitants qualified; of these, 2 were Quakers, William Alexander and Henry Ransome.

42 These men were moderate radicals, in that they wanted to overthrow the corrupt, oligarchical rule of the corporation but did not wish to re-order society, although Quakers were obviously opposed to the Established Church.

43 Police Act 6, Geo.IV, c.127, makes special mention of the affirmation to be taken by Quakers, excluding the words 'So help me God'. Quakers had acted as Improvement Commissioners in Birmingham since 1769 and a succession of Lloyds, Cadburys and Joseph Sturge served. See M. H. Bailey, 'The Contribution of Quakers to some aspects of Local Government in Birmingham 1828–1902', unpublished MA thesis (Univ. of Birmingham, 1952).

44 Samuel Tuke commented on the aldermen who 'conceeded so much' to the United Committee in a letter to Priscilla Tuke written from London when he was lobbying with Jonathan Gray for the redrafted Bill. Letter dated 27 January 1825: Tuke family papers, box 21. Samuel Tuke and Jonathan Gray had been political and reforming allies for many years. It was they who exposed the mis-management and ill-treatment of patients at the York Lunatic Asylum in 1813 and led the campaign for its reform. See A. Digby, *From York Lunatic Asylum to Bootham Park Hospital*, Borthwick Paper No.69 (1986), pp.15–27; also, *A Complete Collection of the Papers Respecting the York Lunatic Asylum* (York, 1816), YPL.

45 *Gazette* (12 February 1825); *Herald* (12 February 1825); and *Courant* (8 February 1825).

46 Improvement Commissioners Minute Book, M.18, YA.

47 This was over the improvement rate of one shilling in the pound. The corporation argued that the rate was high because the commissioners had insisted on an Act which cost £2,000 to implement, whereas the corporation supported an Act which would have cost only £800. They also suggested that the commissioners were attending to their own improvements before those of the general public. The recorder and Alderman Peacock led the corporation's attempt to have the rate set by the commissioners quashed: Improvement Commissioners Minute Book, op.cit., f.46.

48 Quakers had refused to join the United Committee that had been formed under the guidance of the Dissenting deputies to agitate for repeal. There were members of the committee with Quaker connections: Edward Grubb was related to the Quaker Grubbs of Clonmel; W. B. Gurney, a Baptist, was a distant relation of J. J. Gurney and Elizabeth Fry. For the Committees of Repeal, see Committees for Repeal of the Test and Corporation Acts, Minutes (1786–90 and 1827–8), in *London Record Society*, 14, ed. T. M. Davis (1978). See also R. G. Cowherd, *The Politics of English Dissent: The Religious Aspects of Liberal and Humanitarian Reform Movements from 1815 to 1848* (London, 1959), p.30; B. Manning, *The Protestant Dissenting Deputies* (Cambridge, 1952).

49 York Corporation House Book, Vol.50, ff.153–4. This gown was scarlet with gold braid.

50 Seth Agar was the first Catholic on the corporation. He was elected a common councilman in June 1829, as a result of the passing of the Catholic Emancipation Act of the same year. York Quakers were not involved in agitation against this Act, although several leading Anglicans were, including Robert Cattle, Hewley Graham, the Revd James Richardson, the Revd William Richardson and Thomas Richardson. Anti-Catholic pamphlets were sold in York, including one entitled 'A Refutation of the Romic Doctrine of the Mass', published by the Protestant Reformation Society: *York Gazette* (21 and 31 January 1829).

51 In November 1830 the corporation processed through the city to celebrate the accession of William VI, and in July 1830 members had attended morning service on the occasion of the funeral of George IV. In April 1831 Benjamin Horner was present at a ceremony presenting the Freedom of the City to Henry, Lord Brougham and Vaux: York Corporation House Book, ff.154, 155, 211.

52 York Council Minutes, Vol.1, f.45.

53 York Council Minutes, op.cit., ff.11, 47, 79. The Ouse Navigation Commissioners had long been suspected of corruption and mismanagement. The old-style commission had consisted of the Lord mayor, aldermen, sheriffs and Anglican Whig Establishment men, who were accused of building elaborate buildings like Naburn Banqueting Hall at the expense of dredging and widening the river for

mercantile traffic: Ouse Navigation Commissioners Minute Books (1772–8); Ouse Navigation Trustees Minute Books (1836–70). Samuel Tuke, Joseph Rowntree and Thomas Backhouse and other York merchants established the Mutual Insurance Co. in 1834 to insure against the loss from delays in transport which were so frequently incurred because of the poor state of the river.

54   York Council Minutes, op.cit., f.148.

55   Ibid., f.99.

56   Total Quaker investment in the company was £14,500: Thomas Backhouse had 90 shares, worth £4,500; Benjamin Horner had 100, worth £5,000; Thomas Mason, 50, worth £2,500 and Samuel Tuke, 50, worth £2,500: *York Gazette* (21 May 1836).

57   York Council Minutes, Vol.2, f.81.

58   Ibid., f.82.

59   A. J. Peacock, 'George Leeman and York Politics, 1833–1880', in C. Feinstein, ed., *York 1831–1981: 150 years of scientific endeavour and social change* (York, 1981), p.237.

60   Ibid., p.239.

61   York Council Minutes, op.cit., f.218; Vol.2, f.293.

62   York Corporation was unusual in being a bastion of Whiggism; most corporations were Tory Anglican strongholds, e.g. Leeds: E. A. Smith, *Whig Principles and Party Politics: Earl Fitzwilliam and the Whig Party 1748–1833* (Manchester, 1975).

63   For more on this election and the Duncombe débâcle, see E. A. Smith, op cit., pp.66–7; also F. C. Price, 'The Parliamentary Elections in York City 1754–1790', unpublished MA thesis (Univ. of Manchester, 1958), pp.177–200; N. C. Phillips, *Yorkshire and English National Politics 1783–84* (Canterbury, NZ, 1961).

64   J. R. Dinwiddy, *Christopher Wyvill and Reform 1790–1820*, Borthwick Paper No.39 (1971); I. R. Christie, 'Sir George Saville, Edmund Burke and The Yorkshire Reform Programme February 1780', *Yorkshire Archaeological Journal*, 40 (1959–62). William Gray, a leading member of the Evangelical Anglican group in the city and an associate of Wilberforce, was appointed clerk to the association in 1780. It was his indefatigable efforts which led to the organization being so effective in its lobbying of the county squirearchy and collecting so many signatories (approx. 8,000) to its petitions. For details of his involvement, see I. R. Christie, 'The Yorkshire Association, 1780–4: A Study in Political Organisation', *Historical Journal*, 3 (1960), pp.150–1; also I. R. Christie, *Wilkes, Wyvill & Reform: The Parliamentary Reform Movement in British Politics 1760–1785* (London, 1962), pp.68–120; N. C. Phillips, 'Country Against Court: Christopher Wyvill, a Yorkshire Champion', *Yorkshire Archaeological Journal*, 40 (1962), pp.588– 603. Only one Quaker signed the petition, John Sanderson: MSS. M32.5. All the letters and petition skins are held at York City Archives.

65   William White's diary, 20 July 1782: Acc.163, YA. See also Woodhouse Wentworth Muniments, Sheffield City Library, MF39, 41/18–1; WWM/MF56, f.115–39. I am grateful to Olive, Countess Fitzwilliam's Wentworth Settlement Trustees and the director of Sheffield City Libraries for permission to use these manuscripts.

66   E. Isichei, *Victorian Quakers* (Oxford, 1970), pp.189–90. Evidence now becoming available suggests that Isichei has underestimated Quaker involvement in local politics: see Bradley, op.cit.

67   York Corporation House Book, Vol.45, ff.110, 137.

68   William White's diary, op.cit., 17 December 1782.

69   See below, Appendix VII, table 1, for William White's involvement in the affairs of the Meeting. See also list of those appointed to accompany Public Friends 1785, YMM-PM, MF/187 (1787–1842).

70   *Epistles from Yearly Meeting of Friends, 1681–1857* (London, 1858), pp.85, 97. These fears were fuelled by the radical Dissenters, who had established political clubs in every city. Influenced by the ideas of the Enlightenment and driven by the French Revolution, they all emphasized political reform. The York Society for Political Information was founded in 1795 to spread political knowledge because '... the more ignorant men are of the nature of civil and political government, the more they will be in danger of suffering by impositions and oppression ... It is the duty of every man to furnish himself...with political information.' Pamphlet, YPL. York Quakers were interested in political radicalism and William Tuke described Samuel Taylor Coleridge's radical newspaper, *The Watchman* (first published March 1796), as a 'publication to sympathise with if not to approve of': William Tuke to Henry Tuke, letter dated 5 May 1796. Tuke family papers, box 4, BI.

71   Davis, op.cit., p.73.

72   Lindley Murray to Henry Tuke, letter dated 10 October 1803: Tuke family papers, box 73.

73   *A Brief Memoir of the late Rev. William Richardson, sub-chanter of York Cathedral, etc* (York, 1822), p.53. *The Christian Observer* (1802), p.162, quoted in J. D. Walsh, 'The Yorkshire Evangelicals in the Eighteenth Century with especial reference to Methodism', unpublished Ph.D. thesis (University of Cambridge, 1956), p.334.

74   R. Porter, *English Society in the Eighteenth Century* (Penguin, 1982), p.196. For further analysis of radicalism and its relationship to Nonconformity, see Seed, op.cit., pp.299–325, and J. Bradley, 'Whigs and Non-conformists: "Slumbering Radicalism" in English Politics 1739–1789', *Eighteenth Century Studies*, 9 (1975), pp.1–27.

75   Draft of a speech to Yearly Meeting, 1796: Tuke family papers, box 73.

76   Lindley Murray to Henry Tuke, undated 1796: Tuke family papers, box 74.

77   William Tuke to Henry Tuke, letter dated 1804: Tuke family papers, box 2. William Tuke published an election broadside in 1784 and gave

a speech decrying bribery in elections and declaring that he would give his vote to the Whig candidates, Gallway and Milnes.

78   E. Royle and J. Walvin, *English Radicals and Reformers 1760–1848* (Brighton, 1982), pp.32–42; Cowherd, op.cit., pp.46–63.

79   J. Pollock, *Wilberforce* (Tring, 1977), pp.55–8.

80   The London abolitionists were supported by the French/American Quaker anti-slave campaigner, Brissot: see L. Loft, 'Quakers, Brissot and Eighteenth Century Abolitionists', *Journal of the Friends Historical Society*, 55, 8 (1989), pp.277–89.

81   H. J. Cadbury, 'John Woolman in England 1772', *Journal of the Friends Historical Society*, a documentary pamphlet (1971), p.116.

82   Ibid.

83   YQMM, 24 June 1784.

84   York Corporation House Book, Vol.45 (1780–92), f. 283.

85   *Epistles from the Yearly Meeting of Friends*, op.cit., p.78.

86   Henry Tuke to Samuel Tuke, undated letter: Tuke family papers, box 5. In May 1807 Samuel Tuke contributed £50 and Lindley Murray £20 to Wilberforce's campaign fund: W. K. and E. M. Sessions, *The Tukes of York* (York, 1987), p.80. Also Tuke family papers, box 73.

87   Lindley Murray to Henry Tuke, letter dated 23 May 1807: Tuke family papers, box 73.

88   Lindley Murray to Samuel Tuke, letter dated 24 May 1807: Tuke family papers, box 73.

89   Henry Tuke to Lindley Murray, letter dated 25 May 1807: Tuke family papers, box 73.

90   *York Gazette* (1 and 4 August 1823). The first collection in York Meeting for the Anti-Slavery Society was in 1821 and raised £22; another in 1825 raised £89. 15s.

91   W. Alexander, *Address to the Public on the Present State of the Question relative to Negro Slavery in the British Colonies* (York, 1828).

92   H. Richard, *Memoirs of Joseph Sturge* (London, 1864), p.87.

93   *York Gazette* (30 October 1830).

94   *York Gazette* (29 April 1826 and 3 November 1832).

95   Manuscript letter from the Anti-Slavery Society to the lord mayor, dated 20 March 1824: YPL. Quakers throughout Yorkshire continued the abolition campaign. In Leeds, Wilson Armistead, a leading member of Leeds Meeting campaigned on behalf of the slaves; see I. R. Goodyear, 'Wilson Armistead and The Leeds Antislavery Movement', *The Thoresby Miscellany*, 16 (1979), pp.113–30.

96   *York Gazette* (8 August 1840). This was one of the many Meetings held in the Friends Meeting House.

97   The Revd J. Parsons (Independent) and the Revd Thomas Richardson (Evangelical Anglican) were also present. Priscilla Tuke to Elizabeth Hack, letter dated 1825: Tuke family papers, box 24. Eliza Cropper married Joseph Sturge in 1834. She had acted as her father's secretary and was an enthusiastic abolitionist, travelling to anti-slavery meetings

and well suited to Sturge's brand of radical Quakerism. She died in childbirth, ten months after her marriage: see A. Tyrell, *Joseph Sturge and the Moral Radical Party in Early Victorian Britain* (London, 1987), pp.61–2.

98 K. Corfield, 'Elizabeth Heyrick: Radical Quaker', in G. Malmgreen, ed., *Religion in the Lives of English Women 1760–1930* (Croomhelm, 1986) p.43. Quakers were divided on the role that women should take in the anti-slavery movement. J. J. Gurney and Elizabeth Fry had doubts about the correctness of women speaking at public Meetings and Joseph Sturge was amongst the committee of men who excluded American female delegates from the Anti-Slavery Convention in 1840: A. Tyrell, 'Woman's Mission and Pressure Group Politics in Britain 1825–60', *Bulletin of John Rylands Library*, 63 (1980–1), pp.199–200; see also L. and R. Billington, 'A Burning Zeal for Righteousness: Women and the British Anti-Slavery Movement, 1820–1860', in J. Rendall, ed., *Equal or Different: Women's Politics 1800–1914* (Oxford, 1987), pp.82–111.

99 *York Gazette* (22 January and 12 February 1825). For Quaker involvement in Burke's political campaign in Bristol in 1774, see Bradley, op.cit., pp.197–99.

100 The Quaker Joseph Sturge was a member of the Birmingham Political Union, of which York had no equivalent. For his role in the BPU and the CSU, see T. R. Tholfsen, 'The Origins of the Birmingham Caucus', *Historical Journal*, 2 (1959), pp.162–3, and Tyrell, op.cit., pp.67–72.

101 C. Tylor, ed., *Samuel Tuke: His Life, Work and Thoughts*, p.111. Expenses included entertainments, payments to officials, printing, etc. Edward Baines, a Congregationalist, was the wealthy owner of the *Leeds Mercury* and well able to afford the expense entailed in getting himself elected an MP in 1832. For details of Baines, see C. Binfield, *So Down to Prayers: Studies in English Nonconformity 1780–1920* (London, 1977), pp.54–100.

102 *Courant* (12 November 1833) and *Herald* (23 November 1833).

103 Quoted in N. Gash, *Politics in the Age of Peel* (London, 1953), p.112.

104 John Clemesha was also a member of the York Society for the Diffusion of Political Knowledge, founded in January 1838. Other members included George Leeman and Thomas Watkinson, an Independent who was Charles Barkley's election campaign chairman: *York Gazette* (10 June 1825).

105 Barkley came third in the poll, collecting 919 votes.

106 *Courant* (2 September 1835).

107 *Yorkshireman* (11 September 1835).

108 See A. Peacock, 'York in the Age of Reform', unpublished D.Phil. thesis (University of York, 1973), p.301.

109 Tholfsen, op.cit., p.164.

110 *Gazette* (21 January 1844).

111 *Gazette* (3 June 1848). He was a supporter of Joseph Sturge, but his Quakerism was always a bit suspect and, cynics might suggest, adopted for political gain.

112 *Herald*, *Gazette* and *Yorkshireman* (26 January 1850). John Briggs was a members of the York Reform Association.

113 Lewin had been brought in as a stalking-horse for Joseph Brown-Westhead, a Methodist class leader from Manchester who was supported by George Leeman.

114 Peacock, op.cit., p.246.

115 York was a freeman borough with an extensive franchise and there were numerous political associations and organizations within the city, e.g. the radical York Society for Political Information, founded 1795; the York Whig Club, founded 1818 (see P. Brett, *The Rise and Fall of the York Whig Club 1818–1830*, Borthwick Paper No.76 (1989)); the York Political Protestant Association; the Tory York King and Constitution Club.

116 J. Barry, 'The parish in civic life: Bristol and its churches 1640–1750', in S. Wright, ed., *Parish Church and People* (London, 1988), p.161.

CHAPTER 7

1 See D. A. Scott, 'Dissent, Politics and Quakerism in York, 1640–1700', unpublished D.Phil. thesis (University of York, 1990), for an analysis of the socio-economic standing of York's Quakers in the seventeenth century. The table has been compiled from YMM membership lists, Vol.1 (1790–1841); Vol.2 (1842–59). See also York Trade Directories, 1781, 1784, 1796, 1805, 1809–11, 1816–17, 1818, 1828–9, 1843, 1849, 1851.

2 These analyses are based on occupations given by D. H. Pratt, *English Quakers and the First Industrial Revolution: A Study of the Quaker Community in Four Industrial Counties: Lancashire, Yorkshire, Warwickshire and Gloucestershire, 1750–1830* (New York, 1985), p.119.

3 E. Isichei, *Victorian Quakers* (Oxford, 1970); L. Davidoff and C. Hall, *Family Fortunes: Men and Women of the English Middle-class, 1780–1850* (London, 1987).

4 Baptismal registers: St Michael le Belfrey (1779–1838), PRY/MB/7, 8. Marriage registers: St Michael le Belfrey (1772–1812), PRY/MB/11; (1813–34), PRY/MB/12; (1837–53), PRY/MB/14. Register of Burials (1780–1812), PRY/MB/7; (1813–54), PRY/MB/21.BI. Baptismal registers: St Mary's, Castlegate (1773–1860), PRY/MC/137, 138. Marriage registers (1799–1859), PRY/MC/141, 143, 142.

5 A. Armstrong, *Stability & Change in an English Country Town* (Cambridge, 1974), pp.208–12. Statistical Appendix III gives the population of St Mary's, Castlegate, in 1841 as 952 and St Michael's as 1,238; column 'h' shows the annual value of houses assessed for property and

income tax, 1842–3: St Mary's, £2,722 and St Michael's, £6,188; column 'j' details the number of people with property of a rateable value of over £10 in 1850–1: St Mary's, 64; St Michael's, 128.

6   Armstrong, op.cit., pp.179–80. In York 19.7% of households had servants in 1851; in Norwich 13.3%. See: P. J. Corfield, 'The Social and Economic History of Norwich 1650–1850: A Study in Urban Growth', Ph.D. thesis (University of London, 1975), p.562.

7   Armstrong, op.cit., p.69.

8   J. S. Rowntree, *Quakerism Past and Present* (London, 1859).

9   YMM, list of members, Vol.1 (1790–1841), MFR/19; Vol.2 (1842–59), Brotherton Library (BL).

10   D. E. C. Eversley, 'The Demography of the Irish Quakers, 1650–1850', in J. M. Goldstrom and L. A. Clarkson, eds, *Irish Population, Economy and Society, Essays in honour of the late K. H. Connell* (Oxford, 1981), p.84. 'SRUR Quakers' comprised the Quaker Meetings sampled by Eversley: Norfolk, Cambridgeshire and Huntingdonshire, Bedfordshire and Hertfordshire, Buckinghamshire, Berkshire and Oxford Quarterly Meetings. See also R. T. Vann and D. E. C. Eversley, *Friends in Life and Death: The British and Irish Quakers in the Demographic Transition 1650–1900* (Cambridge, 1992).

11   Ibid., pp.79–82.

12   There is a continuing debate amongst historians of population as to the validity of various methods for calculating birth and death rates and the reliability of the various parish registers as a source: see J. T. Krause, 'The Changing Adequacy of English Registration 1650–1837', in D. V. Glass and D. E. C. Eversley, eds, *Population in History: Essays in Historical Demography* (London, 1965), pp.379–93.

13   The only known death from smallpox was that of the American Quaker minister John Woolman, who died at Thomas Priestman's house in Marygate, York in 1772.

14   Eversley, 'Demography of the Irish Quakers', op.cit., p.60.

15   Armstrong, op.cit., p.167.

16   D. E. C. Eversley, 'A Survey of the Population in an Area of Worcestershire from 1660–1850 on the basis of Parish Registers', in Glass and Eversley, op.cit., p.418.

17   Similar demographic work needs to be done on other Meetings to establish how typical or atypical York Meeting was.

18   Davidoff and Hall, op.cit., p.222.

19   Eversley has shown that Quaker women in the SRUR sample were most fertile between the ages of 20–29: see Eversley, 'Demography of the Irish Quakers', op.cit., p.67.

20   Ibid., p.404.

21   The small sample size has resulted in fluctuating marriage rates, but these figures do suggest that the marriage rate was probably lower than the general population and nearer those calculated by John S. Rowntree for the Society.

22   All BMM records are held at Bristol City Archives.

23   BMM, lists of members, SF/R3/4; SF/R3/5; SF/R3/6.

24   John S. Rowntree statistics: marriage regulations; documents and correspondence, no.1. Temp. MSS, Box 93: Friends' House Library.

25   Rowntree, op.cit., pp.80, 88.

26   Ibid., pp.144–58.

27   There was inconsistency in the regulations governing disownment. In 1821 Hannah and David Hall were admitted to York Meeting from Hull Meeting and it was noted that although she was a member of the Society, he was not.

28   William Richardson, bankruptcy papers (in private hands).

29   YMM Certificates of Removals, Vol.3 (1826–51); Vol.4 (1852–1911).

30   Baptismal register for St Mary's, Castlegate (1771–1813), PRY/MC/137. There is no admonition for this breach of rule by York Meeting.

31   BMM disownments (1786–1864): SF/A1/17a–e to SF/A1/28.

32   John S. Rowntree statistics, op.cit.

33   Five members of YMM married in a Registrar's Office after 1852 and were not disowned.

34   John S. Rowntree papers: letter dated 14 August 1858: port. 42/56, FHL.

35   YMM Certificates of Removal, Vol.2.

36   Samuel Tuke carried out a statistical exercise on the movement of members within YMM. He looked at the years 1824–43 and found that, between 1824 and 1833, 465 members (both newly 'convinced' and those already in membership) entered the Meeting and 332 left; between 1824 and 1843 the total number of members entering the Meeting was 449 and 375 left.

37   Patients at the Retreat were not listed as members of YMM while under treatment.

38   There were 20 assistant teachers at Bootham School, 1842–59. Most stayed for between one and three years. The population of York rose from approx. 12,000 in 1760 to 17,000 in 1801, 26,000 in 1831 and 36,303 in 1851: see C. H. Feinstein, 'Population, Occupations and Economic Development 1831–1981', in C. H. Feinstein, ed., *York 1831–1981* (York, 1981), pp.110–11.

39   See Appendix III.

40   YMM membership lists, op.cit., vol.2.

CONCLUSION

1   J. S. Rowntree, *Quakerism Past and Present* (London, 1959).

2   See pp.102–21.

3   See pp.121–8.

4   See pp.128–30.

5   Ackworth School was not a York Meeting project, but without the

encouragement and work of Esther and William Tuke, it would never have been founded and, as John Rowntree wrote, they '… converted the task of founding Ackworth School into a work of reformation': J. Rowntree, ed., *Essays and Addresses* (1905), p.66.

6 Both Ackworth School and Rawdon School in Leeds were run by joint committees of men and women Quakers elected by the individual Meetings which composed the Yorkshire Quarterly Meeting.

7 See p.109.

8 P. J. Corfield, 'The Social and Economic History of Norwich 1650–1850', unpublished Ph.D. thesis (University of London, 1975), p.573; A. Armstrong, *Stability and Change in an English Country Town* (Cambridge, 1974).

9 C. H. Feinstein, 'Population, Occupations and Economic Development 1831–1981', in C. H. Feinstein, ed., *York 1831–1981* (York, 1981), pp.128–9. Traffic through York station increased from 76 trains per day in 1854 to 94 per day in 1868 and 154 in 1878. In 1877 a new station was completed and employees of the North Eastern rose from 500 in 1851 to 6,000 by 1905. By 1900, 2,600 were employed in the company's workshops.

10 See Chap. 7, table 5.

11 Corfield, op.cit., p.547.

12 Norwich had a smaller class I and II percentage of 18.25%, and a larger class III at 53.39%: Corfield, op.cit.

13 A.J. Peacock, 'George Leeman and York Politics 1833–1880', in Feinstein, op.cit., pp.234–54.

14 B. R. Wilson, 'An Analysis of Sect Development', *American Sociological Review*, 24 (1959), pp.3–5; M. Mullett, 'From Sect to Denomination? Social Developments in Eighteenth-Century English Quakerism', *Journal of Religious History*, 13 (1984), pp.168–91.

15 E. A. Isichei, 'From Sect to Denomination in English Quakerism with Special Reference to the Nineteenth Century', *British Journal of Sociology*, 15 (1964).

APPENDICES

1 A. Armstrong, *Stability and Change in an English Country Town* (Cambridge, 1974).

2 Ibid.

3 D. E. C. Eversley, 'The Demography of the Irish Quakers, 1650–1850', in J. M. Goldstrom and L. A. Clarkson, eds, *Irish Population, Economy and Society* (Oxford, 1981), p.76.

Index

GENERAL

Anglican Church   13, 14

Beacon, The   31
Bristol Monthly Meeting   31, 110
  disownment and removals   123–6
  disownment and marriage out
    126–8
  membership   135
    growth and decline   129–30
  socio-economic profile   110–12

Clapham Sect   23, 73

Dissenters
  and conversion   42–3
Dissenting sects
  Bible Christian Connexion   39
    women preaching   43, 45–6
  Congregationalists   13
  Independents   40
  Methodists   13, 14
  Primitive Methodists   39
    women preaching   43–4, 45, 48
  Roman Catholics   13–14
  Unitarians   14
  Wesleyan Methodists   13
    women preaching   43–4
  Wesleyan Reformers   13

Evangelicalism
  domesticity   51, 54, 66
  philanthropy   69–71

Friends, Society of   13, 14–15
  adult education   80–1
  Anti-Corn Law League   106
  anti-slavery campaign   100–3
  Anti-Slavery Society   103
  beliefs   21–2
  breast-feeding   63
  British and Foreign Schools
    Society   79
  chamberlains   92
  children   62–4
  church rates   88–9
  Corporation (York)   91–6
  Corporation Act, 1828   95
  Council (York)   96–8
  death of children   65
  domesticity   53–4
  education   53, 77–80
  Evangelicalism   21–30, 70
  finance and marriage   59–60
  guilds, the   92
  incomes   52–3
  literacy   111–12
  Lothersdale prisoners, the   93–4
  marriage and courtship   55–62
  men
    conversion   41–2
    marriage   56, 57, 119–21
  motherhood   62–4
  Municipal Corporation Act, 1835
    96
  parliamentary elections   104–7
  parliamentary politics   98–107
  petition to Parliament   105–6

philanthropy   69–71
Police Act, 1825   94–5
politics   85–90
poor relief   34–6
Quietism   86–7
radicalism   99
railways   96–7
Rockingham Club, the   98
schools
  Ackworth   24
  British Girls'   78–9
  Hope Street Boys' School   80–1
  (First Day Sabbath School)
  The Mount   12
  Rawdon School, Leeds   35
  Trinity Lane   24, 53
  employment   129
teetotalism   76
temperance   76
voting behaviour   104–5
wills   58, 129
women   31–51
  Anti-Slavery Society   104
  conversion   32, 40–1
  disownment   36–8
  Evangelicalism   31
  marriage   56, 119–21
  the ministry   31, 39–49
  the organization   32–9
  philanthropy   72
  poor relief   34–5
  travel in the ministry   46
  servants   37
  tithe testimony   32
Yorkshire Committee of
  Association   98

Nonconformity   12–13

Retreat, The   23, 69
Reform Bill, 1832   105

Quakers, see Friends, Society of

Sessions, printers   12
slavery
  Anti-Slavery Society   23
societies

Auxiliary Bible Society   29
British and Foreign Bible Society
  29
Religious Tract Society   29
Society for the Reformation of
  Manners   29
Society for the Suppression of Vice
  29, 73–4
Society for the Prevention and
  Discouragement of Vice and
  Profaneness   73–4
York Temperance Society   76
St Mary's, Castlegate   110
infant and child mortality   117
literacy   112
mortality   115
St Michael le Belfrey   110
infant and child mortality   117
literacy   112
mortality   115

Tuke Tea and Coffee Business   11

York
  Dispensary   72
  economy   13, 14
  industrialization   51
  Mechanics Institute   80
  Penitentiary, The   74, 135
    ladies committee   74
  population   13
  Reform Association   106
  schools:
    Archbishop Holdgate's   12
    Bar Convent   12
    Blue Coat Boys'   12, 77
    Grey Coat Girls'   12, 77
    St Peter's   12
    Ragged School   79
  Vagrancy Office   74
York Monthly Meeting   16–17
  adult mortality rates   115
  birth and marriage rates   118–21
  deaths and births   114–18
  demographic profile   112–18
  disownment and marriage out
    126–7
  disownment and removal   121–6

infant and child mortality rates
   116
marriage rates   121
Meeting of Ministers and Elders
   43
membership   113, 135

growth and decline   128
Men's Meeting   32–4
socio-economic profile   109-12
Women's Meeting   33–9
Yorkshire
Committe of Association   98

NAME INDEX

Abraham, Ellen   44
Alexander
   Anne (née Tuke)   14, 45, 74
      marriage   47
      in America   47
   Mary   41, 45
   William   12, 14, 74, 90, 93, 95,
      103
Agar, Seth   96
Allen, William   23
Allis, Mary   33
Anderson, Robert Henry   97
Armitage, Mary   33, 36, 37
Awmack
   Ann   44
   Joseph   73, 80
   Mary   36
Backhouse
   Deborah   44
   Elizabeth   74
   James   11, 14, 89, 93, 95, 103, 106
   Sarah   44, 74
   Thomas   11, 14, 89
Baker
   Ann   37
   James   106, 129
   John   129
   Sarah   44
Bell
   Ann Mercy   17, 44
   Nathaniel   44, 58, 59, 88
Bissell, Mary Ann   35
Bleckley
   Mary Ann   35
   William   92

Briggs
   Caroline (née Jackson)   59
   John   59, 106
   William   106
Cadbury, Richard   76
Cappe, Catherine   72, 77
Cattle, Robert   94, 95, 96, 103
Chivers, Sarah   34
Clarkson, Thos.   23
Clemesha, John   105
Copsie, Favilla   78
Cranswick, Mary   35
Crewdson, Isaac   31
Doeg
   David   33, 73
   Esther   33
Dudley
   Elizabeth   32, 44
   Mary   44
Ellerton, Mary   17
Fletcher, Martha   33, 78
Flower, Francis   93
Forbes, Charles   93
Fothergill
   Elizabeth   37
   John   72, 93
   Rebecca   33, 34
Fox, George   16, 17
Fowler, Rachel   32
Frankland, Henry   17
Fry, Elizabeth   23, 25, 42
Galilee, Hannah   78
Gibson
   Elizabeth (née Tuke)   60
   George   60

Graham, John, the Revd   103
Gray
  Faith 73
  Jonathan 73, 93–4, 96, 103
  William 73, 96, 103
Grubb
  John 25
  Robert 46
  Sarah (née Tuke) 41, 46, 56
    marriage 46
    preaching 46–7
  Sarah Lynes 25
Gurney, Joseph John 25, 42
Hardy, Joseph 35
Hessay, James 37
Hood, Jane (née Casson) 37
Horner, Benjamin 74, 95–6
  alderman 97, 103
Hudson, George 14, 136
  lord mayor 96
Hustler, Mary 44
James, John Angell 32
Janson, Elizabeth 44
Jepson
  George 33
  Katherine (née Allen) 33
Johnson
  Ann 35
  Jane (née Ventress) 59
  John 59
  Peter (city recorder) 72, 98
King, Sarah 33, 78
Knowles
  George 36, 93, 97
  Mary (née Nicholson) 36
Lee, Mary 34
Leeman, George 97, 106, 136
Mason
  John 73
  Thomas 90–1, 97
Meek, James 76, 93, 97, 136
Mennell, Hannah 74
Mildred, Mary 78
More, Hannah 32
Murray
  Hannah 32, 77
  Lindley 14, 17, 59, 73, 74, 77
    anti-slavery 102–4

early life 24
  Evangelicalism 24–5
  moves to York 24
  politics 99–100
Oddy
  Ann 35
  Mary 35
Park, Rachel 35
Peacock
  Daniel 43
  George 93
Pemberton, John 95
Penny, Ann 37
Petre, Edward (lord mayor) 95
Prest, Edward 73
Priestman
  Ann 33, 44, 78
  David 14, 58–9, 73, 103
  Elizabeth 32, 61
  Sarah 44
  Stephen 92
  Thomas 44, 61, 88–9
Procter, Rebecca 35
Oldfield, William 96
Ransome, Henry 90
Richardson
  Hannah (née Procter) 59
  Isabel 44
  John 59
  Martha 33, 37
  Samuel 14, 73
  William 11–12, 14, 73, 93
Richardson, William, the Revd 73
Rockingham, the Marquis of 12, 98
Rowntree
  Henry 11
  John Stephenson 10, 133
  Joseph 14, 80, 96–7, 105, 106,
    129, 136
  Sarah 14, 33, 44, 74
Sanderson, John 37
Savery, William 42
Scarr
  Hannah 76
  Mary 34
Scott, Ann 42
Sharp, Granville 23
Simeon, Charles 40

Spence
  Jemima   44, 74
  Joseph   11, 14, 76, 80, 93
Stears
  Mary   36, 38
  Samuel   38
Stone, Benjamin   17
Storr, Jonathan   88, 90–1
Sturge, Eliza   31
Thurnam, Elizabeth   32
Towse, Elizabeth   35
Tuke
  Ann (see Alexander)   17
  Daniel   94
  Elizabeth   17
  Esther (née Maud)   14–15, 17–18,
    44–6, 78, 133–4
    marriage to William   21, 53, 56
  Esther jun. (see Priestman)   61, 78
  Guilielma   33
  Henry   14, 17, 48, 73
    Anti-Slavery Society   101–2
    education   25
    Evangelicalism   26–8
    marriage to Mary Maria Scott
      25, 60
    politics   99–100
  John   73, 74
  Mable   24

  Maria   74
  Mary   11
  Mary Maria (née Scott)   17
  Priscilla (née Hack)   33, 76, 78
  Samuel   14, 17, 94, 96, 105–6
    anti-slavery   102–4
    marriage to Priscilla Hack   5
  Sarah (see Grubb)   17
  William   11, 14, 88
    anti-slavery   73, 101–2
    Anti-Slavery Society   103–4
    The Dispensary   72
    marriage to Esther Maud   21,
      53, 56
    The Retreat   69
Vincent, Henry   106
Waller
  Hannah   33, 80
  Robert   59
Wellbeloved, Charles   73, 106
Wilcoxs, Celia   76
Withers, Cordelia   77
White
  Martha   78
  William, Dr   77, 98
Wilberforce, William   12, 23, 73,
    101–2
Williams, Caleb   62, 89
Wyvill, Christopher   12, 98